Arthur Sidgwick

Aeschylus Agamemnon

Part I: Introduction and Text

Arthur Sidgwick

Aeschylus Agamemnon
Part I: Introduction and Text

ISBN/EAN: 9783744729543

Printed in Europe, USA, Canada, Australia, Japan

Cover: Foto ©Thomas Meinert / pixelio.de

More available books at **www.hansebooks.com**

Clarendon Press Series

AESCHYLUS

AGAMEMNON

WITH INTRODUCTION AND NOTES

BY

A. SIDGWICK, M.A.

*Fellow and Tutor of Corpus Christi College, Oxford
Late Fellow of Trinity College, Cambridge, and Assistant Master of
Rugby School*

THIRD EDITION, REVISED

PART I.—INTRODUCTION AND TEXT

Oxford

AT THE CLARENDON PRESS

1887

London
HENRY FROWDE

OXFORD UNIVERSITY PRESS WAREHOUSE

AMEN CORNER, E.C.

PREFACE.

THE difficulty of editing Aeschylus' Agamemnon for schools is due to the fact that the play is in many ways too hard for school-boys, though it will always continue, and rightly continue, to be read at school for the sake of its incomparable grandeur and beauty. For example, much of the difficulty of the Agamemnon is owing to the corruptness of the MSS.; and while it is impossible in editing it to put aside discussion of the text, it is not desirable with beginners to enter much into such points, nor even with more advanced students, except to a limited extent. At the same time the better boys in the Upper Form of a public school ought to be taught the elements of text criticism;—and the Agamemnon is not at all a bad play for the purpose.

Under these circumstances I have thought it best to give all the important MS. variations in the text, and to give reasons in the notes for the readings adopted. The teacher can use this as much or as little as he likes.

The mass of literature on the Agamemnon is so great that it is almost impossible to mention all one's obligations. The list of editors and emendators consulted or quoted is given at page xxi; but I may add that I have studied, more fully than the rest, the editions of Dindorf, Paley, Schneidewin, Enger, Hermann, and Kennedy: and that to all I owe much, especially to Enger for interpretation, and Hermann for text. Besides these I have tried to master the main contributions of Schütz, Weil, Wellauer, Klausen, Hartung, Karsten, Schömann, and Madvig. Hartung, Karsten, and Schömann are all very ingenious and suggestive, especially Hartung: and all too much given to emendation. Madvig, though I believe he has got the right reading in one hard passage by a brilliant conjecture (1228), is not usually happy in his suggestions in this play.

I also owe not a little to suggestions in casual papers; amongst which I must mention Zeyss on the religious ideas of Aeschylus, Göttingen 1829, Professor Campbell's paper in the American Journal of Philology, Dec. 1880, and Professor Goodwin's paper on Agamemnon, read before the American Philological Association, 1877, the last two kindly sent me by the authors.

In the Introduction and Notes I have mostly abandoned the meaningless custom of writing the Greek names according to their Latin corruptions. I perhaps ought to apologise for not having done this completely: but some names are so naturalised in their Latin dress that I have not changed them.

Oxford, 1881.

NOTE TO THE SECOND EDITION.

In issuing this revised edition, I wish to express my thanks to several friends and critics for suggestions, especially to Mr. H. A. J. Munro, whose remarks have modified my view of one or two passages: also to Mr. E. S. Shuckburgh, Mr. E. D. A. Morshead, and Professor Mahaffy. Mr. Margoliouth's Agamemnon, unfortunately for me, did not appear in time for me to make any use of it in preparing this edition.

NOTE TO THE THIRD EDITION.

In this revision I have had the advantage of using the edition of Wecklein, who has collected and sifted all the corrections and suggested emendations of the text of Aeschylus, up to the date 1880. I have with the aid of this careful and laborious work corrected a few of the emendations recorded at the foot of my text, which had been wrongly attributed, and added several more notes on the text in an appendix (No. 5). In this appendix I have also included what seemed to me the best of Mr. Margoliouth's numerous and ingenious suggestions. A few misprints have also been corrected in the notes, which I have been enabled to do by the kindness of friends who have detected and pointed out the errors.

Oxford, *Sept.* 1887.

CONTENTS.

PART I.

	PAGE
INTRODUCTION	vii
THE ORESTEIA	vii
STORY AND PLOT OF AGAMEMNON	viii
EARLIER VERSIONS OF THE STORY	viii
MODIFICATIONS OF THE STORY	x
THE DRAMA OF THE AGAMEMNON	xi
THE MORAL AND RELIGIOUS IDEAS	xiii
THE CHARACTERS	xiv
THE CHORIC SONGS	xvii
THE MANUSCRIPTS	xix
THE EDITIONS	xxi
THE TEXT	xxii
TRANSLATIONS	xxii
TEXT	1–61

PART II.

NOTES	1–79
APPENDICES	80
INDICES	86

INTRODUCTION.

THE ORESTEIA.

THE Agamemnon is one of a set of three plays which all dealt with the same story, each constituting as it were one act of a great drama. Such sets were called trilogies, and according to the ordinary theory were acted on the same occasion, and were usually followed by a fourth play of a lighter cast (called Satyric dramas, from the Satyr or attendant of Dionysos, which originally was a leading part in it): the whole four being called a tetralogy. The subject of the Satyric play in this instance is traditionally recorded to have been 'Proteus.' Considerable doubt has been thrown upon this theory of trilogies or tetralogies; but it is at least clear that the three plays in this case were all composed by the poet with reference to each other. The Agamemnon relates the return and murder of the king (the Crime); in the second play, the Choëphoroe, Orestes comes back and slays his mother Klytaemnestra (the Vengeance); while in the third, the Eumenides, the matricide is released from the furies who have pursued him, and acquitted by divine interposition before the Areiopagos at Athens (the Reconciliation). About the Proteus we know nothing[1].

The date of the Agamemnon is given as B.C. 458, and the poet won the first prize.

The presumable division of parts is as follows in the Agamemnon:—

Chief actor or Protagonist: Klytaemnestra.
Second actor or Deuteragonist: Kassandra.
Third actor or Tritagonist: Agamemnon.
Watchman, Herald, Aegisthos, divided among the others.
Chorus of Argive elders.

---

[1] Except three fragmentary lines and a few words, preserved by grammarians and scholiasts, and printed among the fragments of Aeschylus.

THE STORY AND THE PLOT OF THE AGAMEMNON.

The story is the return and murder of Agamemnon by Klytaemnestra his wife, aided by her lover Aegisthos; Agamemnon is accompanied by a captive, the princess and prophetess Kassandra, and she is murdered by the same hands at the same time. The story is as old as Homer, and Aeschylus gives it, as will be seen below, with some differences.

The action of the play in detail is as follows:—

Agamemnon has been absent for ten years at Troy. Meanwhile his wife Klytaemnestra has been ruling Argos (not Mykenae, see note on line 1), in conjunction with her lover Aegisthos. The news of the capture of Troy is daily expected, and the play opens with the appearance of the night-watchman on the roof, waiting (as he has been for a year past) for the beacon fire which is to announce the victory. While the watchman is complaining of his troubles, the flame flashes out, and he goes to tell his mistress (Prologue). The chorus enter and sing; meanwhile the queen comes out, and is seen lighting the altar fires and preparing for a festal display in honour of the event. The leader of the chorus learns from her the tidings, and after describing the beacon-race, she imagines the scene in Troy, and expresses a hope that all will end well (Scene 1). After another choric song the Herald appears, who describes, first, the sufferings before Troy, and, finally, the storm which scattered the fleet; the queen sends by him a welcome to her lord (Scene 2). In Scene 3 Agamemnon returns, with Kassandra; Klytaemnestra greets her lord, and persuades him to step into the palace over purple carpets. In Scene 4 the queen orders in Kassandra, but as the prophetess sits mute and disregards her, she retires. Kassandra then delivers herself of her visions, and announces the murder of the king and of herself. The groans are heard behind the scenes; the doors open, and Klytaemnestra is seen with the dead. She justifies her deed, and afterward Aegisthos comes forth and exults; and just as the Argives are about to assail him, the queen steps in and stays the tumult.

EARLIER VERSIONS OF THE STORY.

The earliest version of the story must be gathered from the following passages in Homer[1]:—

---

[1] Quoted from the beautiful translation by Butcher and Lang.

(1) Od. i. 35. 'Even as of late Aegisthos, beyond that which was ordained, took to him the wedded wife of Atreides, and killed her lord on his return, and that with sheer doom before his eyes, since we [the gods, Zeus is speaking] had warned him by the mouth of Hermes . . . that he should neither kill the man nor woo his wife. For from Orestes shall there be vengeance for Atreides so soon as he shall come to man's estate and long for his own country. So spake Hermes, yet he prevailed not on the heart of Aegisthos.'

(2) Od. iii. 263. '[Aegisthos] living in peace in the heart of Argos . . . spake oftentimes to the wife of Agamemnon and tempted her. Verily at the first she would none of the foul deed, the fair Klytaemnestra, for she had a good understanding. Moreover there was with her a minstrel, whom the son of Atreus straitly charged as he went to Troy to have a care of his wife. But when at last the doom of the gods bound her to her ruin, then did Aegisthos carry the minstrel to a lonely isle, and left him there to be the prey and spoil of birds; while, as for her, he led her to his house, a willing lover with a willing lady . . . . . [304] and for seven years he ruled over Mykenae, rich in gold, after he slew the son of Atreus, and the people were subdued unto him. But in the eighth year came upon him goodly Orestes back from Athens to be his bane, and slew the slayer of his father.'

(3) Od. iv. 521. 'Then verily did Agamemnon set forth with joy upon his country's soil, ... and the watchman spied him from his tower, whom crafty Aegisthos had led and posted there, promising him for a reward two talents of gold. Now he kept watch for a year, lest Agamemnon should pass by him when he looked not, and mind him of his wild prowess. So he went to the house to bear the tidings to the shepherd of the people. And straightway Aegisthos contrived a cunning treason. He chose out twenty of the best men in the township, and set an ambush, and on the further side of the hall he bade prepare a feast. Then with chariot and horses he went to bid to the feast Agamemnon, shepherd of the people: but caitiff thoughts were in his heart. He brought him up to his house all unwitting of his doom, and when he had feasted him, slew him, as one slayeth an ox at the stall. And none of the company of Atreides were left, nor any of the men of Aegisthos, but they were all killed in the halls.'

(4) Od. xi. 409. [Shade of Agamemnon speaks.] 'Aegisthos slew me, with the aid of my accursed wife .... after he had bidden me to his house .... Even so I died, and round me my company likewise were slain without ceasing .... And most pitiful of all, I heard the voice of the daughter of Priam, of Kassandra, whom the traitorous Klytaemnestra slew hard by me; but as for me, as I strove to raise my hands I dropped them to the earth as I lay dying .... Naught is more shameless than a woman who imagines such evil in her heart, even as she too planned a foul deed, fashioning death for her gentle lord.'

MODIFICATIONS OF THE STORY.

It will be seen not only that the tale, as Aeschylus gives it, is different in many particulars from the Homeric story, but also that in the different passages of the Odyssey different versions seem to have been current; or at least it is possible to trace a development of the mythus.

In Homer it is *Aegisthos* who does the murder, either alone, as (1) seems to imply, or by an ambuscade, as (3) tells us. Also Aegisthos is not in Agamemnon's palace: he took Klytaemnestra to his own house (2): and there entertained the king (3), and there murdered him. Aegisthos' motive is not mentioned, but seems to be mere ambition.

Klytaemnestra in (1), (2), and (3) is not said to have had anything to do with the murder, but is only described as unfaithful: while in (4) she 'planned the foul deed,' and 'aided' the murderer, and herself killed Kassandra.

The '*minstrel*' who watched over the wife appears in (2) only and is nowhere else alluded to.

Kassandra appears only in (4).

In Aeschylus *Aegisthos* is only secondary in the murder: he is 'a recreant lion wallowing in the couch.' The motive which he alleges is vengeance, arising out of family feuds.

Klytaemnestra is the leading agent: she is the ἀνδρόβουλον κέαρ who devises and executes: and her motive too is vengeance for her child's death, with a touch of jealousy for Kassandra. Of a feast or ambuscade Aeschylus knows nothing: the king is muffled in a cloak and stabbed in a bath. And there is no battle of attendants.

INTRODUCTION.   xi

The *Watchman* in Aeschylus, though, like the Homeric guard in (3), 'he has watched for a year,' is not a spy of Aegisthos watching to catch Agamemnon, but a loyal servant[1] who grieves over the disorders of the house, is watching for the *beacon*, and is overjoyed at the thought of seeing his master. And the murder takes place in the palace of Agamemnon.

Besides these there are minor modifications of the story. The confusion of Argos and Mykenae is mentioned in notes on line 1. In Homer too *Menelaos*[2] is king of Sparta and has nothing to do with the Agamemnon tale: in Aeschylus he is clearly joint-king of Argos with Agamemnon (42 sqq.). The chorus inquire for him, and call him 'loved ruler of the land' (619). The two are 'one in heart,' a 'two-throned power of the Achaioi' (109), and live in the same palace, called δόμος 'Ατρειδᾶν (400). This accounts for the anxious inquiry of the chorus (617), and the re-assurance given by the herald (675) about Menelaos.

THE DRAMA OF THE AGAMEMNON.

How far Aeschylus was following current modifications in the story, and how far he himself modified the tradition for dramatic purposes, we cannot fully tell: nor is the subject one of great importance. It is of far greater interest to notice briefly some of the points that contribute to the extraordinary impressiveness of the poem as a work of art and as a drama.

Of Aeschylus' style it is not necessary to say much: every reader will feel its beauty and power. The principal characteristics of it are obviously its dignity, its strength, and the boldness and wealth of its imagery[3]: and though there are passages in the Agamemnon which are bare, even in bareness it is grand; and on the other hand there are passages which for tenderness and pathos and pure poetic beauty are unmatched even in Greek.

---

[1] This explains a curious note at the beginning of the Medicean manuscript, θεράπων 'Αγαμέμνονος, οὐχ ὁ ὑπὸ Αἰγίσθου ταχθείς.

[2] This is remarked by Prof. Campbell in American Journal of Phil., Dec. 1880.

[3] Thus he speaks of 'the beard of fire,' 'war the gold-merchant,' a hurricane as 'an evil shepherd,' the sea 'flowering with dead,' a lion 'the Priest of Ruin,' 'the net of death,' 'the mixing bowl of wrath,' 'the raging Dam of Hades,' hope 'treading the halls of Fear.'

Such are the descriptions of Iphigeneia in the first chorus, of Helen in the second, and the whole scene with Kassandra. We have, too, much relief in the variety of the characters; and even a touch of humour here and there, as in the helplessness of the Argive elders after the murder [1], and the racy vernacular idiom of the φύλαξ.

Another point is the marvellous power of conception shown in the two leading figures, Klytaemnestra and Kassandra, as is more fully developed below in treating of the characters (p. xiv).

But the effect of the play is largely due to another element, which is quite independent of the grandeur of the style, and the power of presenting character. And this element is what we may call the moralising of the plot. In Homer we have merely a tale of savage ambition and crime. In Aeschylus we have a house tainted with dreadful wickedness in the past, old sin leading to new sin, and that to further retribution, till the family seems haunted by a terrible fate of bloodshed. According to the later tale, Pelops, the ancestor, slew Myrtilus, by whose aid he won his bride: Atreus and Thyestes, his sons, slew their stepbrother Chrysippos: Thyestes seduced his brother's wife Aerope. Atreus served up the slain children of Thyestes for their father to eat: Atreus' son Agamemnon banished Thyestes and his third son Aegisthos, and slew his own daughter Iphigeneia. Aeschylus only mentions the last three of these crimes: but the bloody past is present in his thoughts. And what gives the play its overwhelming effect is the feeling, ever growing, of this past horror and impending retribution. The 'House knows the many deeds of blood:' and the Avenger is always waiting. The justice of the gods may be slow, but it is sure.

This feeling is chiefly aroused and maintained by the choric songs, which will be found analysed below, p. xvii. For, by the necessities of the case, it is the chorus who have to hint the bloodguiltiness of the king. The queen, who is to avenge the deed, cannot charge him with it, since, in order to execute her plot, she must maintain the mask of love and faithfulness [2]. And

---

[1] The contrast between the decisiveness of the heroic personages and the imbecility of the council reveals a glimpse of the anti-democratic tendencies of the poet.

[2] Enger, Preface to Agamemnon.

accordingly these choric songs are not merely splendid lyric poems, they are also as it were the voice of the general conscience sadly foreboding inevitable doom. In the eloquent words of a French critic[1]: 'The idea of impending chastisement is incessantly repeated; it mingles with the joy of victory; a dark cloud, big with the storm, covers the gloomy scene; till the dream, so wearing and so terrible, filled with visions so fearful and mysterious, ends with a peal of thunder.'

The Moral and Religious Ideas.

The leading religious and moral ideas of Aeschylus, as they appear in the Agamemnon, can be summarised in a few sentences.

There is unquestioning faith in the gods: impiety, τὸ δυσσεβές, is the worst of sins (760). The gods are all powerful: Zeus is beyond compare (162), the cause of all and the doer of all (1485). The gods regard men's actions (370), punish transgression (59), avenge bloodshed (461), though the retribution may linger (364).

The leading idea of the gods is their power: human sin comes from resisting or defying this power, ὕβρις (765). The gods are also just: but the justice is a form of their power; it is the humbling of the proud. So wealth is no defence to the wicked (381), and virtue is found among men in humble dwellings (772).

The cruder idea that God resents mere prosperity, he rejects (755): misery always comes from sin (760). Yet prosperity is dangerous, as it engenders pride (372): mortals are insatiate of wealth (1002, 1331) and so come to ill. For human well-being is precarious: 'Disease is behind the party-wall,' and there is always 'the hidden reef' (1002-5). The thunderbolt strikes the famous (470).

Man then who has sinned cannot escape: the doer must suffer' (1564). And in this way God teaches man: 'wisdom comes by suffering' (177).

Aeschylus feels strongly the mysteriousness of human fate and the helplessness of man. Though the gods are omnipotent and just, yet this justice acts inscrutably. Agamemnon was bidden to slay his child, and had to obey (206): yet it was a crime (219-221),

[1] Patin, Étude sur Eschyle.

and produced 'terrible wrath,' rising again (154). It was to the king 'the collar of necessity' (218). In this way there is a fate, an avenger, established in the house (1481, 1507), the house is 'close welded to ruin' (1565). The refrain of human life is the prayer, 'Woe: but let good prevail,' which recurs in the first chorus: and the conclusion of the whole matter is 'it is hard to discern,' δύσμαχά ἐστι κρῖναι (1561).

The Characters.

Klytaemnestra. The character of Klytaemnestra is given with a masterly force and effect in every stroke. There are no fine shades about the drawing, as there are none in the conception. She is the impersonation of the tyrannic self-will, wronged and angered, and turned to vengeance. She is Homer's οὐλομένη ἄλοχος, 'an accursed wife:' pitiless, and contemptuous, and unimpassioned, but resolutely bent on revenge, and concentrating her whole Titanic force upon it without misgiving[1]. There is no womanly passion in her, and no trace of weakness. The murder she is bent on is in revenge for her slain child, but we hear scarcely a word of love[2] for Iphigeneia from her lips: the lovely description of the maiden in her father's halls is from the mouth of the chorus; but the mother scarcely mentions her save in the climax of her bitter triumph, when with dreadful irony she pictures her welcoming her sire in Hades (1555). She is an adulteress, but there is no love for her paramour; her unfaithfulness is merely a form of her vengeance: hatred of her husband is the motive of it, not love of Aegisthos. She is crafty, but hers is the craft of a strong and not a weak nature: it is only the needful means to carry out her purpose completely, and the moment the need is over, the mask is scornfully flung aside.

Let us briefly trace her attitude through the play.

In scene 2 she enters (264) in apparent triumph: but of course the joy is not over the fall of Troy, it is merely grim delight in the coming vengeance. There is irony in her first word εὐάγ-

---

[1] One leading difference between Klytaemnestra and her great rival Lady Macbeth lies in the difference of the effect of the crime upon the two. Klytaemnestra is unshaken: Lady Macbeth is broken by it.

[2] She does call her φιλτάτην ἐμοὶ ὠδῖνα: but this is in a passing justification, and is not really dwelt on by the poet.

γέλος. There is a savage force in her long description of the beacons (281), and the state of Troy (320): she is acting a part all through. And there is a deep irony in her hope (347) 'that no evil desire might bring woe on the host: old ills might wake!'

In scene 3 she scornfully banters the chorus (590) for having doubted her report: and she ends with the terrible prayer, 'May he find a faithful wife, ay, even as he left her' (606).

In scene 4, when she meets her returning husband, she keeps up unflinchingly the part she is acting. She poses audaciously as the chaste matron who does not speak of her wifely love before others (856): laments the loneliness of her lot in her lord's absence (861): half withdraws the mask to jest about the reported wounds of Agamemnon (868), then enlarges on her tears and watchings (888): and describes her joy at his return in fulsome images (896). This masterly speech ends with the thrilling line 'That justice may lead him to an unlooked for home,' and an ambiguous promise that she will 'order aright what is fated' (910–12).

Then follows the effective irony of Agamemnon entering 'the human slaughter-house' over purple carpets.

After the next chorus she has a short scene (sc. 5) with the speechless Kassandra, showing herself as the contemptuous and pitiless tyrant (1055–1068).

In scene 6 the deed is done and she boasts of it, 'I stand where I struck the blow: the deed is done.' We observe her grim talk of decorum (!), which prevents her from pouring libations of triumph (1395), her total disregard of the opinions others have of her act, 'the blame or praise is all one to me' (1403), and her bitter triumph over Kassandra (1440), savouring characteristically far more of contempt than of jealousy.

In the κομμός her cold irony and hardness reaches a climax. She calls herself the Avenger of the House (1500): vents the fearful sarcasm about Iphigeneia mentioned above (1555): and ends with a calm resolve, as though she were the victim and not the criminal, to 'bear her troubles' and a wish for 'a quiet life and a humble competence!' (1574).

In the last scene, true to herself, she just interposes at the end to stop the brawling between Aegisthos and the Chorus: 'We have had enough of trouble,' and to lead off her lover, bidding him not mind 'the vain howlings' of the Chorus.

Kassandra. Kassandra is not strictly speaking a study of *character* at all: the interest comes from her situation, and the extraordinary picturesqueness and impressiveness of the figure she presents. If the object of tragedy is to arouse 'pity and terror' there is no more supremely tragic figure than Kassandra in all the Greek drama.

She comes on, silent and wild-glancing ('like a new-caught beast,' 1063) in the car of Agamemnon. She is a princess, a prophetess, and a captive. She sits motionless on the stage during the long scene between Agamemnon and Klytaemnestra (810–974), and the choric song (975–1034), and hears the queen's reiterated scornful commands without a word of answer. When Klytaemnestra is gone, she replies to the kind and pitying tones of the chorus first with wild exclamations, then with cries of horror, growing slowly more articulate and clear, against the crime-defiled house before her. Then the past deeds of blood rise before her in visions each more startling than the last, till the climax is reached in the terrible ἰδοὺ ἰδού· ἄπεχε τῆς βοὸς τὸν ταῦρον (1125): after which she passes into tender and sad laments of her own fate. Then she sinks from the excited lyric dochmiacs to 'clear prophecy' in the ordinary iambic metre, broken by two spasms of inspiration. Next follows the splendid soliloquy (1255), when she hurls to the ground the badges of her prophetic office, the sacred staff and chaplets; and finally, after one more prophecy of the Retribution of Orestes, she utters the saddest of all laments over human destiny—

> 'Alas for mortal lot! when prosperous
> 'tis but a sketch! and if misfortune comes,
> the wet sponge with its touch blots out the drawing;'

and so passes under the blood-stained portal to her death.

Agamemnon. Though the king gives his name to the play, and though he is in one sense the central figure, he only appears in one short scene. But that suffices for the poet's purpose. Agamemnon is the victorious heroic monarch, returning in triumph to the house which is to be 'a human slaughter-house:' and all that is wanted is what we have, the stately procession, the thanksgiving, the greeting interchanged with his wife, the natural Greek misgiving at the needless waste and display of the purple tapestries, and the royal graciousness with which after a

brief resistance he gives way to Klytaemnestra's wish. The
irony of the situation is brought fully out; even down to the
minor touches, such as his bitter words about false friends (837)
when he is thinking of the Greeks before Troy, and ignorant of
the faithlessness of his wife: and again the almost pathetic
futility of his pious caution in taking off his shoes (945), when at
last he agrees to tread the purple.

Aegisthos is but the 'recreant lion wallowing in the couch'
(1224), or again, 'the wolf that mated with the lioness' (1259),
as Kassandra calls him : or, in the rough vernacular of the chorus,
'a cock proud before his hen' (1671). He simply comes on to
tell the tale of blood (1577), and to boast the deed he has not
dared to do. He is an effective foil to the queen; especially at
the very end, where Aegisthos blusters and threatens the chorus,
whom Klytaemnestra treats with cold and distant scorn. 'Care
not for the vain howls of these men: thou and I will rule the
house and order it well.' In his case, as in the queen's, vengeance is given as the motive for his plot.

The Watchman forms an effective opening to the play, with
the contrast between the rough and almost humorous homeliness
of his speech and the terrible drama that impends: but enough is
said of him in the notes, see 17.

The Herald performs the usual office of the ἄγγελος, varying
the drama with a fine description of the shipwreck (650). His
appearance also serves to heighten the suspense and darken the
forebodings.

THE CHORIC SONGS.

The full analysis of the choric songs will be found in the notes:
but it is desirable to take a general view of them, in order to see
their dramatic effect.

(1) 40-257. The chorus do not yet know the good news of
the capture: and in this first song they tell the tale of the
mustering of the fleet for Troy, the sign of the eagles and the
hare, and the adverse gales, and the sacrifice of Iphigeneia. The
opening thought is 'the gods are just, and must punish the sin
of Paris' (59 sqq.). But the hope is mixed with fear (100) and
the refrain (121, 139, 159) echoes the mingled feelings. They
cannot shake off the thought that the slaughter of the maiden
must bring woe : ' it is a lawless sacrifice, a seed of strife' (152):
'the wrath remains terribly doomed to return' (155): Zeus

'teaches men by suffering' (176). And the whole description of the sacrifice (205-246) with its terrible pathos and beauty is meant to enhance the horror of the crime. The song ends with an awful foreboding, based on a sure belief in justice (250): the future is so dark that it is folly to look forward: 'too early knowledge is too early sorrow' (252).

A strain of deep faith runs through it all. 'Zeus is beyond compare' (163), and Retribution is sure.

(2) 355-487. The news has now come of the victory, and we expect a song of joy.

But the tone of the Chorus is again rather a praise of justice which punishes crime. It is the crime of Paris of which they speak chiefly: but one feels all through that there are other sins in the singer's mind which shall also be punished: and at the end there is a clear note of misgiving for Agamemnon on a new ground, namely because he has caused the death of so many warriors.

The description of the wrecked happiness of the home, where the wife has been faithless, and of the horrors of war, as shown in the slaughter of citizens and the consequent wide-spread mourning, are both written with a modern intensity and sympathy, which seem remarkably in advance of ordinary Greek sentiment; quite apart from their imperishable beauty.

(3) 681-809. The messenger has come and confirmed the tidings with details of the victory: but significantly the tale ends with disaster: the returning fleet was wrecked.

The Chorus again dwell on the Retribution to those who wronged Hospitality: the beauty of Helen (which is described in lines of unspeakable loveliness, 740-3) only brings into sharper contrast the curse which came with her: like a lion's whelp, a cherished plaything, grown into a ravager of flocks.

At the end is a remarkable passage, in which the poet repudiates the common Greek doctrine of $\phi\theta\acute{o}\nu os$, which taught that man's prosperity roused the envy of the gods and so brought disaster. 'No,' says Aeschylus, 'it is not Prosperity, but always *sin*, violence, injustice that brings woe.'

Again the application is apparently to Paris: again we feel that the sin of Agamemnon is present in the thought.

(4) 975-1034. The king has returned, been greeted, and entered the palace in triumph over the purple tapestry. The success is apparently complete.

The choric song is however one long foreboding of ill: a foreboding 'which they cannot explain, but cannot dismiss' (975-80). But the reason comes out: the sin is there, and so there is no safety. 'The black and murdered blood once shed who can recall?' (1019). They can only take refuge in vague and feeble hopes. One feels impending calamity in the very air.

(5) 1072-1177. In this astonishing scene we have the inspired Kassandra and her visions of past and impending deeds of blood. But this is fully explained in the notes, and the chorus has only a secondary part to play: and accordingly we may pass on.

(6) 1448-1576. The deed has been done: the foreboding is fulfilled, and the chorus in despair can only pray for death, and lament the woe that Helena caused. There is a Fate on the house (1467), it is the will of Heaven, of Zeus (1485): and when the queen urges that it is the requital for the murder of Iphigeneia (the very deed which the chorus all through had expected to bring woe) they can only express sad perplexity: the justice, if it be justice, will demand yet another victim: the blood is falling ever faster (1534). And they end with again striking the note of Justice: 'it is the will of God that the doer shall suffer' (1563).

The Manuscripts.

The MSS. which contain the Agamemnon, the whole or part, are as follows:—

1. M. Much the oldest and most important is the *Medicean*, in the library of Lorenzo dei Medici at Florence, written on parchment in the 10th or 11th century; a facsimile of this has been published by the Clarendon Press at Oxford, 1871. The MS. contains Agamemnon 1-310, and 1067-1159, the middle and end of the play being lost.

2. G. *Guelferbytanus*, at Wolfenbüttel, written on paper in the 15th century, contains the same parts of the Agamemnon as M., of which it is clearly a copy. Dindorf calls it 'a most faulty manuscript.'

3. Ma. *Marcianus* (once in the monastery of San Marco), now in the library of Lorenzo at Florence, written on silk in the 15th century, also clearly a copy of M., containing the same parts of the play.

4. B. *Bessarionis*, in the library of St. Mark at Venice, written on paper about the 13th century, containing Ag. 1-348: probably a copy of M. before the loss of the central leaves (Moritz Haupt, preface to Hermann, 1859).

The above four are practically not independent authorities.

5. V. The *Venetian* (*Venetus* B), in the library of St. Mark at Venice, written on parchment in the 13th[1] century, containing Ag. 1-45, and 1095 to end.

6. Fl. *Florentinus*, in the library of Lorenzo at Florence, written on paper in the 14th century, containing Agamemnon entire.

7. Fa. *Farnesianus* (once in the Farnese library), now in the Museum at Naples, written in the 14th century. It contains the revision of Demetrius Triclinius, who has done a good deal in the way of emendation, though often erroneously.

The exact relation of these three MSS. to the first four is not easy to determine: but there is no doubt that many obvious corruptions are common to all existing manuscripts.

It will perhaps be useful to put these facts about the MSS. in a tabular form as under:—

Name.	Sign.	Contents.	Place.	Century.	Remarks.
Mediceus	M.	1-311, 1067-1159	Florence	10 or 11	
Guelferbytanus	G.	do.	Wolfbtl.	15	Clearly copies of M.
Marcianus	Ma.	do.	Florence	15	
Bessarionis	B.	1-348	Venice	13	Prob. copied from M. before loss of leaves
Venetus	V.	1-45, 1095-end	Venice	13	
Florentinus	Fl.	all	Florence	14	
Farnesianus	Fa.	all	Naples	14	

The following table shows what MS. authority there is for each part of the play:—

    1-45 ...M. G. Ma. B. V. Fl. Fa.
    46-311 ...M. G. Ma. B. Fl. Fa.
    312-348 ...B. Fl. Fa.
    349-1066...Fl. Fa.
    1067-1094...M. G. Ma. Fl. Fa.
    1095-1159...M. G. Ma. V. Fl. Fa.
    1160-end ...V. Fl. Fa.

[1] 15th, according to Wecklein.

The Editions.

The editions of the Agamemnon have been extremely numerous, and the text, which in the MSS. is very corrupt and has often suffered from hasty emendation, has been gradually improved by a perfect host of scholars. There still remain however many places where the true reading is very doubtful, and a few which seem hopeless.

The following are the principal editors and correctors: those who have been consulted or quoted are given with the abbreviations used:—

Abbrev.	Date.	Name.	
	1518	Aldine.	⎧ These give only the fragments of Ag., which are found in M and G. The play is confused with the Choëphoroe.
	1552	Turnebus, Paris.	
Rob.	1552	Robortelli, Venice.	{ This gives the same fragments, but separate.
Vict.	1557	Victorius. This is the first ed. which gives Ag. whole.	
Cant.	1580	Canter, Antwerp.	
Stanl.	1663	Stanley, London.	
	1745	Pauw, Hague.	
Ask.	1746	Askew, Leyden.	
Schütz.	1784	Schütz, Halle.	
Pors.	1794	Porson.	
Butl.	1809	Butler.	
Blom.	1822	Blomfield, Cambridge.	
Tyrr.	1822	Tyrrwhitt (published by Elmsley), Oxford.	
Well.	1823	Wellauer, Leipzig.	
Schol.	1830	Scholefield, Cambridge.	
Klaus.	1833	Klausen, Gotha.	
Con.	1848	Conington, Oxford.	
Dind. D.	1851	Dindorf, Oxford.	
Hart.	1852	Hartung, Leipzig.	
Schöm.	1854	Schömann, Gryphiswald.	
Karst.	1855	Karsten, Traj. ad. Rhen.	
Pal. or P.	1855-79	Paley, London.	
Eng.	1855	Enger, Leipzig.	
Schn.	1856	Schneidewin, Berlin.	
H.	1859	Hermann, Berlin.	
Weil.	1861	Weil, Giessa.	
Keck.	1863	Keck, Leipzig.	
	1864	Van Heusde, Hague.	
Dav.	1868	Davies, Utrecht.	
Gilb.	1874	Gilbert (edited Enger).	
K.	1878	Kennedy, Cambridge.	
Kirch.	1880	Kirchhoff, Berlin.	
Marg.	1884	Margoliouth, Oxford.	
Weck.	1885	Wecklein, Berlin.	

Besides these, the following have contributed emendations:—

Aur.	Auratus.	Heath.	Heath.
Cas.	Is. Casaubon.	Franz.	Franz.
Scal.	Scaliger.	Musgr.	Musgrave.
Ahr.	Ahrens.	Madv.	Madvig.
Dobr.	Dobree.	Both.	Bothe.

I use the common abbreviation L. S. for Liddell and Scott.

The Text.

In the text I have aimed at giving (at the foot of the pages) the MSS. reading of all the doubtful places, where the MSS. differ among themselves, or are all wrong; except in the numerous instances where the corrections are quite obvious and generally accepted; and even of these latter I have given all which can be called important. The MSS. are very corrupt, and the number of such small but necessary corrections is very much greater than any one would suppose who had not studied the full apparatus criticus of the play.

Where the reading adopted occurs in any of the MSS. and any other MS. differs, and the question is doubtful or important, the readings are given in a note at the bottom of the text, but there is no mark in the text.

Where the reading adopted is conjectural, and appears in no MS., it is marked with an asterisk, the MS. reading (or readings) given in the note, and usually the corrector or editor, to whom the emendation is due, named. Thus, line 69, *in the text*, *ὑποκαίων: *in the note* ὑποκλαίων MSS. corr. Cas. i. e. 'the manuscripts read ὑποκλαίων; the correction in the text is due to Casaubon.'

Where neither MSS. nor proposed readings are satisfactory, the passage is marked with †. Thus line 14, †ἐμήν.

Translations.

The Agamemnon has been done into English in nearly a score of translations. Those which I have consulted, and occasionally taken the liberty to quote, are the following; I give the abbreviations in italics, by which they are quoted in my notes:—

   Professor Conington (*Con.*).
   Miss Swanwick (*Swan.*).
   Dean Milman (*Mil.*).
   Mr. R. Browning (*Br.*).
   Professor Kennedy (*Ken.*).
   Mr. E. D. A. Morshead (*Mors.*).

The last is the one to which I owe most.

ΑΓΑΜΕΜΝΩΝ.

ΤΑ ΤΟΥ ΔΡΑΜΑΤΟΣ ΠΡΟΣΩΠΑ.

ΦΥΛΑΞ.
ΧΟΡΟΣ ΑΡΓΕΙΩΝ
ΚΛΥΤΑΙΜΝΗΣΤΡΑ.
ΤΑΛΘΥΒΙΟΣ ΚΗΡΥΞ.
ΑΓΑΜΕΜΝΩΝ.
ΚΑΣΣΑΝΔΡΑ.
ΑΙΓΙΣΘΟΣ.

× Πρ. so firm in its read in a woman's manly-counselling hopeful heart

by way of providing a musical remedy vs. sleep

ΑΓΑΜΕΜΝΩΝ.

ΦΥΛΑΞ.

Θεοὺς μὲν αἰτῶ τῶνδ' ἀπαλλαγὴν πόνων,
φρουρᾶς ἐτείας μῆκος, ἣν κοιμώμενος
στέγαις 'Ατρειδῶν ἄγκαθεν, κυνὸς δίκην,
ἄστρων κάτοιδα νυκτέρων ὁμήγυριν,
καὶ τοὺς φέροντας χεῖμα καὶ θέρος βροτοῖς   5
λαμπροὺς δυνάστας, ἐμπρέποντας αἰθέρι·
[ἀστέρας, ὅταν φθίνωσιν, ἀντολάς τε τῶν·]
καὶ νῦν φυλάσσω λαμπάδος τὸ σύμβολον,
αὐγὴν πυρὸς φέρουσαν ἐκ Τροίας φάτιν;
ἁλώσιμόν τε βάξιν· ὧδε γὰρ κρατεῖ   10
γυναικὸς ἀνδρόβουλον ἐλπίζον κέαρ.
εὖτ' ἂν δὲ νυκτίπλαγκτον ἔνδροσόν τ' ἔχω
εὐνὴν ὀνείροις οὐκ ἐπισκοπουμένην
† ἐμήν,—φόβος γὰρ ἀνθ' ὕπνου παραστατεῖ,
τὸ μὴ βεβαίως βλέφαρα συμβαλεῖν ὕπνῳ·—   15
ὅταν δ' ἀείδειν ἢ μινύρεσθαι δοκῶ,
ὕπνου τόδ' ἀντίμολπον ἐντέμνων ἄκος,
κλαίω τότ' οἴκου τοῦδε συμφορὰν στένων,
οὐχ ὡς τὰ πρόσθ' ἄριστα διαπονουμένου.
νῦν δ' εὐτυχὴς γένοιτ' ἀπαλλαγὴ πόνων   20
εὐαγγέλου φανέντος ὀρφναίου πυρός.

7. Probably spurious.   17. ἐκτέμνων V. Fl.

ΑΙΣΧΥΛΟΥ

ὦ χαῖρε λαμπτὴρ, νυκτός, ἡμερήσιον
φάος πιφαύσκων καὶ χορῶν κατάστασιν
πολλῶν ἐν Ἄργει, τῆσδε συμφορᾶς χάριν.
ἰοῦ ἰοῦ.   25
Ἀγαμέμνονος γυναικὶ σημαίνω τορῶς,
εὐνῆς ἐπαντείλασαν ὡς τάχος δόμοις
ὀλολυγμὸν εὐφημοῦντα τῇδε λαμπάδι
ἐπορθιάζειν, εἴπερ Ἰλίου πόλις
ἑάλωκεν, ὡς ὁ φρυκτὸς ἀγγέλλων πρέπει·   30
αὐτός τ' ἔγωγε φροίμιον χορεύσομαι.
τὰ δεσποτῶν γὰρ εὖ-πεσόντα θήσομαι
τρὶς ἐξ βαλούσης τῆσδέ μοι φρυκτωρίας.
γένοιτο δ' οὖν μολόντος εὐφιλῆ χέρα
ἄνακτος οἴκων τῇδε βαστάσαι χερί.   35
τὰ δ' ἄλλα σιγῶ· βοῦς ἐπὶ γλώσσῃ μέγας
βέβηκεν· οἶκος δ' αὐτός, εἰ φθογγὴν λάβοι,
σαφέστατ' ἂν λέξειεν· ὡς ἑκὼν ἐγὼ
μαθοῦσιν αὐδῶ, κοὐ μαθοῦσι λήθομαι.

ΧΟΡΟΣ.

δέκατον μὲν ἔτος τόδ' ἐπεὶ Πριάμου   40
μέγας ἀντίδικος,
Μενέλαος ἄναξ ἠδ' Ἀγαμέμνων,
διθρόνου Διόθεν καὶ δισκήπτρου
τιμῆς ὀχυρὸν ζεῦγος Ἀτρειδᾶν,
στόλον Ἀργείων χιλιοναύταν   45
τῆσδ' ἀπὸ χώρας
ἦραν, στρατιῶτιν ἀρωγήν,
μέγαν ἐκ θυμοῦ κλάζοντες Ἄρη,

---

26. σημαίνω M.G.   σημανῶ B.V.Fl.Fa.   30. ἀγγέλλων V.Fa.
ἀγγέλων M.Ma.B.Fl.   40. Πριάμω M.

ΑΓΑΜΕΜΝΩΝ.

τρόπον αἰγυπιῶν,
οἵτ' ἐκπατίοις ἄλγεσι παίδων
ὕπατοι λεχέων στροφοδινοῦνται,   50
πτερύγων ἐρετμοῖσιν ἐρεσσόμενοι,
δεμνιοτήρη
πόνον ὀρταλίχων ὀλέσαντες·
ὕπατος δ' ἀΐων ἤ τις Ἀπόλλων,   55
ἢ Πάν, ἢ Ζεύς, οἰωνόθροον
γόον ὀξυβόαν τῶνδε μετοίκων
ὑστερόποινον
πέμπει παράβασιν Ἐρινύν.
οὕτω δ' Ἀτρέως παῖδας ὁ κρείσσων   60
ἐπ' Ἀλεξάνδρῳ πέμπει ξένιος
Ζεύς, πολυάνορος ἀμφὶ γυναικός,
πολλὰ παλαίσματα καὶ γυιοβαρῆ,
γόνατος κονίαισιν ἐρειδομένου
διακναιομένης τ' ἐν προτελείοις   65
κάμακος, θήσων Δαναοῖσι
Τρωσί θ' ὁμοίως. ἔστι δ' ὅπη νῦν
ἔστι· τελεῖται δ' ἐς τὸ πεπρωμένον·
οὔθ' *ὑποκαίων οὔθ' ὑπολείβων
οὔτε δακρύων ἀπύρων ἱερῶν   70
ὀργὰς ἀτενεῖς παραθέλξει.
ἡμεῖς δ' ἀτίται σαρκὶ παλαιᾷ
τῆς τότ' ἀρωγῆς ὑπολειφθέντες
μίμνομεν ἰσχὺν
ἰσόπαιδα νέμοντες ἐπὶ σκήπτροις.   75
ὅ τε γὰρ νεαρὸς μυελὸς στέρνων
ἐντὸς *ἀνάσσων
ἰσόπρεσβυς, Ἄρης δ' οὐκ ἔνι χώρᾳ,

69. ὑποκλαίων MSS. corr. Cas.   77. ἀνάσσων MSS. corr. II.

ΑΙΣΧΥΛΟΥ

τό θ' ὑπεργήρων φυλλάδος ἤδη
κατακαρφομένης τρίποδας μὲν ὁδοὺς   80
στείχει, παιδὸς δ' οὐδὲν ἀρείων
ὄναρ ἡμερόφαντον ἀλαίνει.
σὺ δέ, Τυνδάρεω
θύγατερ, βασίλεια Κλυταιμνήστρα,
τί χρέος; τί νέον; τί δ' ἐπαισθομένη,   85
τίνος ἀγγελίας
* πευθοῖ περίπεμπτα θυοσκεῖς;
πάντων δὲ θεῶν τῶν ἀστυνόμων,
ὑπάτων, χθονίων,
τῶν τ' οὐρανίων τῶν τ' ἀγοραίων,   90
βωμοὶ δώροισι φλέγονται·
ἄλλη δ' ἄλλοθεν οὐρανομήκης
λαμπὰς ἀνίσχει,
φαρμασσομένη χρίματος ἁγνοῦ
μαλακαῖς ἀδόλοισι παρηγορίαις,   95
πελάνῳ μυχόθεν βασιλείῳ.
τούτων λέξασ' ὅ τι καὶ δυνατὸν
καὶ θέμις αἰνεῖν,
παιών τε γενοῦ τῆσδε μερίμνης,
ἣ νῦν τοτὲ μὲν κακόφρων τελέθει,   100
τοτὲ δ' ἐκ θυσιῶν ἀγανὰ φαίνουσ'
ἐλπὶς ἀμύνει φροντίδ' ἄπληστον
* τῆς θυμοβόρου φρένα λύπης.   [στρ. α'.
κύριός εἰμι θροεῖν ὅδιον κράτος αἴσιον ἀνδρῶν
ἐκτελέων. (ἔτι γὰρ θεόθεν καταπνείει   105

79. τίθιπεργήρως M. G.   τίθι περ γήρως Ma.   τόθι περγήρως B.
τόθιπερ γήρως Fl.   τόθ' ὑπεργήρων Fa.   87. πυθοῖ Fl.   πειθοῖ cet.
θυοσκινεῖς MSS. corr. Turn.   101. φαίνεις M.G.   φαίνει B.   φαίνουσ' Fl. Fa.   103. τὴν θυμοφθόρον λύπης φρένα M. G. B.   τὴν
θυμοβόρον λυποφρένα Fa.   τὴν θυμοβόρον λύπης φρένα Fl.

πειθώ, *μολπᾶν
ἀλκάν, σύμφυτος αἰών,
ὅπως Ἀχαιῶν δίθρονον κράτος, Ἑλλάδος ἥβας
ξύμφρονα τᾱγαν, 110
πέμπει ξὺν δορὶ καὶ χερὶ πράκτορι
θούριος ὄρνις Τευκρίδ' ἐπ' αἶαν,
οἰωνῶν βασιλεὺς βασιλεῦσι νεῶν, ὁ κελαινός, ὅ τ'
ἐξόπιν ἀργᾶς, 115
φανέντες ἴκταρ μελάθρων, χερὸς ἐκ δοριπάλτου,
παμπρέπτοις ἐν ἕδραισι,
βοσκόμενοι λαγίναν, ἐρικύμονα *φέρματα, γένναν,
βλαβέντα λοισθίων δρόμων. 120
αἴλινον αἴλινον εἰπέ, τὸ δ' εὖ νικάτω. [ἀντ. α'.
κεδνὸς δὲ στρατόμαντις ἰδὼν δύο *λήμασιν ἴσους
Ἀτρείδας μαχίμους ἐδάη λαγοδαίτας
πομπούς τ' ἀρχάς·
οὕτω δ' εἶπε τεράζων· 125
χρόνῳ μὲν ἀγρεῖ Πριάμου πόλιν ἅδε κέλευθος,
πάντα δὲ πύργων
κτήνη πρόσθε τὰ δημιοπληθῆ
Μοῖρ' ἀλαπάξει πρὸς τὸ βίαιον. 130
οἷον μή τις *ἄγα θεόθεν κνεφάσῃ προτυπὲν στόμιον
μέγα Τροίας
στρατωθέν. *οἴκτῳ γὰρ ἐπίφθονος Ἄρτεμις ἁγνὰ
πτανοῖσιν κυσὶ πατρός, 136
αὐτότοκον πρὸ λόχου μογερὰν πτάκα θυομένοισι·
στυγεῖ δὲ δεῖπνον αἰετῶν.
αἴλινον αἴλινον εἰπέ, τὸ δ' εὖ νικάτω.
τόσον περ εὔφρων, καλά, μεσῳδ. 140

106. πειθοῖ Campbell. μολπὰν MSS. 118. ἐρικύματα φέρματι M.G. ἐρικύμονα φέρματι B. ἐρικύμονα φέρβοντο Fl. Fa. 122. λήμασι δισσούς MSS. 131. ἄτα MSS. corr. H. 135. οἴκῳ MSS. corr. Scal. 140. ἁ καλά Fa.

8 ΑΙΣΧΥΛΟΥ

δρόσοισι λέπτοις μαλερῶν λεόντων,
πάντων τ' ἀγρονόμων φιλομάστοις
θηρῶν ὀβρικάλοισι τερπνά,
τούτων * αἴνει ξύμβολα κρᾶναι,
δεξιὰ μέν, κατάμομφα δὲ φάσματα [στρουθῶν].   145
ἰήιον δὲ καλέω Παιᾶνα,
μή τινας ἀντιπνόους Δαναοῖς χρονίας ἐχενῇδας
ἀπλοίας τεύξῃ,   150
σπευδομένα θυσίαν ἑτέραν, ἄνομόν τιν', ἄδαιτον,
νεικέων τέκτονα σύμφυτον,
οὐ δεισήνορα. μίμνει γὰρ φοβερὰ παλίνορτος,
οἰκονόμος δολία, μνάμων μῆνις τεκνόποινος.   155
τοιάδε Κάλχας ξὺν μεγάλοις ἀγαθοῖς ἀπέκλαγξεν
μόρσιμ' ἀπ' ὀρνίθων ὁδίων οἴκοις βασιλείοις·
τοῖς δ' ὁμόφωνον
αἴλινον αἴλινον εἰπέ, τὸ δ' εὖ νικάτω.
Ζεύς, ὅστις ποτ' ἐστίν, εἰ τόδ' αὐ-   στρ. β'.   160
τῷ φίλον κεκλημένῳ,
τοῦτό νιν προσεννέπω.
οὐκ ἔχω προσεικάσαι,
πάντ' ἐπισταθμώμενος,
πλὴν Διός, εἰ τὸ μάταν ἀπὸ φροντίδος ἄχθος   165
χρὴ βαλεῖν ἐτητύμως.
οὐδ' ὅστις πάροιθεν ἦν μέγας,   ἀντ. β'.
παμμάχῳ θράσει βρύων,
* οὐδὲ λέξεται πρὶν ὤν,   170
ὃς δ' ἔπειτ' ἔφυ, τρια-
κτῆρος οἴχεται τυχών.

141. ἀέπτοις B. Fl.   ἀέλπτοις M.G.   ἀέπτοισι Fa. corr. Well.
ὄντων M. Fl.   144. αἰτεῖ MSS. corr. Gilbert.   170. οὐδὲν λέξαι
M G.B.Fl.   οὐδέν τι λέξαι Fa. corr. Ahrens.

ΑΓΑΜΕΜΝΩΝ.

Ζῆνα δέ τις προφρόνως ἐπινίκια κλάζων
τεύξεται φρενῶν τὸ πᾶν· 175
τὸν φρονεῖν βροτοὺς ὁδώ- στρ. γ΄.
σαντα, *τὸν πάθει μάθος
θέντα κυρίως ἔχειν.
στάζει δ᾽ ἔν θ᾽ ὕπνῳ πρὸ καρδίας
μνησιπήμων πόνος· καὶ παρ᾽ ἄ- 180
κοντας ἦλθε σωφρονεῖν.
δαιμόνων δέ που χάρις *βίαιος,
σέλμα σεμνὸν ἡμένων.
καὶ τόθ᾽ ἡγεμὼν ὁ πρέσ- ἀντ. γ΄.
βυς νεῶν Ἀχαϊκῶν, 185
μάντιν οὔτινα ψέγων,
ἐμπαίοις τύχαισι συμπνέων,
εὖτ᾽ ἀπλοίᾳ κεναγγεῖ βαρύ-
νοντ᾽ Ἀχαϊκὸς λεώς,
Χαλκίδος πέραν ἔχων παλιρρόχ- 190
θοις ἐν Αὐλίδος τόποις,
πνοαὶ δ᾽ ἀπὸ Στρυμόνος μολοῦσαι στρ. δ΄.
κακόσχολοι, νήστιδες, δύσορμοι
βροτῶν ἄλαι, νεῶν τε καὶ πεισμάτων ἀφειδεῖς, 195
παλιμμήκη χρόνον τιθεῖσαι
τρίβῳ κατέξαινον ἄνθος *Ἄργους
ἐπεὶ δὲ καὶ πικροῦ
χείματος ἄλλο μῆχαρ
βριθύτερον προμοισιν
μάντις ἔκλαγξεν, προφέρων Ἄρτεμιν, ὥστε χθόνα βά-
κτροις ἐπικρούσαντας Ἀτρείδας δάκρυ μὴ κατασχεῖν.
ἄναξ δ᾽ ὁ πρέσβυς *τότ᾽ εἶπε φωνῶν· ἀντ. δ΄. 205

177. τῷ MSS. 182. βιαίως MSS. corr. Turn. 197. Ἀργείων MSS. corr. H. 205. τόδ᾽ MSS. corr. Stanl.

βαρεῖα μὲν κὴρ τὸ μὴ πιθέσθαι,
βαρεῖα δ', εἰ τέκνον δαΐξω, δόμων ἄγαλμα,
μιαίνων παρθενοσφάγοισι
ῥείθροις πατρῴους χέρας *πρὸ βωμοῦ.   210
τί τῶνδ' ἄνευ κακῶν;
πῶς λιπόναυς γένωμαι,
ξυμμαχίας ἁμαρτών;
παυσανέμου γὰρ θυσίας παρθενίου θ' αἵματος ὀργᾷ *περιόργῳ σφ' ἐπιθυμεῖν θέμις. εὖ γὰρ εἴη.   216
ἐπεὶ δ' ἀνάγκας ἔδυ λέπαδνον,   στρ. ε'.
φρενὸς πνέων δυσσεβῆ τροπαίαν
ἄναγνον, ἀνίερον, τόθεν   220
τὸ παντότολμον φρονεῖν μετέγνω.
*βροτοὺς θρασύνει γὰρ αἰσχρόμητις
τάλαινα παρακοπὰ
πρωτοπήμων. ἔτλα δ' οὖν
θυτὴρ γενέσθαι θυγατρὸς γυναικοποίνων πολέμων
    ἀρωγὰν   225
καὶ προτέλεια ναῶν·
λιτὰς δὲ καὶ κληδόνας πατρῴους   ἀντ. ε'.
παρ' οὐδὲν αἰῶνα παρθένειόν τ'
ἔθεντο φιλόμαχοι βραβῆς,   230
φράσεν δ' ἀόζοις πατὴρ μετ' εὐχάν,
δίκαν χιμαίρας ὕπερθε βωμοῦ
πέπλοισι περιπετῆ,
παντὶ θυμῷ προνωπῆ   234
λαβεῖν ἀέρδην, στόματός τε καλλιπρῴρου *φυλακᾷ
    κατασχεῖν
φθόγγον ἀραῖον οἴκοις,

210. βωμοῦ πέλας MSS. corr. Schöm.   212. τε γένωμαι M. G. Fl.
216. περιόργως MSS. corr. Schöm.   222. βροτοῖς MSS.   235.
φυλακάν MSS.

ΑΓΑΜΕΜΝΩΝ.

βίᾳ χαλινῶν τ' ἀναύδῳ μένει.   στρ. ς'.
κρόκου βαφὰς δ' ἐς πέδον χέουσα
ἔβαλλ' ἕκαστον θυτήρων ἀπ' ὄμματος βέλει φιλοίκτῳ, 240
πρέπουσά θ' ὡς ἐν γραφαῖς, προσεννέπειν
θέλουσ', ἐπεὶ πολλάκις
πατρὸς κατ' ἀνδρῶνας εὐτραπέζους
ἔμελψεν, *ἁγνᾷ δ' ἀταύρωτος αὐδᾷ πατρὸς
φίλου τριτόσπονδον εὔποτμον   245
*παιᾶνα φίλως ἐτίμα.
τὰ δ' ἔνθεν οὔτ' εἶδον οὔτ' ἐννέπω·   ἀντ. ς'.
τέχναι δὲ Κάλχαντος οὐκ ἄκραντοι.
δίκα δὲ τοῖς μὲν παθοῦσιν μαθεῖν ἐπιρρέπει· τὸ
μέλλον *δ'   250
ἐπεὶ γένοιτ' ἂν κλύοις, *πρὸ χαιρέτω·
ἴσον δὲ τῷ προστένειν.
τορὸν γὰρ ἥξει *σύνορθρον αὐγαῖς.
πέλοιτο δ' οὖν τἀπὶ τούτοισιν εὔπραξις, ὡς   255
θέλει τόδ' ἄγχιστον Ἀπίας
γαίας μονόφρουρον ἕρκος.
ἥκω σεβίζων σόν, Κλυταιμνήστρα, κράτος·
δίκη γάρ ἐστι φωτὸς ἀρχηγοῦ τίειν
γυναῖκ' ἐρημωθέντος ἄρσενος θρόνου.   260
σὺ δ' *εἴ τι κεδνὸν εἴτε μὴ πεπυσμένη
εὖα, γέλοισιν ἐλπίσιν θυηπολεῖς,
κλύοιμ' ἂν εὔφρων· οὐδὲ σιγώσῃ φθόνος.

ΚΛΥΤΑΙΜΝΗΣΤΡΑ.

εὐάγγελος μέν, ὥσπερ ἡ παροιμία,

244. ἀγνά M. ἀγνᾷ Fa.   246. αἰῶνα MSS. corr. Hart.
250. τὸ δὲ προκλύειν after μέλλον B. Fl. G. and M. by later hand.
251. προχαιρέτω MSS. corr. Eng.   254. συνορθὸν αὐταῖς G. B. M.
σύναρθρον Fl. Fa. corr. Well. H.   261. εἴτε MSS.

ΑΙΣΧΥΛΟΥ

ἕως γένοιτο μητρὸς εὐφρόνης πάρα. 265
πεύσει δὲ χάρμα μεῖζον ἐλπίδος κλύειν.
Πριάμου γὰρ ᾑρήκασιν Ἀργεῖοι πόλιν.
ΧΟ. πῶς φής; πέφευγε τοὔπος ἐξ ἀπιστίας.
ΚΛ. Τροίαν Ἀχαιῶν οὖσαν· ἢ τορῶς λέγω;
ΧΟ. χαρά μ' ὑφέρπει δάκρυον ἐκκαλουμένη. 270
ΚΛ. εὖ γὰρ φρονοῦντος ὄμμα σοῦ κατηγορεῖ.
ΧΟ. τί γὰρ τὸ πιστόν; ἔστι τῶνδέ σοι τέκμαρ;
ΚΛ. ἔστιν, τί δ' οὐχί; μὴ δολώσαντος θεοῦ.
ΧΟ. πότερα δ' ὀνείρων φάσματ' εὐπειθῆ σέβεις;
ΚΛ. οὐ δόξαν ἂν λάβοιμι βριζούσης φρενός. 275
ΧΟ. ἀλλ' ἦ σ' ἐπίανέν τις ἄπτερος φάτις;
ΚΛ. παιδὸς νέας ὡς κάρτ' ἐμωμήσω φρένας.
ΧΟ. ποίου χρόνου δὲ καὶ πεπόρθηται πόλις;
ΚΛ. τῆς νῦν τεκούσης φῶς τόδ' εὐφρόνης λέγω.
ΧΟ. καὶ τίς τόδ' ἐξίκοιτ' ἂν ἀγγέλων τάχος; 280
ΚΛ. Ἥφαιστος Ἴδης λαμπρὸν ἐκπέμπων σέλας.
φρυκτὸς δὲ φρυκτὸν δεῦρ' ἀπ' ἀγγάρου πυρὸς
ἔπεμπεν· Ἴδη μὲν πρὸς Ἑρμαῖον λέπας
Λήμνου· μέγαν δὲ πανὸν ἐκ νήσου τρίτον
Ἄθωον αἶπος Ζηνὸς ἐξεδέξατο, 285
ὑπερτελής τε, πόντον ὥστε νωτίσαι,
† ἰσχὺς πορευτοῦ λαμπάδος πρὸς ἡδονὴν
*πέμπει τὸ χρυσοφεγγὲς ὥς τις ἥλιος
σέλας παραγγείλασα Μακίστου *σκοπαῖς·†
ὁ δ' οὔτι μέλλων οὐδ' ἀφρασμόνως ὕπνῳ 290
νικώμενος παρῆκεν ἀγγέλου μέρος·
ἑκὰς δὲ φρυκτοῦ φῶς ἐπ' Εὐρίπου ῥοὰς
Μεσσαπίου φύλαξι σημαίνει μολόν.
οἱ δ' ἀντέλαμψαν καὶ παρήγγειλαν πρόσω

282. ἀγγέλου MSS.   288. πεύκη MSS. πέμπει Eng. προὔκειτο
K. ἐπέσυτο Keck.   289. σκοπάς MSS.

ΑΓΑΜΕΜΝΩΝ.

γραίας ἐρείκης θωμὸν ἄψαντες πυρί. 295
σθένουσα λαμπὰς δ' οὐδέπω μαυρουμένη,
ὑπερθοροῦσα πεδίον Ἀσωποῦ, δίκην
φαιδρᾶς σελήνης, πρὸς Κιθαιρῶνος λέπας
ἤγειρεν ἄλλην ἐκδοχὴν πομποῦ πυρός.
φάος δὲ τηλέπομπον οὐκ ἠναίνετο 300
φρουρά, † πλέον καίουσα τῶν εἰρημένων·
λίμνην δ' ὑπὲρ Γοργῶπιν ἔσκηψεν φάος·
ὄρος τ' ἐπ' Αἰγίπλαγκτον ἐξικνούμενον
ὤτρυνε θεσμὸν *μὴ χατίζεσθαι πυρός.
πέμπουσι δ' ἀνδαίοντες ἀφθόνῳ μένει
φλογὸς μέγαν πώγωνα, καὶ Σαρωνικοῦ
πορθμοῦ *κάτοπτον πρῶν' ὑπερβάλλειν πρόσω
φλέγουσαν, *ἔστ' ἔσκηψεν, *εὖτ' ἀφίκετο
Ἀραχναῖον αἶπος, ἀστυγείτονας σκοπάς·
κἄπειτ' Ἀτρειδῶν ἐς τόδε σκήπτει στέγος 310
φάος τόδ' οὐκ ἄπαππον Ἰδαίου πυρός.
τοιοίδε τοί μοι λαμπαδηφόρων νόμοι,
ἄλλος παρ' ἄλλου διαδοχαῖς πληρούμενοι·
νικᾷ δ' ὁ πρῶτος καὶ τελευταῖος δραμών.
τέκμαρ τοιοῦτο ξύμβολόν τε σοὶ λέγω, 315
ἀνδρὸς παραγγείλαντος ἐκ Τροίας ἐμοί.
ΧΟ. θεοῖς μὲν αὖθις, ὦ γύναι, προσεύξομαι.
λόγους δ' ἀκοῦσαι τούσδε κἀποθαυμάσαι
διηνεκῶς θέλοιμ' ἂν ὡς λέγοις πάλιν.
ΚΛ. Τροίαν Ἀχαιοὶ τῇδ' ἔχουσ' ἐν ἡμέρᾳ. 320
οἶμαι βοὴν ἄμικτον ἐν πόλει πρέπειν.
ὄξος τ' ἄλειφά τ' ἐγχέας ταὐτῷ κύτει
διχοστατοῦντ' ἂν οὐ φίλως προσεννέποις.

---

301. sic MSS. 304. δὴ χαρίζεσθαι Fa. μὴ χαρίζεσθαι M.G.B.
Fl. 307. κάτοπτρον MSS. 308. εἶτ'... εἶτ' MSS. 319. λέγεις B.

14 ΑΙΣΧΥΛΟΥ

καὶ τῶν ἁλόντων καὶ κρατησάντων δίχα
φθογγὰς ἀκούειν ἐστὶ συμφορᾶς διπλῆς. 325
οἱ μὲν γὰρ ἀμφὶ σώμασιν πεπτωκότες
ἀνδρῶν κασιγνήτων τε καὶ φυταλμίων
παῖδες γερόντων, οὐκέτ' ἐξ ἐλευθέρου
δέρης ἀποιμώζουσι φιλτάτων μόρον·
τοὺς δ' αὖτε νυκτίπλαγκτος ἐκ μάχης πόνος 330
νήστεις πρὸς ἀρίστοισιν ὧν ἔχει πόλις
τάσσει, πρὸς οὐδὲν ἐν μέρει τεκμήριον,
ἀλλ' ὡς ἕκαστος ἔσπασεν τύχης πάλον,
ἐν δ' αἰχμαλώτοις Τρωικοῖς οἰκήμασι
ναίουσιν ἤδη, τῶν ὑπαιθρίων πάγων 335
δρόσων τ' ἀπαλλαγέντες, ὡς * δ' εὐδαίμονες
ἀφύλακτον εὐδήσουσι πᾶσαν εὐφρόνην.
εἰ δ' εὖ σέβουσι τοὺς πολισσούχους θεοὺς
τοὺς τῆς ἁλούσης γῆς θεῶν θ' ἱδρύματα,
οὔ * τὰν ἑλόντες αὖθις * ἀνθαλοῖεν ἄν. 340
ἔρως δὲ μή τις πρότερον ἐμπίπτῃ στρατῷ
πορθεῖν ἃ μὴ χρή, κέρδεσιν νικωμένους.
δεῖ γὰρ πρὸς οἴκους νοστίμου σωτηρίας
κάμψαι διαύλου θάτερον κῶλον πάλιν·
θεοῖς δ' ἀναμπλάκητος εἰ μόλοι στρατός, 345
ἐγρηγορὸς τὸ πῆμα τῶν ὀλωλότων
γένοιτ' ἄν, εἰ πρόσπαια μὴ τύχοι κακά.
τοιαῦτά τοι γυναικὸς ἐξ ἐμοῦ κλύεις·
τὸ δ' εὖ κρατοίη, μὴ διχορρόπως ἰδεῖν.
πολλῶν γὰρ ἐσθλῶν *τήνδ' ὄνησιν εἱλόμην· 350
ΧΟ. γύναι, κατ' ἄνδρα σώφρον' εὐφρόνως λέγεις.
ἐγὼ δ' ἀκούσας πιστά σου τεκμήρια

331. νήστισι B. νῆστις Fl. 336. δυσδαίμονες MSS. 340. ἄν
γ' ἑλόντες or ἀνελόντες and ἂν θάνοιεν or αὖ θάνοιεν MSS. corr. Aur. II.
341. ἐμπίπτει B. -ει Fa. -ῃ corrected to -ῃ Fl. 350. τὴν MSS.

θεοὺς προσειπεῖν εὖ παρασκευάζομαι,
χάρις γὰρ οὐκ ἄτιμος εἴργασται πόνων.
ὦ Ζεῦ βασιλεῦ καὶ νὺξ φιλία   355
μεγάλων κόσμων κτεάτειρα,
ἥτ' ἐπὶ Τροίας πύργοις ἔβαλες
στεγανὸν δίκτυον, ὡς μήτε μέγαν
μήτ' οὖν νεαρῶν τιν' ὑπερτελέσαι
μέγα δουλείας   360
γάγγαμον, ἄτης παναλώτου.
Δία τοι ξένιον μέγαν αἰδοῦμαι
τὸν τάδε πράξαντ', ἐπ' Ἀλεξάνδρῳ
τείνοντα πάλαι τόξον, ὅπως ἂν
μήτε πρὸ καιροῦ μήθ' ὑπὲρ ἄστρων   365
βέλος ἠλίθιον σκήψειεν.
| Διὸς πλαγὰν ἔχουσιν εἰπεῖν,   στρ. α'.
πάρεστιν τοῦτό γ' ἐξιχνεῦσαι.
*ἔπραξαν ὡς ἔκρανεν. οὐκ ἔφα τις
θεοὺς βροτῶν ἀξιοῦσθαι μέλειν   370
ὅσοις ἀθίκτων χάρις
πατοῖθ'· ὁ δ' οὐκ εὐσεβής.
πέφανται δ' *ἐκτίνου-
σα τόλμα τῶν Ἄρη   375
πνεόντων μεῖζον ἢ δικαίως,
φλεόντων δωμάτων ὑπέρφευ
ὑπὲρ τὸ βέλτιστον. ἔστω δ' ἀπή-
μαντον, ὥστ' ἀπαρκεῖν
εὖ πραπίδων λαχόντα.   380
οὐ γάρ ἐστιν ἔπαλξις

368. πάρεστι MSS. πάρεστιν Eng.   369. ὡς ἔπραξεν ὡς ἔκρανεν
MSS. corr. Franz.   374. ἐγγόνους ἀτολμήτων MSS. ἐκγόνοις ἀτολμήτως H. text Hart.   379. ὥστε κἀπαρκεῖν Fa. text Fl.

πλούτου πρὸς κόρον ἀνδρὶ
λακτίσαντι μέγαν δίκας βωμὸν εἰς ἀφάνειαν.
βιᾶται δ' ἁ τάλαινα πειθώ, ἀντ. α'. 385
*προβούλου παῖς ἄφερτος ἄτας.
ἄκος δὲ πᾶν μάταιον. οὐκ ἐκρύφθη,
πρέπει δέ, φῶς αἰνολαμπές, σίνος·
κακοῦ δὲ χαλκοῦ τρόπον 390
τρίβῳ τε καὶ προσβολαῖς
μελαμπαγὴς πέλει
δικαιωθείς, (ἐπεὶ
διώκει παῖς ποτανὸν ὄρνιν,)
πόλει πρόστριμμ' ἄφερτον ἐνθείς. 395
λιτᾶν δ' ἀκούει μὲν οὔτις θεῶν·
τὸν δ' ἐπίστροφον *τῶν
φῶτ' ἄδικον καθαιρεῖ.
οἷος καὶ Πάρις ἐλθὼν
ἐς δόμον τὸν Ἀτρειδᾶν 400
ᾔσχυνε ξενίαν τράπεζαν κλοπαῖσι γυναικός.
λιποῦσα δ' ἀστοῖσιν ἀσπίστορας στρ. β'.
*τε καὶ κλόνους λογχίμους ναυβάτας *θ' ὁπλισμούς,
ἄγουσά τ' ἀντίφερνον Ἰλίῳ φθοράν, 406
βέβακεν ῥίμφα διὰ πυλᾶν,
ἄτλητα τλᾶσα· πολλὰ δ' ἔστενον
τόδ' ἐννέποντες δόμων προφῆται·
ἰὼ ἰὼ δῶμα δῶμα καὶ πρόμοι, 410
ἰὼ λέχος καὶ στίβοι φιλάνορες.
†* πάρεστι σιγὰς ἀτίμους ἀλοιδόρους
* αἴσχιστ' ἀφειμένων ἰδεῖν.†

386. προβουλόπαις MSS. corr. Hart. 397. τῶνδ' MSS. corr. Klaus.
405. κλόνους λογχίμους τε καὶ MSS. omit θ' MSS. corr. H. 412.
σιγᾶσ' ἄτιμος ἀλοίδορος ἄδιστος ἀφεμένων MSS. corr. H.

ΑΓΑΜΕΜΝΩΝ.

πόθῳ δ' ὑπερποντίας
φάσμα δόξει δόμων ἀνάσσειν. 415
εὐμόρφων δὲ κολοσσῶν
ἔχθεται χάρις ἀνδρί.
ὀμμάτων δ' ἐν ἀχηνίαις ἔρρει πᾶσ' Ἀφροδίτα.
ὀνειρόφαντοι δὲ πενθήμονες ἀντ. β'. 420
πάρεισι δόξαι φέρουσαι χάριν ματαίαν.
μάταν γάρ, εὖτ' ἂν ἐσθλά τις δοκῶν * ὁρᾷ,
παραλλάξασα διὰ χερῶν,
βέβακεν ὄψις οὐ-μεθύστερον 425
πτεροῖς ὀπαδοῖς ὕπνου κελεύθοις.
τὰ μὲν κατ' οἴκους ἐφ' ἑστίας ἄχη
τάδ' ἐστὶ καὶ τῶνδ' ὑπερβατώτερα.
τὸ πᾶν δ' ἀφ' *Ἕλλανος αἴας συνορμένοις
πένθεια τλησικάρδιος 430
δόμων ἑκάστου πρέπει.
πολλὰ γοῦν θιγγάνει πρὸς ἧπαρ·
οὓς μὲν γάρ * τις ἔπεμψεν
οἶδεν· ἀντὶ δὲ φωτῶν
τεύχη καὶ σποδὸς εἰς ἑκάστου δόμους ἀφικνεῖται.
ὁ χρυσαμοιβὸς δ' Ἄρης σωμάτων στρ. γ'. 436
καὶ ταλαντοῦχος ἐν μάχῃ δορὸς
πυρωθὲν ἐξ Ἰλίου 440
φίλοισι πέμπει βαρὺ
ψῆγμα δυσδάκρυτον ἀν-
τήνορος σποδοῦ γεμί-
ζων λέβητας * εὐθέτους.
στένουσι δ' εὖ λέγοντες ἄνδρα τὸν μὲν ὡς 445

---

423. ὁρᾶν MSS. ὁρᾷ Eng. K. 426. ὑπαδοῦσ' Dobr. 429.
Ἑλλάδος MSS. corr. Bamberg. 433. τις om. MSS. corr. Pors.
444. εὐθέτου MSS. corr. Aur.

C

μάχης ἴδρις· τὸν δ' ἐν φοναῖς καλῶς πεσόντ'
ἀλλοτρίας *διαὶ γυναικός· *τὰ δὲ σῖγά τις βαΰ-
ζει· φθονερὸν δ' ὑπ' ἄλγος ἕρπει προδίκοις Ἀτρείδαις.
οἱ δ' αὐτοῦ περὶ τεῖχος·   450
θήκας Ἰλιάδος γᾶς
εὔμορφοι κατέχουσιν· ἐχθρὰ δ' ἔχοντας ἔκρυψεν.
βαρεῖα δ' ἀστῶν φάτις ξὺν κότῳ·   ἀντ. γ'. 456
δημοκράντου δ' ἀρᾶς τίνει χρέος.
μένει δ' ἀκοῦσαί τί μου
μέριμνα νυκτηρεφές.   460
τῶν πολυκτόνων γὰρ οὐκ
ἄσκοποι θεοί· κελαι-
ναὶ δ' Ἐρινύες χρόνῳ
τυχηρὸν ὄντ' ἄνευ δίκας (παλιντυχεῖ
τριβᾷ βίου) τιθεῖσ' ἀμαυρόν, ἐν δ' ἀΐ-   465
στοις τελέθοντος οὔτις ἀλκά· τὸ δ' *ὑπερκόπως
κλύειν
εὖ βαρύ· βάλλεται γὰρ ὄσσοις διόθεν κεραυνός.   470
κρίνω δ' ἄφθονον ὄλβον.
μήτ' εἴην πτολιπόρθης
μήτ' οὖν αὐτὸς ἁλοὺς ὑπ' ἄλλων βίον κατίδοιμι.
πυρὸς δ' ὑπ' εὐαγγέλου   ἐπῳδ.   475
πόλιν διήκει θοὰ
βάξις· εἰ δ' ἐτητύμως,
τίς οἶδεν, ἢ *τι θεῖόν ἐστι *πῃ ψύθος.
τίς ὧδε παιδνὸς ἢ φρενῶν κεκομμένος,
φλογὸς παραγγέλμασιν   480
νέοις πυρωθέντα καρδίαν, ἔπειτ'
ἀλλαγᾷ λόγου καμεῖν;

447. διὰ MSS. τάδε MSS. corr. H.   467. ὑπερκότας MSS.
478. τοι... μὴ MSS. corr. Ahr.   482. λόγους Fl. text Fa.

Clarendon Press Series

AESCHYLUS

AGAMEMNON

WITH INTRODUCTION AND NOTES

BY

A. SIDGWICK, M.A.

*Fellow and Tutor of Corpus Christi College, Oxford
Late Fellow of Trinity College, Cambridge, and Assistant Master of
Rugby School*

THIRD EDITION, REVISED

PART II.—NOTES

Oxford

AT THE CLARENDON PRESS

1887

[*All rights reserved*]

𝔏𝔬𝔫𝔡𝔬𝔫
HENRY FROWDE

OXFORD UNIVERSITY PRESS WAREHOUSE

AMEN CORNER, E.C.

ΑΓΑΜΕΜΝΩΝ.

γυναικὸς αἰχμᾷ πρέπει,
πρὸ τοῦ φανέντος χάριν ξυναινέσαι.
πιθανὸς ἄγαν ὁ θῆλυς ὅρος ἐπινέμεται   485
ταχύπορος· ἀλλὰ ταχύμορον
γυναικογήρυτον ὄλλυται κλέος.
τάχ' εἰσόμεσθα λαμπάδων φαεσφόρων
φρυκτωριῶν τε καὶ πυρὸς παραλλαγάς,   490
εἴτ' οὖν ἀληθεῖς εἴτ' ὀνειράτων δίκην
τερπνὸν τόδ' ἐλθὸν φῶς ἐφήλωσεν φρένας.
κήρυκ' ἀπ' ἀκτῆς τόνδ' ὁρῶ κατάσκιον
κλάδοις ἐλαίας· μαρτυρεῖ δέ μοι κάσις
πηλοῦ ξύνουρος διψία κόνις τάδε,   495
ὡς οὔτ' ἄναυδος οὔτε σοι δαίων φλόγα
ὕλης ὀρείας σημανεῖ καπνῷ πυρός,
ἀλλ' ἢ τὸ χαίρειν μᾶλλον ἐκβάξει λέγων·
τὸν ἀντίον δὲ τοῖσδ' ἀποστέργω λόγον·
εὖ γὰρ πρὸς εὖ φανεῖσι προσθήκη πέλοι.   500
ὅστις τάδ' ἄλλως τῇδ' ἐπεύχεται πόλει,
αὐτὸς φρενῶν καρποῖτο τὴν ἁμαρτίαν.

ΚΗΡΥΞ.

ἰὼ πατρῷον οὖδας Ἀργείας χθονός,
δεκάτῳ σε φέγγει τῷδ' ἀφικόμην ἔτους,
πολλῶν ῥαγεισῶν ἐλπίδων μιᾶς τυχών.   505
οὐ γάρ ποτ' ηὔχουν τῇδ' ἐν Ἀργείᾳ χθονὶ
θανὼν μεθέξειν φιλτάτου τάφου μέρος.
νῦν χαῖρε μὲν χθών, χαῖρε δ' ἡλίου φάος,
ὕπατός τε χώρας Ζεύς, ὁ Πύθιός τ' ἄναξ,
τόξοις ἰάπτων μηκέτ' εἰς ἡμᾶς βέλη·   510

483. ἐν γυναικὸς MSS. corr. Scal.

ἅλις παρὰ Σκάμανδρον *ἦσθ' ἀνάρσιος·
νῦν δ' αὖτε σωτὴρ ἴσθι *καὶ παιώνιος,
ἄναξ Ἄπολλον. τούς τ' ἀγωνίους θεοὺς
πάντας προσαυδῶ, τόν τ' ἐμὸν τιμάορον
Ἑρμῆν, φίλον κήρυκα, κηρύκων σέβας,   515
ἥρως τε τοὺς πέμψαντας, εὐμενεῖς πάλιν
στρατὸν δέχεσθαι τὸν κελειμμένον δορός.
ἰὼ μέλαθρα βασιλέων, φίλαι στέγαι,
σεμνοί τε θᾶκοι, δαίμονές τ' ἀντήλιοι,
*εἴ που πάλαι, φαιδροῖσι τοισίδ' ὄμμασι   520
δέξασθε κόσμῳ βασιλέα πολλῷ χρόνῳ.
ἥκει γὰρ ὑμῖν φῶς ἐν εὐφρόνῃ φέρων
καὶ τοῖσδ' ἅπασι κοινὸν Ἀγαμέμνων ἄναξ.
ἀλλ' εὖ νιν ἀσπάσασθε, καὶ γὰρ οὖν πρέπει,
Τροίαν κατασκάψαντα τοῦ δικηφόρου   525
Διὸς μακέλλῃ, τῇ κατείργασται πέδον.
βωμοὶ δ' ἄϊστοι καὶ θεῶν ἱδρύματα,
καὶ σπέρμα πάσης ἐξαπόλλυται χθονός.
τοιόνδε Τροίᾳ περιβαλὼν ζευκτήριον
ἄναξ Ἀτρείδης πρέσβυς εὐδαίμων ἀνὴρ   530
ἥκει, τίεσθαι δ' ἀξιώτατος βροτῶν
τῶν νῦν· Πάρις γὰρ οὔτε συντελὴς πόλις
ἐξεύχεται τὸ δρᾶμα τοῦ πάθους πλέον.
ὀφλὼν γὰρ ἁρπαγῆς τε καὶ κλοπῆς δίκην
τοῦ ῥυσίου θ' ἥμαρτε καὶ πανώλεθρον   535
αὐτόχθονον πατρῷον ἔθρισεν δόμον.
διπλᾶ δ' ἔτισαν Πριαμίδαι θἀμάρτια.
ΧΟ. κῆρυξ Ἀχαιῶν χαῖρε τῶν ἀπὸ στρατοῦ.
ΚΗ. χαίρω *γε· τεθνάναι δ' οὐκ ἔτ' ἀντερῶ θεοῖς.

511. ἦλθες Fa. ἦλθ', with -ες superscribed Fl.   512. καὶ παγώ-
νιος Fl. κἀπαγώνιος Fa. corr. Dobr. Ahr.   520. ἦπου MSS.   539.
χαίρω τεθνάναι MSS. corr. Eng.

ΧΟ. ἔρως πατρῴας τῆσδε γῆς σ' ἐγύμνασεν; 540
ΚΗ. ὥστ' ἐνδακρύειν γ' ὄμμασιν χαρᾶς ὕπο.
ΧΟ. τερπνῆς ἄρ' ἦτε τῆσδ' ἐπήβολοι νόσου.
ΚΗ. πῶς δή; διδαχθεὶς τοῦδε δεσπόσω λόγου.
ΧΟ. τῶν ἀντερώντων ἱμέρῳ *πεπληγμένοι.
ΚΗ. ποθεῖν ποθοῦντα τήνδε γῆν στρατὸν λέγεις; 545
ΧΟ. ὡς πόλλ' ἀμαυρᾶς ἐκ φρενός μ' ἀναστένειν.
ΚΗ. πόθεν τὸ δύσφρον τοῦτ' ἐπῆν στύγος *φρενῶν;
ΧΟ. πάλαι τὸ σιγᾶν φάρμακον βλάβης ἔχω.
ΚΗ. καὶ πῶς; ἀπόντων κοιράνων ἔτρεις τινάς;
ΧΟ. *ὡς νῦν τὸ σὸν δή, καὶ θανεῖν πολλὴ χάρις. 550
ΚΗ. εὖ γὰρ πέπρακται. ταῦτα δ' ἐν πολλῷ χρόνῳ
τὰ μέν τις *ἂν λέξειεν εὐπετῶς ἔχειν,
τὰ δ' αὖτε κἀπίμομφα. τίς δὲ πλὴν θεῶν
ἅπαντ' ἀπήμων τὸν δι' αἰῶνος χρόνον;
μόχθους γὰρ εἰ λέγοιμι καὶ δυσαυλίας, 555
σπαρνὰς παρήξεις καὶ κακοστρώτους, τί δ' οὐ
στένοντες, οὐ †λαχόντες ἤματος μέρος;
τὰ δ' αὖτε χέρσῳ καὶ προσῆν, πλέον στύγος·
εὐναὶ γὰρ ἦσαν δαΐων πρὸς τείχεσιν·
ἐξ οὐρανοῦ δὲ κἀπὸ γῆς λειμώνιαι 560
†δρόσοι κατεψάκαζον, ἔμπεδον σίνος
ἐσθημάτων, τιθέντες ἔνθηρον τρίχα.
χειμῶνα δ' εἰ λέγοι τις οἰωνοκτόνον,
οἷον παρεῖχ' ἄφερτον Ἰδαία χιών,
ἢ θάλπος, εὖτε πόντος ἐν μεσημβριναῖς 565
κοίταις ἀκύμων νηνέμοις εὕδοι πεσών·
τί ταῦτα πενθεῖν δεῖ; παροίχεται πόνος·

541. ἐκδ. Fa. 542. ἴστε Fl. 544. πεπληγμένος MSS. 547. στρατῷ MSS. corrupt. φρενῶν H. 550. ὧν MSS. corr. Scal. 552. εὖ MSS. 557. λαχόντες corrupt. Perhaps πάσχοντες or κλαίοντες, or ἀσχάλλοντες for οὐ λαχόντες Marg.

παροίχεται δέ, τοῖσι μὲν τεθνηκόσιν
τὸ μήποτ' αὖθις μηδ' ἀναστῆναι μέλειν.
τί τοὺς ἀναλωθέντας ἐν ψήφῳ λέγειν, 570
τὸν ζῶντα δ' ἀλγεῖν χρὴ τύχης παλιγκότου;
καὶ πολλὰ χαίρειν ξυμφοραῖς καταξιῶ.
ἡμῖν δὲ τοῖς λοιποῖσιν Ἀργείων στρατοῦ
νικᾷ τὸ κέρδος, πῆμα δ' οὐκ ἀντιρρέπει.
ὡς κομπάσαι τῷδ' εἰκὸς ἡλίου φάει, 575
ὑπὲρ θαλάσσης καὶ χθονὸς ποτωμένοις·
Τροίαν ἑλόντες δήποτ' Ἀργείων στόλος
θεοῖς λάφυρα ταῦτα τοῖς καθ' Ἑλλάδα
δόμοις ἐπασσάλευσαν ἀρχαῖον γάνος.
τοιαῦτα χρὴ κλύοντας εὐλογεῖν πόλιν 580
καὶ τοὺς στρατηγούς· καὶ χάρις τιμήσεται
Διὸς τόδ' ἐκπράξασα. πάντ' ἔχεις λόγον.

ΧΟ. νικώμενος λόγοισιν οὐκ ἀναίνομαι.
ἀεὶ γὰρ ἡβᾷ τοῖς γέρουσιν εὖ μαθεῖν.
δόμοις δὲ ταῦτα καὶ Κλυταιμνήστρᾳ μέλειν 585
εἰκὸς μάλιστα, ξὺν δὲ πλουτίζειν ἐμέ.

ΚΛ. ἀνωλόλυξα μὲν πάλαι χαρᾶς ὕπο,
ὅτ' ἦλθ' ὁ πρῶτος νύχιος ἄγγελος πυρός,
φράζων ἅλωσιν Ἰλίου τ' ἀνάστασιν.
καί τίς μ' ἐνίπτων εἶπε, φρυκτωρῶν δία 590
πεισθεῖσα Τροίαν νῦν πεπορθῆσθαι δοκεῖς;
ἦ κάρτα πρὸς γυναικὸς αἴρεσθαι κέαρ.
λόγοις τοιούτοις πλαγκτὸς οὖσ' ἐφαινόμην.
ὅμως δ' ἔθυον· καὶ γυναικείῳ νόμῳ
ὀλολυγμὸν ἄλλος ἄλλοθεν κατὰ πτόλιν 595
ἔλασκον εὐφημοῦντες, ἐν θεῶν ἕδραις
θυηφάγον κοιμῶντες εὐώδη φλόγα.
καὶ νῦν τὰ μάσσω μὲν τί δεῖ σ' ἐμοὶ λέγειν;
ἄνακτος αὐτοῦ πάντα πεύσομαι λόγον.

ΑΓΑΜΕΜΝΩΝ. 23

ὅπως δ' ἄριστα τὸν ἐμὸν αἰδοῖον πόσιν 600
σπεύσω πάλιν μολόντα δέξασθαι—τί γὰρ
γυναικὶ τούτου φέγγος ἥδιον δρακεῖν,
ἀπὸ στρατείας ἀνδρὶ σώσαντος θεοῦ
πύλας ἀνοῖξαι;—ταῦτ' ἀπάγγειλον πόσει·
ἥκειν ὅπως τάχιστ' ἐράσμιον πόλει. 605
γυναῖκα πιστὴν δ' ἐν δόμοις εὕροι μολὼν
οἵανπερ οὖν ἔλειπε, δωμάτων κύνα
ἐσθλὴν ἐκείνῳ, πολεμίαν τοῖς δύσφροσιν,
καὶ τἄλλ' ὁμοίαν πάντα, σημαντήριον
οὐδὲν διαφθείρασαν ἐν μήκει χρόνου. 610
οὐδ' οἶδα τέρψιν, οὐδ' ἐπίψογον φάτιν,
ἄλλου πρὸς ἀνδρὸς μᾶλλον ἢ χαλκοῦ βαφάς.
τοιόσδ' ὁ κόμπος τῆς ἀληθείας γέμων
οὐκ αἰσχρὸς ὡς γυναικὶ γενναίᾳ λακεῖν.
ΧΟ. αὕτη μὲν οὕτως εἶπε μανθάνοντί σοι 615
τοροῖσιν ἑρμηνεῦσιν εὐπρεπῶς λόγον.
σὺ δ' εἰπέ, κῆρυξ, Μενέλεων δὲ πεύθομαι,
εἰ νόστιμός γε καὶ σεσωσμένος πάλιν
ἥξει ξὺν ὑμῖν, τῆσδε γῆς φίλον κράτος.
ΚΗ. οὐκ ἔσθ' ὅπως λέξαιμι τὰ ψευδῆ καλὰ 620
ἐς τὸν πολὺν φίλοισι καρποῦσθαι χρόνον.
ΧΟ. πῶς δῆτ' ἂν εἰπὼν κεδνὰ τἀληθῆ *τύχοις;
σχισθέντα δ' οὐκ εὔκρυπτα γίγνεται τάδε.
- ΚΗ. ἀνὴρ ἄφαντος ἐξ Ἀχαϊκοῦ στρατοῦ,
αὐτός τε καὶ τὸ πλοῖον. οὐ ψευδῆ λέγω. 625
ΧΟ. πότερον ἀναχθεὶς ἐμφανῶς ἐξ Ἰλίου,
ἢ χεῖμα, κοινὸν ἄχθος, ἥρπασε στρατοῦ;
ΚΗ. ἔκυρσας ὥστε τοξότης ἄκρος σκοποῦ·

613. ΚΗ. MSS. 622. τύχης Fl. τυχ⁵ Fa. 624. ἀνήρ MSS.
corr. H.

μακρὸν δὲ πῆμα ξυντόμως ἐφημίσω.
ΧΟ. πότερα γὰρ αὐτοῦ ζῶντος ἢ τεθνηκότος 630
φάτις πρὸς ἄλλων ναυτίλων ἐκλῄζετο;
ΚΗ. οὐκ οἶδεν οὐδεὶς ὥστ' ἀπαγγεῖλαι τορῶς,
πλὴν τοῦ τρέφοντος Ἡλίου χθονὸς φύσιν.
ΧΟ. πῶς γὰρ λέγεις χειμῶνα ναυτικῷ στρατῷ
ἐλθεῖν τελευτῆσαί τε δαιμόνων κότῳ; 635
ΚΗ. εὔφημον ἦμαρ οὐ πρέπει κακαγγέλῳ
γλώσσῃ μιαίνειν· χωρὶς ἡ τιμὴ θεῶν.
ὅταν δ' ἀπευκτὰ πήματ' ἄγγελος πόλει
στυγνῷ προσώπῳ πτωσίμου στρατοῦ φέρῃ,
πόλει μὲν ἕλκος ἓν τὸ δήμιον τυχεῖν, 640
πολλοὺς δὲ πολλῶν ἐξαγισθέντας δόμων
ἄνδρας διπλῇ μάστιγι, τὴν Ἄρης φιλεῖ,
δίλογχον ἄτην, φοινίαν ξυνωρίδα·
τοιῶνδε μέντοι πημάτων *σεσαγμένον
πρέπει λέγειν παιᾶνα τόνδ' Ἐρινύων· 645
σωτηρίων δὲ πραγμάτων εὐάγγελον
ἥκοντα πρὸς χαίρουσαν εὐεστοῖ πόλιν,
πῶς κεδνὰ τοῖς κακοῖσι συμμίξω, λέγων
χειμῶν' *Ἀχαιοῖς οὐκ ἀμήνιτον *θεῶν;
ξυνώμοσαν γάρ, ὄντες ἔχθιστοι τὸ πρίν, 650
πῦρ καὶ θάλασσα, καὶ τὰ πίστ' ἐδειξάτην,
φθείροντε τὸν δύστηνον Ἀργείων στρατόν.
ἐν νυκτὶ δυσκύμαντα δ' ὠρώρει κακά.
ναῦς γὰρ πρὸς ἀλλήλαισι Θρῄκιαι πνοαὶ
ἤρεικον· αἱ δὲ κεροτυπούμεναι βίᾳ 655
χειμῶνι τυφῶ σὺν ζάλῃ τ' ὀμβροκτύπῳ
ᾤχοντ' ἄφαντοι, ποιμένος κακοῦ στρόβῳ.

644. σεσαγμένων MSS. 649. Ἀχαιῶν ... θεοῖς MSS. corr.
Dobr. H.   655. ἤρειπον Fa. κερωτυπούμεναι MSS.

ΑΓΑΜΕΜΝΩΝ.

ἐπεὶ δ' ἀνῆλθε λαμπρὸν ἡλίου φάος,
ὁρῶμεν ἀνθοῦν πέλαγος Αἰγαῖον νεκροῖς
ἀνδρῶν Ἀχαιῶν ναυτικοῖς τ' ἐρειπίοις. 660
ἡμᾶς γε μὲν δὴ ναῦν τ' ἀκήρατον σκάφος
ἤτοι τις ἐξέκλεψεν ἢ 'ξῃτήσατο
θεός τις, οὐκ ἄνθρωπος, οἴακος θιγών.
τύχῃ δὲ σωτὴρ ναῦν θέλουσ' ἐφέζετο,
ὡς μήτ' ἐν ὅρμῳ κύματος ζάλην ἔχειν 665
μήτ' ἐξοκεῖλαι πρὸς κραταίλεων χθόνα.
ἔπειτα δ' Ἅιδην πόντιον πεφευγότες,
λευκὸν κατ' ἦμαρ, οὐ πεποιθότες τύχῃ,
ἐβουκολοῦμεν φροντίσιν νέον πάθος,
στρατοῦ καμόντος καὶ κακῶς σποδουμένου. 670
καὶ νῦν ἐκείνων εἴ τις ἐστὶν ἐμπνέων,
λέγουσιν ἡμᾶς ὡς ὀλωλότας, τί μή;
ἡμεῖς τ' ἐκείνους ταῦτ' ἔχειν δοξάζομεν.
γένοιτο δ' ὡς ἄριστα. Μενέλεων γὰρ οὖν
πρῶτόν τε καὶ μάλιστα προσδόκα μολεῖν. 675
εἰ δ' οὖν τις ἀκτὶς ἡλίου νιν ἱστορεῖ
καὶ ζῶντα καὶ βλέποντα, μηχαναῖς Διός,
οὔπω θέλοντος ἐξαναλῶσαι γένος,
ἐλπίς τις αὐτὸν πρὸς δόμους ἥξειν πάλιν.
τοσαῦτ' ἀκούσας ἴσθι τἀληθῆ κλύων. 680

ΧΟ. τίς ποτ' ὠνόμαζεν ὧδ' στρ. α'.
ἐς τὸ πᾶν ἐτητύμως—
μή τις ὅντιν' οὐχ ὁρῶ-
μεν προνοίαισι τοῦ πεπρωμένου
γλῶσσαν ἐν τύχᾳ νέμων;— 685
τὰν δορίγαμβρον ἀμφινεικῆ θ' Ἑλέναν;
ἐπεὶ πρεπόντως

---

660. ναυτικῶν τ' ἐριπίων MSS. corr. Aur.   673. ταῦτ' MSS.
corr. Stanl.

ΑΙΣΧΥΛΟΥ

ἑλένας, ἕλανδρος, ἑλέπτολις,
ἐκ τῶν ἁβροτίμων   690
προκαλυμμάτων ἔπλευσε
ζεφύρου γίγαντος αὔρᾳ,
πολύανδροί τε φεράσπιδες
κυναγοὶ κατ' ἴχνος
* πλατᾶν ἄφαντον   695
κέλσαντες Σιμόεντος
ἀκτὰς * ἐπ' ἀεξιφύλλους
δι' ἔριν αἱματόεσσαν.
Ἰλίῳ δὲ κῆδος ὀρ-   ἀντ. α'.
θώνυμον τελεσσίφρων   700
μῆνις ἤλασεν, τραπέ-
ζας * ἀτίμωσιν ὑστέρῳ χρόνῳ
καὶ ξυνεστίου Διὸς
πρασσομένα τὸ νυμφότιμον μέλος ἐκ-   705
φάτως τίοντας,
ὑμέναιον, ὃς τότ' ἐπέρρεπεν
γαμβροῖσιν ἀείδειν.
μεταμανθάνουσα δ' ὕμνον
Πριάμου πόλις γεραιὰ   710
πολύθρηνον μέγα που στένει,
κικλήσκουσα Πάριν
τὸν αἰνόλεκτρον,
* παμπορθῆ πολύθρηνον
αἰῶνα * διαὶ πολιτᾶν   715
μέλεον αἷμ' ἀνατλᾶσα·
ἔθρεψεν δὲ * λέοντος ἶ-   στρ. β'.
νιν δόμοις ἀγάλακτον οὕ-

695. πλάταν MSS. corr. Heath.   697. ἐπ' ἀξιφ. Fl. εἰς ἀεξιφ. Fa.
703. ἀτίμως Fa. ἀρίμως ἴν' Fl. corr. Cant.   714. παμπρόσθη MSS.
715. ἀμφὶ πολίταν MSS.   717. λέοντα σίνιν MSS. corr. Conington.

ΑΓΑΜΕΜΝΩΝ. 27

τως ἀνὴρ φιλόμαστον,
ἐν βιότου προτελείοις 720
ἄμερον, εὐφιλόπαιδα,
καὶ γεραροῖς ἐπίχαρτον.
πολέα δ᾽ *ἔσκ᾽ ἐν ἀγκάλαις,
νεοτρόφου τέκνου δίκαν,
φαιδρωπὸς ποτὶ χεῖρα, σαί- 725
νων τε γαστρὸς ἀνάγκαις.
χρονισθεὶς δ᾽ ἀπέδειξεν * ἦ-   ἀντ. β΄. 727
θος τὸ πρὸς τοκέων· χάριν
γὰρ τροφεῦσιν ἀμείβων,
μηλοφόνοισι *σὺν ἄταις 730
δαῖτ᾽ ἀκέλευστος ἔτευξεν·
αἵματι δ᾽ οἶκος ἐφύρθη·
ἄμαχον ἄλγος οἰκέταις,
μέγα σίνος πολυκτόνον·
ἐκ θεοῦ δ᾽ ἱερεύς τις ἄ- 735
τας δόμοις *προσεθρέφθη.
παρ᾽ αὐτὰ δ᾽ ἐλθεῖν ἐς Ἰλίου πόλιν   στρ. γ΄ 737
λέγοιμ᾽ ἂν φρόνημα μὲν
νηνέμου γαλάνας, 740
ἀκασκαῖον *δ᾽ ἄγαλμα πλούτου,
μαλθακὸν ὀμμάτων βέλος,
δηξίθυμον ἔρωτος ἄνθος.
παρακλίνασ᾽ ἐπέκρανεν
δὲ γάμου πικρὰς τελευτάς,
δύσεδρος καὶ δυσόμιλος

723. ἔσχ᾽ MSS. c   as.   727. ἔθος MSS. ἦθος Con.
729. τροφᾶς γὰρ Fl. Text Fa.   730. μηλοφόνοισιν ἄταις Fa.
μ. ἄταισιν Fl.   735. προσετράφη MSS. corr. Heath.   737.
πάραντα MSS.   δ᾽ Fl.   δ᾽ οὖν Fa.   741. MSS. om. δ᾽.   745.

συμένα Πριαμίδαισιν,
πομπᾷ Διὸς ξενίου,
νυμφόκλαυτος Ἐρινύς.
παλαίφατος δ' ἐν βροτοῖς γέρων λόγος   ἀντ. γ'.   750
τέτυκται, μέγαν τελεσ-
θέντα φωτὸς ὄλβον
τεκνοῦσθαι μηδ' ἄπαιδα θνῄσκειν,
ἐκ δ' ἀγαθᾶς τύχας γένει   755
βλαστάνειν ἀκόρεστον οἰζύν.
δίχα δ' ἄλλων μονόφρων εἰ-
μί. τὸ δυσσεβὲς γὰρ ἔργον
μετὰ μὲν πλείονα τίκτει,
σφετέρα δ' εἰκότα γέννᾳ.   760
οἴκων δ' ἄρ' εὐθυδίκων
καλλίπαις πότμος ἀεί.
φιλεῖ δὲ τίκτειν ὕβρις   στρ. δ'.
μὲν παλαιὰ νεά-
ζουσαν ἐν κακοῖς βροτῶν   765
ὕβριν τότ' ἢ τόθ', *ὅτε τὸ κύριον μόλῃ
*φάος τόκου,
δαίμονά τε *τὰν ἄμαχον, ἀπόλεμον,
ἀνίερον θράσος, μελαίνας μελάθροισιν ἄτας,   770
*εἰδομένας τοκεῦσιν.
δίκα δὲ λάμπει μὲν ἐν   ἀντ. δ'.
δυσκάπνοις δώμασιν,
τὸν δ' ἐναίσιμον τίει [βίον]·
τὰ χρυσόπαστα δ' *ἔδεθλα σὺν πίνῳ χερῶν   775
παλιντρόποις

755. γὰρ δυσσεβές MSS.   766. ὅταν MSS. ὅτε Kl.   767
νεαρὰ φάους κότον Fl. Fa.   νέα δ' ἔφυσεν κύρον Pal.   φάος τόκου
Ahr.   769. τὸν MSS. ἄμαχον om. Fa.   771. εἰδομέναν MSS.
775. βίον MSS. prob. corrupt.   776. ἐσθλὰ MSS. corr. Aurat.

ΑΓΑΜΕΜΝΩΝ.

ὄμμασι λιποῦσ᾽ ὅσια *προσέμολε
δύναμιν οὐ σέβουσα πλούτου παράσημον αἴνῳ· 780
πᾶν δ᾽ ἐπὶ τέρμα νωμᾷ.
ἄγε δή, βασιλεῦ, Τροίας πτολίπορθ᾽,
Ἀτρέως γένεθλον,
πῶς σε προσείπω ; πῶς σε σεβίζω, 785
μήθ᾽ ὑπεράρας μήθ᾽ ὑποκάμψας
καιρὸν χάριτος ;
πολλοὶ δὲ βροτῶν τὸ δοκεῖν εἶναι
προτίουσι δίκην παραβάντες. ?
τῷ δυσπραγοῦντι δ᾽ ἐπιστενάχειν 790
πᾶς τις ἕτοιμος· δῆγμα δὲ λύπης
οὐδὲν ἐφ᾽ ἧπαρ προσικνεῖται,
καὶ ξυγχαίρουσιν ὁμοιοπρεπεῖς
ἀγέλαστα πρόσωπα βιαζόμενοι.
(ὅστις δ᾽ ἀγαθὸς προβατογνώμων,) 795
οὐκ ἔστι λαθεῖν ὄμματα φωτὸς
τὰ δοκοῦντ᾽ εὔφρονος ἐκ διανοίας
ὑδαρεῖ σαίνειν φιλότητι.
σὺ δέ μοι τότε μὲν στέλλων στρατιὰν
Ἑλένης ἕνεκ᾽, οὐ γάρ *σ᾽ ἐπικεύσω, 800
κάρτ᾽ ἀπομούσως ἦσθα γεγραμμένος,
οὐδ᾽ εὖ πραπίδων οἴακα νέμων
θράσος *ἐκ θυσιῶν
ἀνδράσι θνήσκουσι κομίζων.
νῦν δ᾽ οὐκ ἀπ᾽ ἄκρας φρενὸς οὐδ᾽ ἀφίλως· 805
εὔφρων *πνόος εὖ τελέσασι.
γνώσει δὲ χρόνῳ διαπευθόμενος

779. προσέβα τον MSS. corr. H.   791. δεῖγμα Fl.   800. σ᾽
omit. MSS. corr. Musgr.   803. ἑκούσιον MSS. text Franz.   806.
πόνος MSS.   πνόος Weil.

τόν τε δικαίως καὶ τὸν ἀκαίρως
πόλιν οἰκουροῦντα πολιτῶν.

ΑΓΑΜΕΜΝΩΝ.

πρῶτον μὲν Ἄργος καὶ θεοὺς ἐγχωρίους   810
δίκη προσειπεῖν, τοὺς ἐμοὶ μεταιτίους
νόστου δικαίων θ᾽ ὧν ἐπραξάμην πόλιν
Πριάμου. δίκας γὰρ οὐκ ἀπὸ γλώσσης θεοὶ
κλύοντες ἀνδροκμῆτας Ἰλίου φθορὰς
εἰς αἱματηρὸν τεῦχος οὐ διχορρόπως
ψήφους ἔθεντο· τῷ δ᾽ ἐναντίῳ κύτει
ἐλπὶς προσῄει χειρὸς οὐ πληρουμένῳ.
καπνῷ δ᾽ ἁλοῦσα νῦν ἔτ᾽ εὔσημος πόλις.
ἄτης θύελλαι ζῶσι· συνθνῄσκουσα δὲ
σποδὸς προπέμπει πίονας πλούτου πνοάς.   820
τούτων θεοῖσι χρὴ πολύμνηστον χάριν
τίνειν, ἐπείπερ καὶ πάγας ὑπερκότους
ἐφραξάμεσθα, καὶ γυναικὸς οὕνεκα
πόλιν διημάθυνεν Ἀργεῖον δάκος,
ἵππου νεοσσός, ἀσπιδοστρόφος λεώς,   825
πήδημ᾽ ὀρούσας ἀμφὶ Πλειάδων δύσιν·
ὑπερθορὼν δὲ πύργον ὠμηστὴς λέων
ἄδην ἔλειξεν αἵματος τυραννικοῦ.
θεοῖς μὲν ἐξέτεινα φροίμιον τόδε·
τὰ δ᾽ ἐς τὸ σὸν φρόνημα, μέμνημαι κλύων,   830
καὶ φημὶ ταὐτὰ καὶ συνήγορόν μ᾽ ἔχεις.
παύροις γὰρ ἀνδρῶν ἐστι συγγενὲς τόδε,
φίλον τὸν εὐτυχοῦντ᾽ ἄνευ φθόνου σέβειν.
δύσφρων γὰρ ἰὸς καρδίαν προσήμενος

823. ἐπραξάμεσθα MSS. corr. Franck.   831. ταῦτα MSS.

ΑΓΑΜΕΜΝΩΝ. 31

ἄχθος διπλοίζει τῷ πεπαμένῳ νόσον, 835
τοῖς τ' αὐτὸς αὐτοῦ πήμασιν βαρύνεται
καὶ τὸν θυραῖον ὄλβον εἰσορῶν στένει·
εἰδὼς λέγοιμ' ἄν, εὖ γὰρ ἐξεπίσταμαι
ὁμιλίας κάτοπτρον, εἴδωλον σκιᾶς,
δοκοῦντας εἶναι κάρτα πρευμενεῖς ἐμοί. 840
μόνος δ' Ὀδυσσεύς, ὅσπερ οὐχ ἑκὼν ἔπλει,
ζευχθεὶς ἕτοιμος ἦν ἐμοὶ σειραφόρος·
εἴτ' οὖν θανόντος εἴτε καὶ ζῶντος πέρι
λέγω. τὰ δ' ἄλλα πρὸς πόλιν τε καὶ θεοὺς
κοινοὺς ἀγῶνας θέντες ἐν πανηγύρει 845
βουλευσόμεσθα. καὶ τὸ μὲν καλῶς ἔχον
ὅπως χρονίζον εὖ μενεῖ βουλευτέον·
ὅτῳ δὲ καὶ δεῖ φαρμάκων παιωνίων,
ἤτοι κέαντες ἢ τεμόντες εὐφρόνως
πειρασόμεσθα * πῆμ' ἀποστρέψαι νόσου. 850
νῦν δ' ἐς μέλαθρα καὶ δόμους ἐφεστίους
ἐλθὼν θεοῖσι πρῶτα δεξιώσομαι,
οἵπερ πρόσω πέμψαντες ἤγαγον πάλιν.
νίκη δ' ἐπείπερ ἕσπετ', ἐμπέδως μένοι.
Κλ. ἄνδρες πολῖται, πρέσβος Ἀργείων τόδε, 855
οὐκ αἰσχυνοῦμαι τοὺς φιλάνορας τρόπους
λέξαι πρὸς ὑμᾶς· ἐν χρόνῳ δ' ἀποφθίνει
τὸ τάρβος ἀνθρώποισιν. οὐκ ἄλλων πάρα
μαθοῦσ', ἐμαυτῆς δύσφορον λέξω βίον,
τοσόνδ' ὅσονπερ οὗτος ἦν ὑπ' Ἰλίῳ. 860
τὸ μὲν γυναῖκα πρῶτον ἄρσενος δίχα
ἧσθαι δόμοις ἔρημον ἔκπαγλον κακόν,
πολλὰς κλύουσαν * κληδόνας παλιγκότους·

850. πήματος τρέψαι νόσον MSS. corr. Pors. 863. ἡδονὰς MSS.
corr. Aur.

καὶ τὸν μὲν ἥκειν, τὸν δ' ἐπεσφέρειν κακοῦ
κάκιον ἄλλο πῆμα, λάσκοντας δόμοις. 865
καὶ τραυμάτων μὲν εἰ τόσων ἐτύγχανεν
ἀνὴρ ὅδ', ὡς πρὸς οἶκον ὠχετεύετο
φάτις, *τέτρηται δικτύου πλέον λέγειν.
εἰ δ' ἦν τεθνηκώς, ὡς ἐπλήθυον λόγοι,
τρισώματός τἂν Γηρυὼν ὁ δεύτερος 870
[πολλὴν ἄνωθεν, τὴν κάτω γὰρ οὐ λέγω]
χθονὸς τρίμοιρον χλαῖναν ἐξηύχει *λαβεῖν,
ἅπαξ ἑκάστῳ κατθανὼν μορφώματι.
τοιῶνδ' ἕκατι κληδόνων παλιγκότων
πολλὰς ἄνωθεν ἀρτάνας ἐμῆς δέρης 875
ἔλυσαν ἄλλοι πρὸς βίαν λελημμένης.
ἐκ τῶνδέ τοι παῖς ἐνθάδ' οὐ παραστατεῖ,
ἐμῶν τε καὶ σῶν κύριος *πιστωμάτων,
ὡς χρῆν, Ὀρέστης· μηδὲ θαυμάσῃς τόδε·
τρέφει γὰρ αὐτὸν εὐμενὴς δορύξενος 880
Στρόφιος ὁ Φωκεύς, ἀμφίλεκτα πήματα
ἐμοὶ προφωνῶν, τόν θ' ὑπ' Ἰλίῳ σέθεν
κίνδυνον, εἴ τε δημόθρους ἀναρχία
βουλὴν καταρρίψειεν, ὥστε σύγγονον
βροτοῖσι τὸν πεσόντα λακτίσαι πλέον. 885
τοιάδε μέντοι σκῆψις οὐ δόλον φέρει.
ἔμοιγε μὲν δὴ κλαυμάτων ἐπίσσυτοι
πηγαὶ κατεσβήκασιν, οὐδ' ἔνι σταγών.
ἐν ὀψικοίτοις δ' ὄμμασι βλάβας ἔχω,
τὰς ἀμφί σοι κλαίουσα λαμπτηρουχίας 890
ἀτημελήτους αἰέν. ἐν δ' ὀνείρασι

867. ἀνήρ MSS. 868. τέτρωται MSS. text Ahr. 871. No
doubt corrupt. 872. λαβὼν MSS. corr. K. Pal. 878. πιστευμάτων MSS. corr. H.

ΑΓΑΜΕΜΝΩΝ.

λεπταῖς ὑπαὶ κώνωπος ἐξηγειρόμην
ῥιπαῖσι θωΰσσοντος, ἀμφί σοι πάθη
ὁρῶσα πλείω τοῦ ξυνεύδοντος χρόνου.
νῦν ταῦτα πάντα τλᾶσ᾽, ἀπενθήτῳ φρενὶ 895
λέγοιμ᾽ ἂν ἄνδρα τόνδε, τῶν σταθμῶν κύνα,
σωτῆρα ναὸς πρότονον, ὑψηλῆς στέγης
στῦλον ποδήρη, μονογενὲς τέκνον πατρί,
καὶ γῆν φανεῖσαν ναυτίλοις παρ᾽ ἐλπίδα,
κάλλιστον ἦμαρ εἰσιδεῖν ἐκ χείματος, 900
ὁδοιπόρῳ διψῶντι πηγαῖον ῥέος.
τερπνὸν δὲ τἀναγκαῖον ἐκφυγεῖν ἅπαν.
τοιοῖσδέ *τοί νιν ἀξιῶ προσφθέγμασιν.
φθόνος δ᾽ ἀπέστω· πολλὰ γὰρ τὰ πρὶν κακὰ
ἠνειχόμεσθα· νῦν δέ μοι, φίλον κάρα, 905
ἔκβαιν᾽ ἀπήνης τῆσδε, μὴ χαμαὶ τιθεὶς
τὸν σὸν πόδ᾽, ὦναξ, Ἰλίου πορθήτορα.
δμωαί, τί μέλλεθ᾽, αἷς ἐπέσταλται τέλος
πέδον κελεύθου στρωννύναι πετάσμασιν;
εὐθὺς γενέσθω πορφυρόστρωτος πόρος 910
ἐς δῶμ᾽ ἄελπτον ὡς ἂν ἡγῆται δίκη.
τὰ δ᾽ ἄλλα φροντὶς οὐχ ὕπνῳ νικωμένη
θήσει δικαίως σὺν θεοῖς εἱμαρμένα.

ΑΓ. Λήδας γένεθλον, δωμάτων ἐμῶν φύλαξ,
ἀπουσίᾳ μὲν εἶπας εἰκότως ἐμῇ· 915
μακρὰν γὰρ ἐξέτεινας· ἀλλ᾽ ἐναισίμως
αἰνεῖν, παρ᾽ ἄλλων χρὴ τόδ᾽ ἔρχεσθαι γέρας·
καὶ τἆλλα μὴ γυναικὸς ἐν τρόποις ἐμὲ
ἅβρυνε μηδὲ βαρβάρου φωτὸς δίκην
χαμαιπετὲς βόαμα προσχάνῃς ἐμοί, 920
μηδ᾽ εἵμασι στρώσασ᾽ ἐπίφθονον πόρον

903. τοίνυν MSS. corr. Schütz.

τίθει· θεούς τοι τοῖσδε τιμαλφεῖν χρεών·
ἐν ποικίλοις δὲ θνητὸν ὄντα κάλλεσιν
βαίνειν ἐμοὶ μὲν οὐδαμῶς ἄνευ φόβου.
λέγω κατ' ἄνδρα, μὴ θεόν, σέβειν ἐμέ. 925
χωρὶς ποδοψήστρων τε καὶ τῶν ποικίλων
κληδὼν ἀϋτεῖ· καὶ τὸ μὴ κακῶς φρονεῖν
θεοῦ μέγιστον δῶρον. ὀλβίσαι δὲ χρὴ
βίον τελευτήσαντ' ἐν εὐεστοῖ φίλῃ.
εἰ πάντα δ' ὣς πράσσοιμ' ἄν, εὐθαρσὴς ἐγώ. 930
ΚΛ. καὶ μὴν τόδ' εἰπὲ μὴ παρὰ γνώμην ἐμοί.
ΑΓ. γνώμην μὲν ἴσθι μὴ διαφθεροῦντ' ἐμέ.
ΚΛ. ηὔξω θεοῖς δείσας ἂν ὧδ' ἔρδειν τάδε;
ΑΓ. εἴπερ τις, εἰδώς γ' εὖ τόδ' ἐξεῖπον τέλος.
ΚΛ. τί δ' ἂν δοκεῖ σοι Πρίαμος εἰ τάδ' ἤνυσεν; 935
ΑΓ. ἐν ποικίλοις ἂν κάρτα μοι βῆναι δοκεῖ.
ΚΛ. μή νυν τὸν ἀνθρώπειον αἰδεσθῇς ψόγον.
ΑΓ. φήμη γε μέντοι δημόθρους μέγα σθένει.
ΚΛ. ὁ δ' ἀφθόνητός γ' οὐκ ἐπίζηλος πέλει.
ΑΓ. οὔτοι γυναικός ἐστιν ἱμείρειν μάχης. 940
ΚΛ. τοῖς δ' ὀλβίοις γε καὶ τὸ νικᾶσθαι πρέπει.
ΑΓ. ἦ καὶ σὺ νίκην τήνδε δήριος τίεις;
ΚΛ. πιθοῦ· κράτος μέντοι πάρες γ' ἑκὼν ἐμοί.
ΑΓ. ἀλλ' εἰ δοκεῖ σοι ταῦθ', ὑπαί τις ἀρβύλας
λύοι τάχος πρόδουλον ἔμβασιν ποδός, 945
καὶ τοῖσδέ μ' ἐμβαίνονθ' ἁλουργέσιν θεῶν
μή τις πρόσωθεν ὄμματος βάλοι φθόνος.
πολλὴ γὰρ αἰδὼς *δωματοφθορεῖν ποσὶ
φθείροντα πλοῦτον ἀργυρωνήτους θ' ὑφάς.
τούτων μὲν οὕτω· τὴν ξένην δὲ πρευμενῶς 950

930. πράσσοιμεν H. 946. σὺν ταῖσδέ Fa. text Fl. 948.
δωματοφθορεῖν MSS. δωμ. Schütz.

ΑΓΑΜΕΜΝΩΝ.

τήνδ' ἐσκόμιζε· τὸν κρατοῦντα μαλθακῶς
θεὸς πρόσωθεν εὐμενῶς προσδέρκεται.
ἑκὼν γὰρ οὐδεὶς δουλίῳ χρῆται ζυγῷ.
αὕτη δὲ πολλῶν χρημάτων ἐξαίρετον
ἄνθος, στρατοῦ δώρημ', ἐμοὶ ξυνέσπετο. 955
ἐπεὶ δ' ἀκούειν σοῦ κατέστραμμαι τάδε,
εἶμ' ἐς δόμων μέλαθρα, πορφύρας πατῶν.
ΚΛ. ἔστιν θάλασσα, τίς δέ νιν κατασβέσει;
τρέφουσα πολλῆς πορφύρας * ἰσάργυρον
κηκῖδα παγκαίνιστον, εἱμάτων βαφάς. 960
οἶκος δ' ὑπάρχει τῶνδε σὺν θεοῖς, ἄναξ,
ἔχειν· πένεσθαι δ' οὐκ ἐπίσταται δόμος.
πολλῶν πατησμὸν δ' εἱμάτων ἂν ηὐξάμην,
δόμοισι προὐνεχθέντος ἐν χρηστηρίοις,
ψυχῆς κόμιστρα τῆσδε μηχανωμένῃ. 965
ῥίζης γὰρ οὔσης φυλλὰς ἵκετ' ἐς δόμους,
σκιὰν ὑπερτείνασα σειρίου κυνός.
καὶ σοῦ μολόντος δωματῖτιν ἑστίαν,
θάλπος μὲν ἐν χειμῶνι σημαίνεις μολόν·
ὅταν δὲ τεύχῃ Ζεὺς ἀπ' ὄμφακος πικρᾶς 970
οἶνον, τότ' ἤδη ψῦχος ἐν δόμοις πέλει,
ἀνδρὸς τελείου δῶμ' ἐπιστρωφωμένου.
Ζεῦ Ζεῦ τέλειε, τὰς ἐμὰς εὐχὰς τέλει·
μέλοι δέ τοι σοὶ τῶνπερ ἂν μέλλῃς τελεῖν.
ΧΟ. τίπτε μοι τόδ' ἐμπέδως στρ. α'. 975
δεῖμα προστατήριον
καρδίας τερασκόπου ποτᾶται,
μαντιπολεῖ δ' ἀκέλευστος ἄμισθος ἀοιδά·

959. εἰς ἄργυρον MSS.   965. μηχανωμένης MSS. corr. H.
969. μολών MSS.   970. Ζεύς τ' MSS.   976. δεῖγμα Fl. δεῖμα Fa.

36   ΑΙΣΧΥΛΟΥ

οὐδ' ἀποπτύσαι δίκαν   980
δυσκρίτων ὀνειράτων
θάρσος εὔπιθὲς ἵζει
φρενὸς φίλον θρόνον; †χρόνος δ' ἐπὶ
πρυμνησίων *ξυνεμβολαῖς
ψαμμίας ἀκάτας παρή-   985
βησεν, εὖθ' ὑπ' Ἴλιον
ὦρτο ναυβάτας στρατός.
πεύθομαι δ' ἀπ' ὀμμάτων   ἀντ. α'.
νόστον, αὐτόμαρτυς ὤν·
τὸν δ' ἄνευ λύρας *ὅμως ὑμνῳδεῖ   990
θρῆνον Ἐρινύος αὐτοδίδακτος ἔσωθεν
θυμός, οὐ τὸ πᾶν ἔχων
ἐλπίδος φίλον θράσος.
σπλάγχνα δ' *οὔτι ματάζει   995
πρὸς ἐνδίκοις φρεσὶν τελεσφόροις
δίναις κυκλούμενον κέαρ.
εὔχομαι δ' ἀπ' ἐμᾶς *τοιαῦτ'
ἐλπίδος ψύθη πεσεῖν,
ἐς τὸ μὴ τελεσφόρον.   1000
μάλα γέ τοι *τὸ μεγάλας ὑγιείας   στρ. β'.
ἀκόρεστον τέρμα. νόσος γὰρ *ἀεὶ
γείτων ὁμότοιχος ἐρείδει,
καὶ πότμος εὐθυπορῶν   1005
  *   *   *   *   *
ἀνδρὸς ἔπαισεν ἄφαντον ἔρμα.
καὶ τὸ μὲν πρὸ χρημάτων

980. ἀποπτύσας Fl. text Fa.   982. ἵζει MSS. corr. Scal.
983. ἐπεὶ Fl.   984. ξυνεμβόλοις MSS.   990. ὅπως MSS.   991.
Ἐρινύς MSS.   995. οὔτοι MSS.   998. ἐξ ἐμᾶς Fl.   τοι Fa. om.
Fl. τοιαῦτ' K.   1001. γάρ τοι Fl. γέ τοι δὴ Fa. τᾶς πολλᾶς MSS.
text Pal.   τὸ πολέος Enger.   1002. om. ἀεὶ MSS.   1006. line
omitted probably.

ΑΓΑΜΕΜΝΩΝ.

κτησίων ὄκνος βαλών,
σφενδόνας ἀπ' εὐμέτρου,— 1010
οὐκ ἔδυ πρόπας δόμος
πημονᾶς γέμων ἄγαν,
οὐδ' ἐπόντισε σκάφος.
πολλά τοι δόσις ἐκ Διὸς ἀμφιλαφής τε καὶ ἐξ
ἀλόκων ἐπετειᾶν 1015
νῆστιν ὤλεσεν νόσον.
τὸ δ' ἐπὶ γᾶν *πεσὸν ἅπαξ θανάσιμον ἀντ. β'.
προπάροιθ' ἀνδρὸς μέλαν αἷμα τίς ἂν 1020
πάλιν ἀγκαλέσαιτ' ἐπαείδων ;
οὐδὲ τὸν ὀρθοδαῆ
τῶν φθιμένων ἀνάγειν
Ζεὺς *ἀπέπαυσεν ἐπ' εὐλαβείᾳ ; †
εἰ δὲ μὴ τεταγμένα 1025
μοῖρα μοῖραν ἐκ θεῶν
εἶργε μὴ πλέον φέρειν,
προφθάσασα καρδία
γλῶσσαν ἂν τάδ' ἐξέχει.
νῦν δ' ὑπὸ σκότῳ βρέμει 1030
θυμαλγής τε καὶ οὐδὲν ἐπελπομένα ποτὲ καίριον
ἐκτολυπεύσειν,
ζωπυρουμένας φρενός.
ΚΛ. εἴσω κομίζου καὶ σύ, Κασσάνδραν λέγω, 1035
ἐπεί σ' ἔθηκε Ζεὺς ἀμηνίτως δόμοις
κοινωνὸν εἶναι χερνίβων, πολλῶν μετὰ
δούλων, σταθεῖσαν κτησίου βωμοῦ πέλας.
ἔκβαιν' ἀπήνης τῆσδε, μηδ' ὑπερφρόνει.
καὶ παῖδα γάρ τοι φασὶν Ἀλκμήνης ποτὲ 1040

1019. πεσόνθ' ἅπαξ MSS. 1024. αὖτ' ἔπαυσεν MSS. text
Hartung. ἐπ' ἀβλαβείᾳ γε Fa. text Fl.

38   ΑΙΣΧΥΛΟΥ

πραθέντα τλῆναι καὶ ζυγῶν θιγεῖν βίᾳ.
εἰ δ' οὖν ἀνάγκη τῆσδ' ἐπιρρέποι τύχης,
ἀρχαιοπλούτων δεσποτῶν πολλὴ χάρις.
οἳ δ' οὔποτ' ἐλπίσαντες ἤμησαν καλῶς,
ὠμοί τε δούλοις πάντα καὶ παρὰ στάθμην.   1045
ἔχεις παρ' ἡμῶν οἷάπερ νομίζεται.
ΧΟ. σοί τοι λέγουσα παύεται σαφῆ λόγον.
ἐντὸς δ' *ἁλοῦσα μορσίμων ἀγρευμάτων,
πείθοι' ἂν εἰ πείθοι'· ἀπειθοίης δ' ἴσως.
ΚΛ. ἀλλ' εἴπερ ἐστὶ μὴ χελιδόνος δίκην   1050
ἀγνῶτα φωνὴν βάρβαρον κεκτημένη,
ἔσω φρενῶν λέγουσα πείθω νιν λόγῳ.
ΧΟ. ἕπου. τὰ λῷστα τῶν παρεστώτων λέγει.
πείθου, λιποῦσα τόνδ' ἀμαξήρη θρόνον.
ΚΛ. οὔτοι *θυραίᾳ τῇδ' ἐμοὶ σχολὴ πάρα   1055
τρίβειν· τὰ μὲν γὰρ ἑστίας μεσομφάλου
ἕστηκεν ἤδη μῆλα πρὸς σφαγὰς πυρός,
ὡς οὔποτ' ἐλπίσασι τήνδ' ἕξειν χάριν.
σὺ δ' εἴ τι δράσεις τῶνδε, μὴ σχολὴν τίθει.
εἰ δ' ἀξυνήμων οὖσα μὴ δέχει λόγον,   1060
σὺ δ' ἀντὶ φωνῆς φράζε καρβάνῳ χερί.
ΧΟ. ἑρμηνέως ἔοικεν ἡ ξένη τοροῦ
δεῖσθαι· τρόπος δὲ θηρὸς ὡς νεαιρέτου.
ΚΛ. ἦ μαίνεταί γε καὶ κακῶν κλύει φρενῶν,
ἥτις λιποῦσα μὲν πόλιν νεαίρετον   1065
ἥκει, χαλινὸν δ' οὐκ ἐπίσταται φέρειν,
πρὶν αἱματηρὸν ἐξαφρίζεσθαι μένος.
οὐ μὴν πλέω ῥίψασ' ἀτιμωθήσομαι.

1041. τλῆναι δουλείας μάζης βία Fl. text Fa.   1042. ἐπιρρέπει
Fa.   1048. ἂν οὖσα MSS. text Haupt.   1055. θυραίαν τήνδ'
MSS.

ΑΓΑΜΕΜΝΩΝ.

ΧΟ. ἐγὼ δ', ἐποικτείρω γάρ, οὐ θυμώσομαι.
ἴθ', ὦ τάλαινα, τόνδ' ἐρημώσασ' ὄχον, 1070
*εἴκουσ' ἀνάγκῃ τῇδε καίνισον ζυγόν.

ΚΑΣΣΑΝΔΡΑ.

ὀτοτοτοῖ πόποι δᾶ. = γῆ   στρ. α'.
ὤπολλον ὤπολλον.
ΧΟ. τί ταῦτ' ἀνωτότυξας ἀμφὶ Λοξίου;
οὐ γὰρ τοιοῦτος ὥστε θρηνητοῦ τυχεῖν.   1075
ΚΑ. ὀτοτοτοῖ πόποι δᾶ.   ἀντ. α'.
ὤπολλον ὤπολλον.
ΧΟ. ἡ δ' αὖτε δυσφημοῦσα τὸν θεὸν καλεῖ
οὐδὲν προσήκοντ' ἐν γόοις παραστατεῖν.
ΚΑ. Ἄπολλον Ἄπολλον   στρ. β'. 1080
ἀγυιᾶτ' ἀπόλλων ἐμός.
ἀπώλεσας γὰρ οὐ-μόλις τὸ δεύτερον.
ΧΟ. χρήσειν ἔοικεν ἀμφὶ τῶν αὑτῆς κακῶν.
μένει τὸ θεῖον δουλίᾳ *περ ἐν φρενί....
ΚΑ. Ἄπολλον Ἄπολλον   ἀντ. β'. 1085
ἀγυιᾶτ' ἀπόλλων ἐμός.
ἆ ποῖ ποτ' ἤγαγές με; πρὸς ποίαν στέγην;
ΧΟ. πρὸς τὴν Ἀτρειδῶν· εἰ σὺ μὴ τόδ' ἐννοεῖς,
ἐγὼ λέγω σοι· καὶ τάδ' οὐκ ἐρεῖς ψύθη.
ΚΑ. μισόθεον μὲν οὖν, πολλὰ συνίστορα   στρ. γ'. 1090
αὐτόφονα κακὰ *καὶ ἀρτάνας,
ἀνδρὸς *σφαγεῖον καὶ πέδον ῥαντήριον.
ΧΟ. ἔοικεν εὖρις ἡ ξένη κυνὸς δίκην
εἶναι, ματεύει δ' ὧν *ἀνευρήσει φόνον.

1071. ἐκοῦσ' MSS. corr. Rob. 1084. παρ' ἐν M.G. παρὲν Fl.
παρὸν Fa. 1091. κἀρτάνας Fa. κἀρτάναι M.G. Fl. 1092.
σφάγιον MSS. 1094. ὧν ἂν εὑρήσῃ M.G ὧν ἐφευρήσει Fl. Fa.
corr. Pors.

ΑΙΣΧΥΛΟΥ

ΚΑ. μαρτυρίοισι γὰρ τοῖσδ' ἐπιπείθομαι· ἀντ. γ'. 1095
κλαιόμενα τάδε βρέφη σφαγάς,
ὀπτάς τε σάρκας πρὸς πατρὸς βεβρωμένας.
ΧΟ. ἦμεν κλέος σοῦ μαντικὸν πεπυσμένοι·
*τούτων προφήτας δ' οὔτινας ματεύομεν.
ΚΑ. ἰὼ πόποι, τί ποτε μήδεται;   στρ. δ'   1100
τί τόδε νέον ἄχος μέγα
μέγ' ἐν δόμοισι τοῖσδε μήδεται κακὸν
ἄφερτον φίλοισιν, δυσίατον; ἀλκὰ δ'
ἑκὰς ἀποστατεῖ.
ΧΟ. τούτων ἄϊδρίς εἰμι τῶν μαντευμάτων·   1105
ἐκεῖνα δ' ἔγνων· πᾶσα γὰρ πόλις βοᾷ.
ΚΑ. ἰὼ τάλαινα, τόδε γὰρ τελεῖς,   ἀντ. δ'.
τὸν ὁμοδέμνιον πόσιν
λουτροῖσι φαιδρύνασα—πῶς φράσω τέλος;
τάχος γὰρ τόδ' ἔσται. προτείνει δὲ χεὶρ ἐκ   1110
χερὸς *ὀρέγματα.
ΧΟ. οὔπω ξυνῆκα· νῦν γὰρ ἐξ αἰνιγμάτων
ἐπαργέμοισι θεσφάτοις ἀμηχανῶ.
ΚΑ. ἒ ἔ, παπαῖ παπαῖ, τί τόδε φαίνεται;   στρ. ε'.
ἦ δίκτυόν τι Ἅιδου;   1115
ἀλλ' ἄρκυς ἡ ξύνευνος, ἡ ξυναιτία
φόνου. στάσις δ' ἀκόρετος γένει
κατολολυξάτω θύματος λευσίμου.
ΧΟ. ποίαν Ἐρινὺν τήνδε δώμασιν κέλει
ἐπορθιάζειν; οὔ με φαιδρύνει λόγος.   1120
ἐπὶ δὲ καρδίαν ἔδραμε κροκοβαφὴς

1095. μαρτυρίοις μὲν γὰρ Fl. Fa. V. τοῖσδε πεπείθομαι MSS.
1096. τάδε M.G. τὰ Fl. Fa. V. 1098. ἦμεν G. Fl. V. ἦ μὴν M?
ἦ μὲν Fa. 1099. ἦμεν MSS. τούτων Weil. 1111. ὀρεγομένα
M.G. ὀρεγμένα Fl. Fa. V. corr. H. 1117. ἀκόρεστος MSS.

ΑΓΑΜΕΜΝΩΝ. 41

σταγών, † ἄτε * καιρία πτώσιμος
ξυνανύτει βίου δύντος, αὐγαῖς.
ταχεῖα δ' ἄτα πέλει.

ΚΑ. ἆ ἆ. ἰδοὺ ἰδού· ἄπεχε τῆς βοὸς   ἀντ. ε΄. 1125
τὸν ταῦρον· ἐν πέπλοισι
* μελαγκέρῳ λαβοῦσα μηχανήματι
τύπτει· πίτνει δ' * ἐν ἐνύδρῳ * κύτει.
δολοφόνου λέβητος τύχαν σοὶ λέγω.

ΧΟ. οὐ κομπάσαιμ' ἂν θεσφάτων γνώμων ἄκρος 1130
εἶναι, κακῷ δέ τῳ προσεικάζω τάδε.
ἀπὸ δὲ θεσφάτων τίς ἀγαθὰ φάτις
βροτοῖς στέλλεται; κακῶν γὰρ * διαὶ
πολυεπεῖς τέχναι θεσπιῳδὸν
φόβον φέρουσιν μαθεῖν.   1135

ΚΑ. ἰὼ ἰὼ ταλαίνας κακόποτμοι τύχαι.   στρ. ϛ΄.
τὸ γὰρ ἐμὸν θροῶ πάθος * ἐπεγχέαι.
ποῖ δή με δεῦρο τὴν τάλαιναν ἤγαγες;
οὐδέν ποτ' εἰ μὴ ξυνθανουμένην. τί γάρ;

ΧΟ. φρενομανής τις εἶ θεοφόρητος, ἀμ-   1140
φὶ δ' αὑτᾶς θροεῖς
νόμον ἄνομον, οἷά τις ξουθὰ
ἀκόρετος βοᾶς, φεῦ, ταλαίναις φρεσὶν
Ἴτυν Ἴτυν στένουσ' ἀμφιθαλῆ κακοῖς
ἀηδὼν βίον.   1145

ΚΑ. ἰὼ ἰὼ λιγείας μόρον ἀηδόνος·   ἀντ. ϛ΄.
* περιβάλον γὰρ οἱ πτεροφόρον δέμας

1122. καὶ δορία M. καὶ δωρία G. V. Fl.   δωρία Fa. corr. D.
1127. μελάγκερων Fa. Fl. V. and M. originally. μελαγκαίρωνι G.
1128. MSS. om. ἐν. τεύχει MSS. corr. Blom. II.   1133. διὰ M.G.
δὴ αἱ Fl. Fa. V.   1137. ἐπεγχέασα M.G.   ἐπαγχέασα V. Fl. Fa.
ἐπεγχέαι Campbell.   1143. ἀκύρεστος MSS. cf. 1117.   1147.
περεβάλοντο γὰρ M. περεβάλλοντο γὰρ G. περιβαλόντες γὰρ Fa.
Fl. V. corr. Blom.

42 ΑΙΣΧΥΛΟΥ

] θεοί, γλυκύν τ' αἰῶνα κλαυμάτων ἄτερ·
ἐμοὶ δὲ μίμνει σχισμὸς ἀμφήκει δορί.
ΧΟ. πόθεν ἐπισσύτους θεοφόρους τ' ἔχεις   1150
ματαίους δύας,
τὰ δ' ἐπίφοβα δυσφάτῳ κλαγγᾷ
μελοτυπεῖς ὁμοῦ τ' ὀρθίοις ἐν νόμοις;
πόθεν ὅρους ἔχεις θεσπεσίας ὁδοῦ
κακορρήμονας;   1155
ΚΑ. ἰὼ γάμοι γάμοι Πάριδος ὀλέθριοι φίλων· στρ. ζ'.
ἰὼ Σκαμάνδρου πάτριον ποτόν.
τότε μὲν ἀμφὶ σὰς ἀϊόνας τάλαιν'
ἠνυτόμαν τροφαῖς·
νῦν δ' ἀμφὶ Κωκυτόν τε κἀχερουσίους   1160
ὄχθους ἔοικα θεσπιῳδήσειν τάχα.
ΧΟ. τί τόδε τορὸν ἄγαν ἔπος ἐφημίσω;
νεόγονος * ἂν αἰῶν μάθοι.
πέπληγμαι δ' ὑπαὶ * δάκει φοινίῳ,
δυσαλγεῖ τύχᾳ μινύρα κακὰ * θρεὺμένας,   1165
θραύματ' ἐμοὶ κλύειν.
ΚΑ. ἰὼ πόνοι πόνοι πόλεος ὀλομένας τὸ πᾶν. ἀντ. ζ'.
ἰὼ πρόπυργοι θυσίαι πατρὸς
πολυκανεῖς βοτῶν ποιονόμων· ἄκος δ'
οὐδὲν ἐπήρκεσαν   1170
τὸ μὴ πόλιν μὲν ὥσπερ οὖν ἔχει παθεῖν.
ἐγὼ δὲ *θερμὴν οὐ στάγ' ἐν πέδῳ βαλῶ;
ΧΟ. ἑπόμενα προτέροισι τάδ' ἐφημίσω.
καί τίς σε * κακοφρονῶν τίθη-

1148. ἀγῶνα MSS.   1152. ἐπιφόβῳ M.G.   1163. νεογνὸς
ἀνθρώπων μάθοι MSS.   καὶ παῖς νεύγονος ἂν μάθοι II. text Karst.
1164. δήγματι MSS.   1165. θρεομένας MSS.   1166. θαύματ'
Fa. text V. Fl.   1172. θερμόνους τάχ' ἐμπέδῳ MSS. corr.
Miller.   1174. κακοφρονεῖν MSS.

σι δαίμων ὑπερβαρὴς ἐμπίτνων 1175
μελίζειν πάθη γοερὰ θανατηφόρα.
τέρμα δ' ἀμηχανῶ.

ΚΑ. καὶ μὴν ὁ χρησμὸς οὐκέτ' ἐκ καλυμμάτων
ἔσται δεδορκὼς νεογάμου νύμφης δίκην·
λαμπρὸς δ' ἔοικεν ἡλίου πρὸς ἀντολὰς 1180
πνέων ἐσῄξειν, ὥστε κύματος δίκην
*κλύζειν πρὸς αὐγὰς τοῦδε πήματος πολὺ
μεῖζον· φρενώσω δ' οὐκέτ' ἐξ αἰνιγμάτων.
καὶ μαρτυρεῖτε συνδρόμως ἴχνος κακῶν
ῥινηλατούσῃ τῶν πάλαι πεπραγμένων. 1185
τὴν γὰρ στέγην τήνδ' οὔποτ' ἐκλείπει χορὸς
σύμφθογγος, οὐκ εὔφωνος· οὐ γὰρ εὖ λέγει.
καὶ μὴν πεπωκώς γ', ὡς θρασύνεσθαι πλέον,
βρότειον αἷμα κῶμος ἐν δόμοις μένει,
δύσπεμπτος ἔξω συγγόνων Ἐρινύων. 1190
ὑμνοῦσι δ' ὕμνον δώμασιν προσήμεναι
πρώταρχον ἄτην· ἐν μέρει δ' ἀπέπτυσαν
εὐνὰς ἀδελφοῦ τῷ πατοῦντι δυσμενεῖς.
ἥμαρτον, ἢ *θηρῶ τι τοξότης τὶς ὥς;
ἢ ψευδόμαντίς εἰμι θυροκόπος φλέδων; 1195
ἐκμαρτύρησον προὐμόσας τό μ' εἰδέναι
λόγῳ-παλαιὰς τῶνδ' ἁμαρτίας δόμων.

ΧΟ. καὶ πῶς ἂν ὅρκος, *πῆγμα γενναίως παγέν,
παιώνιος γένοιτο; θαυμάζω δέ σε
πόντου πέραν τραφεῖσαν ἀλλόθρουν πόλιν 1200
κυρεῖν λέγουσαν, ὥσπερ εἰ παρεστάτεις.

ΚΑ. μάντις μ' Ἀπόλλων τῷδ' ἐπέστησεν τέλει.

1176. θανατοφόρα V. Fl. text Fa. 1182. κλύειν MSS. corr.
Aur. Schutz. 1194. τηρῶ MSS. corr. Cant. 1196. τὸ μὴ δέναι V.
text Fl. Fa. 1198. πῆμα MSS. 1199. παιώνιον V. Fl. text Fa.

ΧΟ. μῶν καὶ θεός περ ἱμέρῳ πεπληγμένος ;
ΚΑ. προτοῦ μὲν αἰδὼς ἦν ἐμοὶ λέγειν τάδε.
ΧΟ. ἁβρύνεται γὰρ πᾶς τις εὖ-πράσσων πλέον. 1205
ΚΑ. ἀλλ' ἦν παλαιστής, κάρτ' ἐμοὶ πνέων χάριν.
ΧΟ. ἦ καὶ τέκνων εἰς ἔργον ἠλθέτην νόμῳ ;
ΚΑ. ξυναινέσασα Λοξίαν ἐψευσάμην.
ΧΟ. ἤδη τέχναισιν ἐνθέοις ᾑρημένη ;
ΚΑ. ἤδη πολίταις πάντ' ἐθέσπιζον πάθη. 1210
ΧΟ. πῶς δῆτ' *ἄνατος ἦσθα Λοξίου κότῳ ;
ΚΑ. ἔπειθον οὐδέν' οὐδέν, ὡς τάδ' ἤμπλακον.
ΧΟ. ἡμῖν γε μὲν δὴ πιστὰ θεσπίζειν δοκεῖς.
ΚΑ. ἰοὺ ἰού, ὢ ὢ κακά.

ὑπ' αὖ με δεινὸς ὀρθομαντείας πόνος 1215
στροβεῖ, ταράσσων φροιμίοις * δυσφροιμίοις.
ὁρᾶτε, τούσδε τοὺς δόμοις ἐφημένους
νέους, ὀνείρων προσφερεῖς μορφώμασι ;
παῖδες θανόντες ὡσπερεὶ πρὸς τῶν φίλων,
χεῖρας κρεῶν πλήθοντες οἰκείας βορᾶς, 1220
σὺν ἐντέροις τε σπλάγχν', ἐποίκτιστον γέμος,
πρέπουσ' ἔχοντες, ὧν πατὴρ ἐγεύσατο.
ἐκ τῶνδε ποινάς φημι βουλεύειν τινὰ
λέοντ' ἄναλκιν ἐν λέχει στρωφώμενον
οἰκουρόν, οἴμοι, τῷ μολόντι δεσπότῃ 1225
ἐμῷ· φέρειν γὰρ χρὴ τὸ δούλιον ζυγόν.
νεῶν τ' ἔπαρχος Ἰλίου τ' ἀναστάτης
† οὐκ οἶδεν οἵα γλῶσσα μισητῆς κυνὸς
λέξασα, κἀκτείνασα φαιδρόνους, δίκην
ἄτης λαθραίου, τεύξεται κακῇ τύχῃ.† 1230

1203 and 1204 inverted in MSS. H. restored the order. 1211.
ἄνακτος MSS. corr. Cant. 1216. ἐφημένους MSS. text H. 1228.
corrupt. Madv. conj. οἵα γλῶσσα μ. κ. λείξασα κἀκτείνασα φαιδρὸν
ὖς, δ. ἀ. λ., δήξεται κακῇ τύχῃ. (λείξασα Tyrwhitt.)

*τοιᾷδε τόλμῃ θῆλυς ἄρσενος φονεὺς
ἔστιν.— τί νιν καλοῦσα δυσφιλὲς δάκος
τύχοιμ' ἄν; ἀμφίσβαιναν, ἢ Σκύλλαν τινὰ
οἰκοῦσαν ἐν πέτραισι, ναυτίλων βλάβην,
θύουσαν Ἅιδου μητέρ', ἄσπονδόν τ' Ἄρη   1235
φίλοις πνέουσαν; ὡς δ' ἐπωλολύξατο
ἡ παντότολμος, ὥσπερ ἐν μάχης τροπῇ.
δοκεῖ δὲ χαίρειν νοστίμῳ σωτηρίᾳ.
καὶ τῶνδ' ὅμοιον εἴ τι μὴ πείθω· τί γάρ;
τὸ μέλλον ἥξει. καὶ σύ * μ' ἐν τάχει παρὼν   1240
ἄγαν ἀληθόμαντιν οἰκτείρας ἐρεῖς.
ΧΟ. τὴν μὲν Θυέστου δαῖτα παιδείων κρεῶν
ξυνῆκα καὶ πέφρικα· καὶ φόβος μ' ἔχει
κλύοντ' ἀληθῶς οὐδὲν ἐξῃκασμένα.
τὰ δ' ἄλλ' ἀκούσας ἐκ δρόμου πεσὼν τρέχω.   1245
ΚΑ. Ἀγαμέμνονός σέ φημ' ἐπόψεσθαι μόρον.
ΧΟ. εὔφημον, ὦ τάλαινα, κοίμησον στόμα.
ΚΑ. ἀλλ' οὔτι Παιὼν τῷδ' ἐπιστατεῖ λόγῳ.
ΧΟ. οὔκ, * εἴπερ ἔσται γ'· ἀλλὰ μὴ γένοιτό πως.
ΚΑ. σὺ μὲν κατεύχει, τοῖς δ' ἀποκτείνειν μέλει.   1250
ΧΟ. τίνος πρὸς ἀνδρὸς τοῦτ' ἄχος πορσύνεται;
ΚΑ. ἦ κάρτα * τἄρ' ἂν παρεκόπης χρησμῶν ἐμῶν.
ΧΟ. τοῦ γὰρ τελοῦντος οὐ ξυνῆκα μηχανήν.
ΚΑ. καὶ μὴν ἄγαν γ' Ἕλλην' ἐπίσταμαι φάτιν.
ΧΟ. καὶ γὰρ τὰ πυθόκραντα· δυσμαθῆ δ' ὅμως.   1255
ΚΑ. παπαῖ, οἷον τὸ πῦρ· ἐπέρχεται δέ μοι.
ὀτοτοῖ, Λύκει' Ἄπολλον, οἳ ἐγὼ ἐγώ.
αὕτη δίπους λέαινα συγκοιμωμένη

1231. τοιάδε τολμᾷ V. Fl. τοιαῦτα Fa. corr. Karst.   1235.
ἀρὰν MSS. text Pors. Ἄρην Butler.   1240. μὴν MSS.   1249.
εἰ πάρεσται MSS.   1252. κάρτ' ἄρ' ἂν παρεσκύπης (ει suprascript.)
Fl. V. παρεσκύπ(ης suprasc.) Fa. παρεσκύπεις Vict. κάρτα τἄρα
παρεκόπης Hart.   1258. δίπλους V. Fl. Fa. text Vict.

λύκῳ, λέοντος εὐγενοῦς ἀπουσίᾳ,
κτενεῖ με τὴν τάλαιναν· ὡς δὲ φάρμακον   1260
τεύχουσα κἀμοῦ μισθὸν ἐνθήσειν κότῳ
ἐπεύχεται, θήγουσα φωτὶ φάσγανον,
ἐμῆς ἀγωγῆς ἀντιτίσασθαι φόνον.
τί δῆτ' ἐμαυτῆς καταγέλωτ' ἔχω τάδε,
καὶ σκῆπτρα καὶ μαντεῖα περὶ δέρῃ στέφη;   1265
σὲ μὲν πρὸ μοίρας τῆς ἐμῆς διαφθερῶ.
ἴτ' ἐς φθόρον· πεσόντα * θ' ὧδ' ἀμείψομαι·
ἄλλην τιν' *ἄτης ἀντ' ἐμοῦ πλουτίζετε.
ἰδοὺ δ' Ἀπόλλων αὐτὸς ἐκδύων ἐμὲ
χρηστηρίαν ἐσθῆτ', ἐποπτεύσας δέ με   1270
κἀν τοῖσδε κόσμοις καταγελωμένην *μέγα
φίλων ὑπ' ἐχθρῶν οὐ διχορρόπως μάτην—
καλουμένη δὲ φοιτὰς ὡς ἀγύρτρια,
πτωχὸς τάλαινα λιμοθνὴς ἠνεσχόμην—
καὶ νῦν ὁ μάντις μάντιν ἐκπράξας ἐμὲ   1275
ἀπήγαγ' ἐς τοιάσδε θανασίμους τύχας.
βωμοῦ πατρῴου δ' ἀντ' ἐπίξηνον μένει
θερμῷ κοπείσης φοινίῳ προσφάγματι.
οὐ μὴν ἄτιμοί γ' ἐκ θεῶν τεθνήξομεν.
ἥξει γὰρ ἡμῶν ἄλλος αὖ τιμάορος,   1280
μητροκτόνον φίτυμα, ποινάτωρ πατρός·
φυγὰς δ' ἀλήτης τῆσδε γῆς ἀπόξενος
κάτεισιν, ἄτας τάσδε θριγκώσων φίλοις·
ὀμώμοται γὰρ ὅρκος ἐκ θεῶν μέγας
†ἄξειν νιν ὑπτίασμα κειμένου πατρός.   1285
τί δῆτ' ἐγὼ *κάτοικτος ὧδ' ἀναστένω;

1261. ἐνθήσει V.Fl. text Fa. 1267. ἀγαθῷ δ' ἀμείψομαι
MSS. πεσόντ'· ἐγὼ δ' ἄμ' ἕψομαι H. text A. W. Verrall. 1268.
ἄτην MSS. corr. Stan. 1271. μετὰ MSS. corr. H. 1284. MSS.
read this after 1290. corr. H. 1286. κάτοικος MSS. corr. Scal.

ΑΓΑΜΕΜΝΩΝ.

ἐπεὶ τὸ πρῶτον εἶδον Ἰλίου πόλιν
πράξασαν ὡς ἔπραξεν, οἱ δ' * εἶλον πόλιν,
οὕτως ἀπαλλάσσουσιν ἐν θεῶν κρίσει,
ἰοῦσα πράξω· τλήσομαι τὸ κατθανεῖν. 1290
Ἅιδου πύλας δὲ * τάσδ' ἐγὼ προσεννέπω.
ἐπεύχομαι δὲ καιρίας πληγῆς τυχεῖν,
ὡς ἀσφάδαστος, αἱμάτων εὐθνησίμων
ἀπορρυέντων, ὄμμα συμβάλω τόδε.
ΧΟ. ὦ πολλὰ μὲν τάλαινα, πολλὰ δ' αὖ σοφὴ 1295
γύναι, μακρὰν ἔτεινας. εἰ δ' ἐτητύμως
μόρον τὸν αὑτῆς οἶσθα, πῶς θεηλάτου
βοὸς δίκην πρὸς βωμὸν εὐτόλμως πατεῖς;
ΚΑ. οὐκ ἔστ' ἄλυξις, οὔ, ξένοι, * χρόνον πλέω.
ΧΟ. ὁ δ' ὕστατός γε τοῦ χρόνου πρεσβεύεται. 1300
ΚΑ. ἥκει τόδ' ἦμαρ· σμικρὰ κερδανῶ φυγῇ.
ΧΟ. ἀλλ' ἴσθι τλήμων οὖσ' ἀπ' εὐτόλμου φρενός.
ΚΑ. ἀλλ' εὐκλεῶς τοι κατθανεῖν χάρις βροτῷ.
ΧΟ. οὐδεὶς ἀκούει ταῦτα τῶν εὐδαιμόνων.
ΚΑ. ἰὼ, πάτερ, σοῦ τῶν τε γενναίων τέκνων. 1305
ΧΟ. τί δ' ἐστὶ χρῆμα, τίς σ' ἀποστρέφει φόβος;
ΚΑ. φεῦ φεῦ.
ΧΟ. τί τοῦτ' ἔφευξας; εἴ τι μὴ φρενῶν στύγος.
ΚΑ. φόνον δόμοι πνέουσιν αἱματοσταγῆ.
ΧΟ. καὶ πῶς; τόδ' ὄζει θυμάτων ἐφεστίων. 1310
ΚΑ. ὅμοιος ἀτμὸς ὥσπερ ἐκ τάφου πρέπει.
ΧΟ. οὐ Σύριον ἀγλάϊσμα δώμασιν λέγεις;
ΚΑ. ἀλλ' εἶμι κἀν δόμοισι κωκύσουσ' ἐμὴν
Ἀγαμέμνονός τε μοῖραν. ἀρκείτω βίος.

1288. εἶχον MSS. corr. Musgr. 1291. τὰς λέγω MSS. corr.
Aur. 1299. χρόνῳ MSS. 1309. φόβον MSS., but Fa. has ν
over the β.

ἰὼ ξένοι. 1315
οὔτοι δυσοίζω θάμνον ὡς ὄρνις φόβῳ
ἄλλως· θανούσῃ μαρτυρεῖτέ μοι τόδε,
ὅταν γυνὴ γυναικὸς ἀντ' ἐμοῦ θάνῃ,
ἀνήρ τε δυσδάμαρτος ἀντ' ἀνδρὸς πέσῃ.
ἐπιξενοῦμαι ταῦτα δ' ὡς θανουμένη. 1320
ΧΟ. ὦ τλῆμον, οἰκτείρω σε θεσφάτου μόρου.
ΚΑ. ἅπαξ ἔτ' εἰπεῖν ῥῆσιν, *οὐ θρῆνον θέλω
ἐμὸν τὸν αὐτῆς. ἡλίου δ' ἐπεύχομαι
πρὸς ὕστατον φῶς † τοῖς ἐμοῖς τιμαόροις,
ἐχθροῖς φονεῦσιν τοῖς ἐμοῖς τίνειν ὁμοῦ,† 1325
δούλης θανούσης, εὐμαροῦς χειρώματος.
ἰὼ βρότεια πράγματ'· εὐτυχοῦντα μὲν
*σκιᾷ τις ἂν πρέψειεν· εἰ δὲ δυστυχῇ,
βολαῖς ὑγρώσσων σπόγγος ὤλεσεν γραφήν.
καὶ ταῦτ' ἐκείνων μᾶλλον οἰκτείρω πολύ. 1330
ΧΟ. τὸ μὲν εὖ πράσσειν ἀκόρεστον ἔφυ
πᾶσι βροτοῖσιν· δακτυλοδείκτων δ'
οὔτις ἀπειπὼν εἴργει μελάθρων,
'μηκέτ' ἐσέλθῃς τάδε' φωνῶν.
καὶ τῷδε πόλιν μὲν ἑλεῖν ἔδοσαν 1335
μάκαρες Πριάμου,
θεοτίμητος δ' οἴκαδ' ἱκάνει·
νῦν δ' εἰ προτέρων αἷμ' ἀποτίσει,
καὶ τοῖσι θανοῦσι θανὼν ἄλλων
ποινὰς θανάτων *ἐπικραίνει, 1340
τίς ἂν εὔξαιτο *βροτὸς ὢν ἀσινεῖ

1317. ἀλλ' ὡς θανούσῃ MSS. corr. H.   1322. ᾗ MSS. corr. H.
1323. ἡλίῳ MSS. corr. Jacobs.   1328. σκιά τις ἀντρέψειεν MSS. ἂν
Pors. πρέψειεν H. σκιᾷ Con.   1340. ἐπικρανεῖ Fl. V. ἄγαν
ἐπικρανεῖ Fa. corr. H.   1341. βροτῶν MSS. corr. Bothe.

ΑΓΑΜΕΜΝΩΝ. 49

δαίμονι φῦναι τάδ' ἀκούων;
ΑΓ. ὤμοι, πέπληγμαι καιρίαν πληγὴν ἔσω.

ΗΜΙΧΟΡΟΙ.

ΗΜ. σῖγα· τίς πληγὴν ἀϋτεῖ καιρίως οὐτασμένος;
ΑΓ. ὤμοι μάλ' αὖθις, δευτέραν πεπληγμένος. 1345
ΗΜ. τοὔργον εἰργάσθαι δοκεῖ μοι βασιλέως οἰμώγματι,
ἀλλὰ κοινωσώμεθ' *ἢν πως ἀσφαλῆ βουλεύματ' *ῇ.
ΗΜ. ἐγὼ μὲν ὑμῖν τὴν ἐμὴν γνώμην λέγω,
πρὸς δῶμα δεῦρ' ἀστοῖσι κηρύσσειν βοήν.
ΗΜ. ἐμοὶ δ' ὅπως τάχιστά γ' ἐμπεσεῖν δοκεῖ 1350
καὶ πρᾶγμ' ἐλέγχειν ξὺν νεορρύτῳ ξίφει.
ΗΜ. κἀγὼ τοιούτου γνώματος κοινωνὸς ὢν
ψηφίζομαί τι δρᾶν. τὸ μὴ μέλλειν δ' ἀκμή.
ΗΜ. ὁρᾶν πάρεστι· φροιμιάζονται γὰρ ὡς
τυραννίδος σημεῖα πράσσοντες πόλει. 1355
ΗΜ. χρονίζομεν γάρ. οἱ δὲ *τῆς μελλοῦς κλέος
*πέδοι πατοῦντες οὐ καθεύδουσιν χερί.
ΗΜ. οὐκ οἶδα βουλῆς ἧστινος τυχὼν λέγω.
τοῦ δρῶντός ἐστι καὶ τὸ βουλεῦσαι πέρι.
ΗΜ. κἀγὼ τοιοῦτός εἰμ', ἐπεὶ δυσμηχανῶ 1360
λόγοισι τὸν θανόντ' ἀνιστάναι πάλιν.
ΗΜ. ἦ καὶ βίον *τείνοντες ὧδ' ὑπείξομεν
δόμων καταισχυντῆρσι τοῖσδ' ἡγουμένοις;
ΗΜ. ἀλλ' οὐκ ἀνεκτόν, ἀλλὰ κατθανεῖν κρατεῖ.
πεπαιτέρα γὰρ μοῖρα τῆς τυραννίδος. 1365
ΗΜ. ἦ γὰρ τεκμηρίοισιν ἐξ οἰμωγμάτων·
μαντευσόμεσθα τἀνδρὸς ὡς ὀλωλότος;

1347. ἂν .... βουλεύματα MSS. 1356. μελλούσης Fa. τῆς
μελλούσης Fl. V. 1357. πέδον MSS. corr. II. 1362. κτείνοντες
MSS.

E

50   ΑΙΣΧΥΛΟΥ

ΗΜ. σάφ' εἰδότας χρὴ τῶνδε *θυμοῦσθαι πέρι.
    τὸ γὰρ τοπάζειν τοῦ σάφ' εἰδέναι δίχα.
ΗΜ. ταύτην ἐπαινεῖν πάντοθεν πληθύνομαι,   1370
    τρανῶς 'Ἀτρείδην εἰδέναι κυροῦνθ' ὅπως.
ΚΛ. πολλῶν πάροιθεν καιρίως εἰρημένων
    τἀναντί' εἰπεῖν οὐκ ἐπαισχυνθήσομαι.
    πῶς γάρ τις ἐχθροῖς ἐχθρὰ πορσύνων, φίλοις
    δοκοῦσιν εἶναι, *πημονῆς ἀρκύστατ' ἂν   1375
    φράξειεν ὕψος κρεῖσσον ἐκπηδήματος;
    ἐμοὶ δ' ἀγὼν ὅδ' οὐκ ἀφρόντιστος πάλαι
    *νείκης παλαιᾶς ἦλθε, σὺν χρόνῳ γε μήν·
    ἕστηκα δ' ἔνθ' ἔπαισ' ἐπ' ἐξειργασμένοις.
    οὕτω δ' ἔπραξα, καὶ τάδ' οὐκ ἀρνήσομαι   1380
    ὡς μήτε φεύγειν μήτ' ἀμύνασθαι μόρον.
    ἄπειρον ἀμφίβληστρον, ὥσπερ ἰχθύων,
    περιστιχίζω, πλοῦτον εἵματος κακόν.
    παίω δέ νιν δίς· κἂν δυοῖν οἰμώγμασι
    μεθῆκεν αὐτοῦ κῶλα· καὶ πεπτωκότι   1385
    τρίτην ἐπενδίδωμι, τοῦ κατὰ χθονὸς
    †"Ἀιδου νεκρῶν σωτῆρος εὐκταίαν χάριν.
    οὕτω τὸν αὐτοῦ θυμὸν ὁρμαίνει πεσών·
    κἀκφυσιῶν ὀξεῖαν αἵματος σφαγὴν
    βάλλει μ' ἐρεμνῇ ψακάδι φοινίας δρόσου,   1390
    χαίρουσαν οὐδὲν ἧσσον ἢ *διοσδότῳ
    γάνει σπορητὸς κάλυκος ἐν λοχεύμασιν.
    ὡς ὧδ' ἐχόντων, πρέσβος 'Ἀργείων τόδε,
    χαίροιτ' ἄν, εἰ χαίροιτ', ἐγὼ δ' ἐπεύχομαι.
    εἰ δ' ἦν πρεπόντων ὥστ' ἐπισπένδειν νεκρῷ, 1395

1368. μυθοῦσθαι MSS. corr. E. A. Ahrens.   1375. πημονὴν
ἀρκύστατον MSS.   πημονῆς Aur.   ἀρκύστατ' ἂν Elmsl.   1378.
νίκης MSS. corr. Heath.   1381. ἀμύνασθαι V. Fl. Fa.   ἀμύνεσθαι
Vict. and many edd.   1387. "Ἀιδου MSS.   Διὸς Enger.   1391.
Διὸς νότῳ γᾶν, εἰ MSS. corr. Pors.

ΑΓΑΜΕΜΝΩΝ. 51

*τῷδ' ἂν δικαίως ἦν, ὑπερδίκως μὲν οὖν.
τοσῶνδε κρατῆρ' ἐν δόμοις κακῶν ὅδε
πλήσας ἀραίων, αὐτὸς ἐκπίνει μολών.
ΧΟ. θαυμάζομέν σου γλῶσσαν, ὡς θρασύστομος,
ἥτις τοιόνδ' ἐπ' ἀνδρὶ κομπάζεις λόγον. 1400
ΚΛ. πειρᾶσθέ(μου γυναικὸς)ὡς ἀφράσμονος,
ἐγὼ δ' ἀτρέστῳ καρδίᾳ πρὸς εἰδότας
λέγω· σὺ δ' αἰνεῖν εἴτε με ψέγειν θέλεις
ὅμοιον. οὗτός ἐστιν Ἀγαμέμνων, ἐμὸς
πόσις, νεκρὸς δέ, τῆσδε δεξιᾶς χερὸς 1405
ἔργον δικαίας τέκτονος. τάδ' ὧδ' ἔχει.
ΧΟ. τί κακόν, ὦ γύναι, χθονοτρεφὲς ἐδανὸν στρ.
ἢ ποτὸν πασαμένα *ῥυτᾶς ἐξ ἁλὸς ὄρμενον
τόδ' ἐπέθου θύος δημοθρόους τ' ἀράς;
ἀπέδικες, ἀπέταμές *τ'· ἀπόπολις δ' ἔσει, 1410
μῖσος ὄβριμον ἀστοῖς.
ΚΛ. νῦν μὲν δικάζεις ἐκ πόλεως φυγὴν ἐμοὶ
καὶ μῖσος ἀστῶν δημόθρους τ' ἔχειν ἀράς,
οὐδὲν *τότ' ἀνδρὶ τῷδ' ἐναντίον φέρων·
ὃς οὐ προτιμῶν, ὡσπερεὶ βοτοῦ μόρον, 1415
μήλων φλεόντων εὐπόκοις νομεύμασιν,
ἔθυσεν αὑτοῦ παῖδα, φιλτάτην ἐμοὶ
ὠδῖν', ἐπῳδὸν Θρῃκίων *ἀημάτων.
οὐ τοῦτον ἐκ γῆς τῆσδε χρῆν σ' ἀνδρηλατεῖν,
μιασμάτων ἄποιν'; ἐπήκοος δ' ἐμῶν 1420
ἔργων δικαστὴς τραχὺς εἶ. λέγω δέ σοι
τοιαῦτ' ἀπειλεῖν, ὡς παρεσκευασμένης
ἐκ τῶν ὁμοίων χειρὶ νικήσαντ' ἐμοῦ

1396. τάδε MSS. 1408. ῥυσᾶς MSS. 1410. ἀπέταμες ἄπολις
MSS. τ' Κ. ἀπόπολις Seid. 1414. τόδ' MSS. 1418. τε λημμάτων
MSS. corr. Cant. 1419. χρή MSS.

E 2

ΑΙΣΧΥΛΟΥ

ἄρχειν· ἐὰν δὲ τοὔμπαλιν κραίνῃ θεός,
γνώσει διδαχθεὶς ὀψὲ γοῦν τὸ σωφρονεῖν. 1425
ΧΟ. μεγαλόμητις εἶ, περίφρονα δ' ἔλακες,
ὥσπερ οὖν φονολιβεῖ τύχᾳ φρὴν ἐπιμαίνεται·
λίβος ἐπ' ὀμμάτων αἵματος *ἐμπρέπει·
ἀτίετον ἔτι σὲ χρὴ στερομέναν φίλων
τύμμα τύμματι τῖσαι. 1430
ΚΛ. καὶ τήνδ' ἀκούεις ὁρκίων ἐμῶν θέμιν·
μὰ τὴν τέλειον τῆς ἐμῆς παιδὸς δίκην,
Ἄτην Ἐρινύν θ', αἷσι τόνδ' ἔσφαξ' ἐγώ,
οὔ μοι φόβου μέλαθρον ἐλπὶς ἐμπατεῖ,
ἕως ἂν αἴθῃ πῦρ ἐφ' ἑστίας ἐμῆς 1435
Αἴγισθος, ὡς τὸ πρόσθεν εὖ φρονῶν ἐμοί.
οὗτος γὰρ ἡμῖν ἀσπὶς οὐ μικρὰ θράσους.
κεῖται γυναικὸς τῆσδε λυμαντήριος,
Χρυσηίδων μείλιγμα τῶν ὑπ' Ἰλίῳ,
ἥ τ' αἰχμάλωτος ἥδε καὶ τερασκόπος, 1440
καὶ κοινόλεκτρος τοῦδε, θεσφατηλόγος
πιστὴ ξύνευνος, ναυτίλων δὲ σελμάτων
*ἰσοτριβής. ἄτιμα δ' οὐκ ἐπραξάτην.
ὁ μὲν γὰρ οὕτως· ἡ δέ τοι κύκνου δίκην
τὸν ὕστατον μέλψασα θανάσιμον γόον 1445
κεῖται φιλήτωρ *τῷδ', ἐμοὶ δ' ἐπήγαγεν
εὐνῆς παροψώνημα τῆς ἐμῆς χλιδῆς.
ΧΟ. φεῦ, τίς ἂν ἐν τάχει, μὴ περιώδυνος,
μηδὲ δεμνιοτήρης,
μόλοι τὸν ἀεὶ φέρουσ' ἐν ἡμῖν 1450
μοῖρ' ἀτέλευτον ὕπνον, δαμέντος

1428. εὖ πρέπει ἀτίετον Fa. εὖ πρέπει ἀντίετον Fl. εὐπρέπειαν τίετον V. ἐμπρέπει Aurat. 1443. ἰσοτριβής. corr. Pauw. 1446. τοῦδ' MSS. corr. H.

ΑΓΑΜΕΜΝΩΝ. 53

φύλακος εὐμενεστάτου
* πολέα τλάντος γυναικὸς διαί·
πρὸς γυναικὸς δ᾽ ἀπέφθισεν βίον.
ἰὼ * ἰὼ * παράνους Ἑλένα   στρ. α΄.   1455
μία τὰς πολλάς, τὰς πάνυ πολλὰς
ψυχὰς ὀλέσασ᾽ ὑπὸ Τροίᾳ.
νῦν δὲ τελείαν   * / *
*   *   *   *   *
*   *   *   *   *
*   *   *   *   *
*   *   *   *   *

† πολύμναστον ἐπηνθίσω [δι᾽] αἷμ᾽ ἄνιπτον.
ἦ τις ἦν τότ᾽ ἐν δόμοις   1460
ἔρις ἐρίδματος, ἀνδρὸς οἰζύς.

ΚΛ. μηδὲν θανάτου μοῖραν ἐπεύχου   στρ. β΄.
τοῖσδε βαρυνθείς·
μηδ᾽ εἰς Ἑλένην κότον ἐκτρέψῃς,
ὡς ἀνδρολέτειρ᾽, ὡς μία πολλῶν   1465
ἀνδρῶν ψυχὰς Δαναῶν ὀλέσασ᾽
ἀξύστατον ἄλγος ἔπραξε.

ΧΟ. δαῖμον, ὃς ἐμπίτνεις δώμασι καὶ * διφυί-
οισι Τανταλίδαισιν,
κράτος τ᾽ ἰσόψυχον ἐκ γυναικῶν   1470
* καρδιόδηκτον ἐμοὶ κρατύνεις.
ἐπὶ δὲ σώματος δίκαν
κόρακος ἐχθροῦ σταθεῖσ᾽ ἐκνόμως
ὕμνον ὑμνεῖν * * ἐπεύχεται.

1453. καὶ πολλὰ MSS. πολέα Haupt. 1455. ἰὼ παρανόμους MSS
ἰὼ ἰὼ Blomf. παράνους H.   1459. δι᾽ MSS.   1460. ἥτις MSS.
corr. Eng.   1468. ἐμπίπτεις MSS. διφυεῖσι MSS. corr H.   1471.
καρδίᾳ δηκτόν MSS.   1472. δίκαν μοι MSS.   1473. σταθεὶς MSS.
corr. Schütz. Pors. ἐννόμως V. Fl. text Fa.

ΚΛ. νῦν δ' ὤρθωσας στόματος γνώμην,   ἀντ. β'. 1475
τὸν *τριπάχυντον
δαίμονα γέννης τῆσδε κικλήσκων.
ἐκ τοῦ γὰρ ἔρως αἱματολοιχὸς
† νείρει τρέφεται, πρὶν καταλῆξαι
τὸ παλαιὸν ἄχος, νέος ἰχώρ. 1480

ΧΟ. ἦ μέγαν *οἰκονόμον   στρ. γ'.
δαίμονα καὶ βαρύμηνιν αἰνεῖς.
φεῦ φεῦ, κακὸν αἶνον ἀτη-
ρᾶς τύχας ἀκορέστου·
ἰώ, ἰὴ διαὶ Διὸς   1485
παναιτίου πανεργέτα,
τί γὰρ βροτοῖς ἄνευ Διὸς τελεῖται;
τί τῶνδ' οὐ θεόκραντόν ἐστιν;
ἰὼ ἰὼ βασιλεῦ βασιλεῦ,
πῶς σε δακρύσω;   1490
φρενὸς ἐκ φιλίας τί ποτ' εἴπω;
κεῖσαι δ' ἀράχνης ἐν ὑφάσματι τῷδ'
ἀσεβεῖ θανάτῳ βίον ἐκπνέων.
ὤμοι μοι κοίταν τάνδ' ἀνελεύθερον
δολίῳ μόρῳ δαμεὶς   1495
ἐκ χερὸς ἀμφιτόμῳ βελέμνῳ.

ΚΛ. αὐχεῖς εἶναι τόδε τοὔργον ἐμόν.
μηδ' ἐπιλεχθῇς
Ἀγαμεμνονίαν εἶναί μ' ἄλοχον.
φανταζόμενος δὲ γυναικὶ νεκροῦ   1500
τοῦδ' ὁ παλαιὸς δριμὺς ἀλάστωρ
Ἀτρέως χαλεποῦ θοινατῆρος

1476. τριπάχυιον MSS. corr. Bamb.   1481. οἴκοις τοῖσδε MSS.
corr. Schn. K.   1486. πανεργέταν Fl. V. text Fa.   1498. text
V. Fl.   μὴ δ' Fa.   μηκέτι λεχθῇ δ' H.

ΑΓΑΜΕΜΝΩΝ.

τόνδ' ἀπέτισεν,
τέλεον νεαροῖς ἐπιθύσας.
ΧΟ. ὡς μὲν ἀναίτιος εἶ   ἀντ. γ΄.   1505
τοῦδε φόνου τίς ὁ μαρτυρήσων;
πῶ πῶ; πατρόθεν δὲ συλλή-
πτωρ γένοιτ' ἂν ἀλάστωρ.
βιάζεται δ' ὁμοσπόροις
ἐπιρροαῖσιν αἱμάτων   1510
μέλας Ἄρης † ὅποι *δίκαν προβαίνων
πάχνᾳ κουροβόρῳ παρέξει.†
ἰὼ ἰὼ βασιλεῦ βασιλεῦ,
πῶς σε δακρύσω;
φρενὸς ἐκ φιλίας τί ποτ' εἴπω;   1515
κεῖσαι δ' ἀράχνης ἐν ὑφάσματι τῷδ'
ἀσεβεῖ θανάτῳ βίον ἐκπνέων.
ὤμοι μοι κοίταν τάνδ' ἀνελεύθερον
δολίῳ μόρῳ δαμεὶς
ἐκ χερὸς ἀμφιτόμῳ βελέμνῳ.   1520
ΚΛ. [οὔτ' ἀνελεύθερον οἶμαι θάνατον
τῷδε γενέσθαι.]
οὐδὲ γὰρ οὗτος δολίαν ἄτην
οἴκοισιν ἔθηκ';
ἀλλ' ἐμὸν ἐκ τοῦδ' ἔρνος ἀερθέν,   1525
τὴν πολύκλαυτόν τ' Ἰφιγενείαν,
*ἄξια δράσας ἄξια πάσχων
μηδὲν ἐν Ἅιδου μεγαλαυχείτω,
ξιφοδηλήτῳ
θανάτῳ τίσας ἅπερ ἦρξεν.
ΧΟ. ἀμηχανῶ φροντίδος στερηθεὶς   στρ. δ΄. 1530

1511. δὲ καὶ προσβαίνων MSS. προβαίνων Cant.   δίκην Butl.
δίκαν Scholef.   1521-2. Probably spurious.   1527. ἀνάξια MSS.

ΑΙΣΧΥΛΟΥ

εὐπάλαμον μέριμναν
ὅπα τράπωμαι, πίτνοντος οἴκου.
δέδοικα δ' ὄμβρου κτύπον δομοσφαλῆ
τὸν αἱματηρόν· ψακὰς δὲ λήγει·
δίκην δ' ἐπ' ἄλλο πρᾶγμα *θηγάνει βλάβης　　1535
πρὸς ἄλλαις θηγάναισι Μοῖρα.
ἰὼ γᾶ γᾶ, εἴθ' ἔμ' ἐδέξω,　　　　　ἀντ. α'.
πρὶν τόνδ' ἐπιδεῖν ἀργυροτοίχου
δροίτας κατέχοντα χαμεύναν.　　　　1540
τίς ὁ θάψων νιν; τίς ὁ θρηνήσων;
ἦ σὺ τόδ' ἔρξαι τλήσει, κτείνασ'
ἄνδρα τὸν αὑτῆς, ἀποκωκῦσαι
ψυχήν, ἄχαριν χάριν ἀντ' ἔργων　　　1545
μεγάλων ἀδίκως ἐπικρᾶναι;
τίς δ' *ἐπιτύμβιον αἶνον ἐπ' ἀνδρὶ θείῳ
σὺν δακρύοις ἰάπτων
ἀλαθείᾳ φρενῶν πονήσει;　　　　　1550
ΚΛ. οὐ σὲ προσήκει τὸ μέλημα λέγειν　　στρ. ε'.
τοῦτο· πρὸς ἡμῶν
κάππεσε, κάτθανε, καὶ καταθάψομεν
οὐχ ὑπὸ κλαυθμῶν τῶν ἐξ οἴκων,
*　*　*　*　*
*　*　*　*　*
ἀλλ' Ἰφιγένειά νιν ἀσπασίως　　　　1555
θυγάτηρ, ὡς χρή,
πατέρ' ἀντιάσασα πρὸς ὠκύπορον
πόρθμευμ' ἀχέων
περὶ *χεῖρε βαλοῦσα φιλήσει.

1535. δίκη MSS. corr. Aur. θήγει MSS. corr H. δίκη ... θηγάναις μάχαιραν Musgr. θηγάναις MSS. 1547. ἐπιτύμβιος αἶνος MSS. corr. Voss. Stanl. 1555. Ἰφιγένειαν· ἵν' MSS. corr. Jacob. 1559. χεῖρα MSS.

ΑΓΑΜΕΜΝΩΝ. 57

ΧΟ. ὄνειδος ἥκει τόδ' ἀντ' ὀνείδους.   ἀντ. δ'.   1560
δύσμαχα δ' ἐστὶ κρῖναι.
φέρει φέροντ', ἐκτίνει δ' ὁ καίνων.
μίμνει δὲ μίμνοντος ἐν *θρόνῳ Διὸς
παθεῖν τὸν ἔρξαντα. θέσμιον γάρ·
τίς ἂν γονὰν *ἀραῖον ἐκβάλοι δόμων;   1565
κεκόλληται γένος *πρὸς ἄτᾳ.

ΚΛ. ἐς τόνδ' ἐνέβη ξὺν ἀληθείᾳ   ἀντ. ε'.
*χρησμός. ἐγὼ δ' οὖν
ἐθέλω δαίμονι τῷ Πλεισθενιδῶν
ὅρκους θεμένη τάδε μὲν στέργειν,   1570
δύστλητά περ ὄνθ'. ὁ δὲ λοιπόν, ἰόντ'
ἐκ τῶνδε δόμων ἄλλην γενεὰν
τρίβειν θανάτοις αὐθένταισι.
κτεάνων τε μέρος
βαιὸν ἐχούσῃ πᾶν ἀπόχρη μοι   1575
μανίας μελάθρων
ἀλληλοφόνους ἀφελούσῃ.

ΑΙΓΙΣΘΟΣ.

ὦ φέγγος εὖφρον ἡμέρας δικηφόρου.
φαίην ἂν ἤδη νῦν βροτῶν τιμαόρους
θεοὺς ἄνωθεν-γῆς ἐποπτεύειν ἄχη,
ἰδὼν ὑφαντοῖς ἐν πέπλοις Ἐρινύων   1580
τὸν ἄνδρα τόνδε κείμενον φίλως ἐμοί,
χερὸς πατρῴας *ἐκτίνοντα μηχανάς.
Ἀτρεὺς γὰρ ἄρχων τῆσδε γῆς, τούτου πατήρ.

1563. χρόνῳ MSS. corr. Schütz.   1565. ῥῖον MSS. corr. H.
1566. προσάψαι MSS. corr. Blomf.   1568. χρησμὸν MSS.   1575.
μοι δ' | ἀλληλοφόνους MSS.   δ' has come from hiatus, hiatus from
wrong order; corr. Erfurdt.   1582. ἐκτείνοντα MSS.

πατέρα Θυέστην τὸν ἐμόν, ὡς τορῶς φράσαι,
αὐτοῦ τ' ἀδελφόν, ἀμφίλεκτος ὢν κράτει, 1585
ἠνδρηλάτησεν ἐκ πόλεώς τε καὶ δόμων.
καὶ προστρόπαιος ἑστίας μολὼν πάλιν
τλήμων Θυέστης μοῖραν εὗρετ' ἀσφαλῆ,
τὸ μὴ θανὼν πατρῷον αἱμάξαι πέδον.
[αὐτοῦ.] ξένια δὲ τοῦδε δύσθεος πατὴρ 1590
['Ατρεύς, προθύμως μᾶλλον ἢ φίλως,] πατρὶ
τὠμῷ, κρεουργὸν ἦμαρ εὐθύμως ἄγειν
δοκῶν, παρέσχε δαῖτα παιδείων κρεῶν.
τὰ μὲν ποδήρη καὶ χερῶν ἄκρους κτένας
† ἔθρυπτ' ἄνωθεν ἀνδρακὰς καθήμενος 1595
* ἄσημ'· ὁ δ' αὐτῶν αὐτίκ' ἀγνοίᾳ λαβὼν †
ἔσθει βορὰν ἄσωτον, ὡς ὁρᾷς, γένει.
κἄπειτ' ἐπιγνοὺς ἔργον οὐ καταίσιον,
ᾤμωξεν, ἀμπίπτει δ' † ἀπὸ * σφαγὴν ἐρῶν,†
μόρον δ' ἄφερτον Πελοπίδαις ἐπεύχεται, 1600
λάκτισμα δείπνου ξυνδίκως τιθεὶς ἀρᾷ,
οὕτως ὀλέσθαι πᾶν τὸ Πλεισθένους γένος.
ἐκ τῶνδέ σοι πεσόντα τόνδ' ἰδεῖν πάρα.
κἀγὼ δίκαιος τοῦδε τοῦ φόνου ῥαφεύς.
τρίτον γὰρ ὄντα μ' ἐπὶ * δυσαθλίῳ πατρὶ 1605
συνεξελαύνει τυτθὸν ὄντ' ἐν σπαργάνοις.
τραφέντα δ' αὖθις ἡ δίκη κατήγαγεν.
καὶ τοῦδε τἀνδρὸς ἡψάμην θυραῖος ὤν,
πᾶσαν συνάψας μηχανὴν δυσβουλίας.
οὕτω καλὸν δὴ καὶ τὸ κατθανεῖν ἐμοί, 1610

1590-1. Bracketed parts in MSS., but very probably spurious.
1595. ἔκρυπτ' Cas.   1596. ἄσημα δ' MSS. text H.D.   1599.
ἄν. πίπτει MSS. corr. Cant.   σφαγῆς MSS. text Hart.   ἐρῶν MSS.
ἐμῶν edd.   1605. ἐπὶ δέκ' ἀθλίῳ MSS. text Schöm. Karst.

ΑΓΑΜΕΜΝΩΝ.

ἰδόντα τοῦτον τῆς δίκης ἐν ἕρκεσιν.
ΧΟ. Αἴγισθ', ὑβρίζειν ἐν κακοῖσιν οὐ σέβω.
σὺ δ' ἄνδρα τόνδε φῂς ἑκὼν κατακτανεῖν,
μόνος δ' ἔποικτον τόνδε βουλεῦσαι φόνον·
οὔ φημ' ἀλύξειν ἐν δίκῃ τὸ σὸν κάρα   1615
δημορριφεῖς, σάφ' ἴσθι, λευσίμους ἀράς.
ΑΙ. σὺ ταῦτα φωνεῖς νερτέρᾳ προσήμενος
κώπῃ, κρατούντων τῶν ἐπὶ ζυγῷ δορύς;
γνώσει γέρων ὢν ὡς διδάσκεσθαι βαρὺ
τῷ τηλικούτῳ, σωφρονεῖν εἰρημένον.   1620
δεσμὸς δὲ καὶ τὸ γῆρας αἵ τε νήστιδες
δύαι διδάσκειν ἐξοχώταται φρενῶν
ἰατρομάντεις. οὐχ ὁρᾷς ὁρῶν τάδε;
πρὸς κέντρα μὴ λάκτιζε, μὴ *παίσας μογῇς.
ΧΟ. γύναι, σὺ τοὺς ἥκοντας ἐκ μάχης *μένων   1625
οἰκουρὸς εὐνὴν ἀνδρὸς *αἰσχύνας ἅμα
ἀνδρὶ στρατηγῷ τόνδ' ἐβούλευσας μόρον;
ΑΙ. καὶ ταῦτα τἄπη κλαυμάτων ἀρχηγενῆ.
Ὀρφεῖ δὲ γλῶσσαν τὴν ἐναντίαν ἔχεις.
ὁ μὲν γὰρ ἦγε πάντ' ἀπὸ φθογγῆς χαρᾷ,   1630
σὺ δ' ἐξορίνας *νηπίοις ὑλάγμασιν
ἄξει· κρατηθεὶς δ' ἡμερώτερος φανεῖ.
ΧΟ. ὡς δὴ σύ μοι τύραννος Ἀργείων ἔσει,
ὃς οὐκ, ἐπειδὴ τῷδ' ἐβούλευσας μόρον,
δρᾶσαι τόδ' ἔργον οὐκ ἔτλης αὐτοκτόνως;   1635
ΑΙ. τὸ γὰρ δολῶσαι πρὸς γυναικὸς ἦν σαφῶς·
ἐγὼ δ' ὕποπτος ἐχθρὸς ἦ παλαιγενής.
ἐκ τῶν δὲ τοῦδε χρημάτων πειράσομαι

1611. ἰδόντι Fa.   1613. τόνδ' ἔφης MSS.   1621. δεσμόν
V. Fl. text Fa.   1624. πήσας MSS.   1625. τοῦδ' ἥκοντος Stanl.
and most edd. text MSS.   μένων Wieseler. νέον MSS.   1626. αἰσχύνουσ' MSS. corr. Wieseler.   1631. ἠπίοις MSS. corr. Jacob.

ἄρχειν πολιτῶν· τὸν δὲ μὴ πειθάνορα
ζεύξω βαρείαις οὔτι μὴ σειραφόρον   1640
κριθῶντα πῶλον· ἀλλ' ὁ δυσφιλὴς *σκότῳ
λιμὸς ξύνοικος μαλθακόν σφ' ἐπόψεται.
ΧΟ. τί δὴ τὸν ἄνδρα τόνδ' ἀπὸ ψυχῆς κακῆς
οὐκ αὐτὸς ἠνάριζες; ἀλλὰ † σὺν γυνὴ
χώρας μίασμα καὶ θεῶν ἐγχωρίων   1645
ἔκτειν'. Ὀρέστης ἆρά που βλέπει φάος,
ὅπως κατελθὼν δεῦρο πρευμενεῖ τύχῃ
ἀμφοῖν γένηται τοῖνδε παγκρατὴς φονεύς;
ΑΙ. ἀλλ' ἐπεὶ δοκεῖς τάδ' ἔρδειν καὶ λέγειν, γνώσει τάχα.
ΧΟ.   *   *   *   *   *   1650
ΑΙ. εἶα δὴ φίλοι λοχῖται, τοὔργον οὐκ ἑκὰς τόδε.
ΧΟ. εἶα δή, ξίφος πρόκωπον πᾶς τις εὐτρεπιζέτω.
ΑΙ. ἀλλὰ μὴν κἀγὼ πρόκωπος οὐκ ἀναίνομαι θανεῖν.
ΧΟ. δεχομένοις λέγεις θανεῖν σε· τὴν τύχην δ' *αἱρούμεθα.   1653
Κ.Λ. μηδαμῶς, ὦ φίλτατ' ἀνδρῶν, ἄλλα *δράσωμεν κακά.
ἀλλὰ καὶ τάδ' ἐξαμῆσαι πολλὰ, δύστηνον *θέρος·
πημονῆς δ' ἅλις γ' ὑπάρχει· μηδὲν αἱματώμεθα.
† *στεῖχε καὶ σὺ χοἰ γέροντες πρὸς δόμους,
*πεπρωμένοις
πρὶν παθεῖν *εἴξαντες. ἄρκειν χρῆν τάδ' ὡς ἐπρά-
ξαμεν. †
εἰ δέ τοι μόχθων γένοιτο τῶνδ' ἅλις, *δεχοίμεθ' ἄν,
δαίμονος χολῇ βαρείᾳ δυστυχῶς πεπληγμένοι. 1660

1641. κότῳ MSS. Perhaps δυσφιλεῖ σκότῳ is right.   1644. σὺν
MSS. νιν most edd. σοὶ Sch.   1653. ἐρούμεθα MSS.   1654.
δράσομεν MSS.   1655. ὁ ἔρως MSS. corr. Schütz.   1656. ὕπαρχε
MSS. ἦματ. MSS.   1657. στείχετε δ' οἱ γέροντες πρὸς δόμους
πεπρωμένους τούσδε MSS. στεῖχε καὶ σὺ χοἰ Franz.   πεπρωμένοις
Madv. 1658. παθεῖν. ἔρξαντες καιρὸν Fl. παθεῖν. ἔρξαντα κ. V. Fa.
ἔρξαντες. ἀρκεῖν H. text Madv. 1659. γ' ἐχοίμεθ ἄν MSS. corr. H.

ΑΓΑΜΕΜΝΩΝ.

ὧδ' ἔχει λόγος γυναικός, εἴ τις ἀξιοῖ μαθεῖν.
ΑΙ. ἀλλὰ τούσδ' ἐμοὶ ματαίαν γλῶσσαν ὧδ' <u>ἀπανθίσαι</u>,
κἀκβαλεῖν ἔπη τοιαῦτα δαίμονος πειρωμένους,
σώφρονος γνώμης δ' ἁμαρτεῖν, τὸν κρατοῦντά * θ'
ὑβρίσαι. 1664
ΧΟ. οὐκ ἂν Ἀργείων τόδ' εἴη, φῶτα προσσαίνειν κακόν.
ΑΙ. ἀλλ' ἐγώ σ' ἐν ὑστέραισιν ἡμέραις μέτειμ' ἔτι.
ΧΟ. οὔκ, ἐὰν δαίμων Ὀρέστην δεῦρ' ἀπευθύνῃ μολεῖν.
ΑΙ. οἶδ' ἐγὼ φεύγοντας ἄνδρας ἐλπίδας σιτουμένους.
ΧΟ. πρᾶσσε, πιαίνου, μιαίνων τὴν δίκην· ἐπεὶ πάρα.
ΑΙ. ἴσθι μοι δώσων ἄποινα τῆσδε μωρίας χάριν. 1670
ΧΟ. κόμπασον θαρσῶν, ἀλέκτωρ ὥστε θηλείας πέλας.
ΚΛ. μὴ προτιμήσῃς ματαίων τῶνδ' ὑλαγμάτων· *ἐγὼ
καὶ σὺ θήσομεν κρατοῦντε τῶνδε δωμάτων *καλῶς.

1664. MSS. have 3 syllables wanting. θ' ὑβρίσαι Blomf. 1672.
ἐγώ Cant. Wanting in MSS. 1673. καλῶς Aur. Wanting in
MSS.

NOTES.

[PROLOGUE. *The palace of Agamemnon at Argos, at night. Enter on the roof a watchman, who reclines head on arm, and soliloquises:*
(ll. 1-39.) 'For a year I have been watching for the fire to tell of Troy's capture; the life here is one of sadness and anxiety: now I hope for better things.' The light then appears, and he bursts into a shout of joy, broken by gloomy hints at the close.]

l. 1. The place is called Argos, and the people Argeioi, all through the play. According to the old tradition, however, Agamemnon was king of Mykenae, a town about six miles from Argos. Homer (2. 569) enumerates the towns which formed his kingdom. The use of the name Argos for Mykenae was nevertheless common in the Greek poets, and it was all the more natural now, as about B.C. 463 (five years before 458, the date of the play) Argos had defeated and dismantled Mykenae and sold or expelled the inhabitants. Soon after this the Argeioi became allied with Athens.

The watchman is a loyal servant of Agamemnon, sent to watch for the beacon-fire which is to tell of the capture of Troy. It is possible, however, that the queen wishes for her own purposes to have early tidings of her lord's return. (Patin, Eschyle, 314.)

l. 2. 'Through this long year of watching,' lit. 'through the length of a year's watch.' μῆκος, acc. of duration. (It is possible to take φρουρᾶς as app. to πόνων, and μῆκος acc. of respect, 'these toils, my watch a year in length,' but it makes a rougher, more artificial, construction. The conjecture μῆχος, 'cure,' which D. adopted, is ingenious, but quite unnecessary.) ἣν κοιμώμενος, 'wherein resting.' ἣν cognate or internal acc.

l. 3. στέγαις Ἀτρειδῶν ἄγκαθεν, κυνὸς δίκην, 'on the roof of the Atreidae couched head on arm, like a dog.' ἄγκαθεν from ἄγκη, 'bent arm' (like the common Homeric ἀγκάς in ἀγκὰς ἑλεῖν, ἀγκὰς ἔχειν, κ.τ.λ. 'to hold, or take in the arm'), found Eum. 80 ἄγκαθεν λαβὼν βρέτας: quite a different word from ἀνέκαθεν (from ἄνω, ἔκαθεν,) 'from above,' which is clearly the right reading in Eum. 369.

Eng., Schn., Dind., read στέγης, and construe ἄγκαθεν, 'above,' con-

AGAMEMNON.

tracted from ἀνέκαθεν, which makes good sense, but it is unlikely that Aeschylus should have used the rare word ἀνέκαθεν in a form syncopated so as to confuse it with the different word ἄγκαθεν, which we know he also uses in Eum. 80.

l. 4. κάτοιδα, 'I know well,' 'I have learnt to know.'

l. 6. δυνάστας, bright 'rulers,' as he finely calls the leading constellations whose rise marks the seasons; not 'the sun and moon,' as Pal., which in no sense bring summer and winter.

l. 7. Is no doubt a gloss. ἀστέρας is rough rhythm, a dull repetition after ἄστρων, superfluous to the construction with δυνάστας in the line before; and the whole line rather produces the effect of bathos.

l. 8. Notice the rhetorical repetitions, λαμπάδος .. πυρός, φάτιν .. βάξιν. φυλάσσω, 'I watch for.'

l. 10. ἀλώσιμον .. βάξιν, 'tidings of capture,' a rare use of the adj.; in poetry, however, there is hardly any relation to the substantive which the adj. cannot express. ὧδε γάρ, best taken simply, 'for such sway she bears, my mistress' manly heart, nursing her hope,' i.e. for I am forced to obey her. (So Eng., Schn.; Paley's κρατεῖ ἐλπίζον, 'confident in hope,' is forced and unusual; and the order is against it.) The phrase is slightly strained but not unnatural. Others take it 'for so she orders' simply: but κρατεῖ is not so used.

l. 12. The clause εὖτ' ἂν .. ἔχω, is interrupted by the parenthesis ὕβος γὰρ .. ὕπνῳ, and taken up again loosely but naturally by ὅταν δέ .., so that the general sense is 'and when I keep my weary watch (for fear prevents my sleeping), and try to while away the time by song.'

l. 14. ἐμήν, with the double emphasis of being last word of the sentence and first word of the line, is very weak, and is perhaps a corruption of εὐνήν in the line before, as Hartung suggests: though neither Bentley's ἐμοί, nor Schn.'s τί μήν; is satisfactory: and we do find weak words in that position, cf. 1231, 1589. φόβος, 'the fear,' is of what will follow when the king returns; but it is only a hint, as in 19 and 31.

l. 15. τὸ μὴ .. συμβαλεῖν, a common Greek idiom, being one form of the consecutive infinitive, expressing the *result*, the sense being 'so that I cannot,' 'preventing me from.'

l. 16. ἀείδειν. There is a proverb 'singing on watch,' (φρουρᾶς ᾄδων) Arist. Clouds, 720. μινύρομαι, 'to hum,' or 'warble,' properly 'to sing in a low tone,' used often of birds. The full phrase is found Ar. Eccl. 880 μινυρομένη πρὸς ἐμαυτὴν μέλος (of a woman waiting and humming a tune to while away the time). δοκῶ, 'I think to,' as we say. So Ar. Vesp. 177 τὸν ὄνον ἐξάγειν δοκῶ, Αν. 671 φιλῆσαί μοι δοκῶ. (The construction is really an attraction into the *personal* from the *impersonal*, instead of saying δοκεῖ μοι... So the Greeks say δίκαιός εἰμι ποιεῖν for δίκαιόν μοι ἐστὶ ποιεῖν. See 1079.)

NOTES. LINES 4–34.

l. 17. 'Shredding in this vocal cure in place of sleep.' ἐντέμνω, 'to slice or shred in,' is used of putting (medicinal) herbs into a potion; so here metaphorically. (K.'s ἐν τέμνω is not happy; if τέμνω is admitted, what more natural than ἐντέμνω?) Observe the mixture of sententiousness and forcible homeliness in the speech of this servant: his repetitions (8–10), and antithesis (11, 21–22), and dark hints (39), and his homely metaphors from watchdogs (3), drugs (71), dicing (32–33), oxen (36), are all characteristic.

l. 19. This cautious phrase might simply mean that the 'absence of the king was felt;' but 'to those who know' (39) it meant the unfaithfulness of Klytaemnestra.

l. 21. 'When with glad tidings shines the fire of darkness,' a sententious antithesis such as the rustic wit delights in. So νυκτός, ἡμερήσιον, 22. [*At this point the beacon he is watching for flashes out.* He is supposed to be looking northward toward the Argolic mountain, Arachnaion, which was the last beacon before Argos, 309.]

l. 22. 'Thou blaze of night, a daylight glare revealing,' is another of his antitheses.

l. 24. συμφορά, 'hap,' 'event,' a neutral word, here in good sense, though mostly used in a bad one.

l. 25. ἰοῦ, ἰοῦ. 'Hurrah!' exclamation of joy here; though more often of horror and woe, as 1214.

l. 26. The MSS. vary between σημαίνω (M. G.) and σημανῶ: the latter expresses his *intention* of telling Klytaemnestra; the former means 'by this cry ἰοῦ I signify to K.,' and that is rather more vigorous, and also suits τορῶς, 'loudly,' better.

l. 27. The constr. is the acc. inf. of the oblique petition, 'I signify that she should rise from her bed and upraise a shout,' etc. ἐπαντείλασαν (notice the syncope, for ἐπ-ανα-τείλασαν), a picturesque word suggesting the rise of sun or star. δόμοις might be dat. recip. 'for the house;' but more likely it is the *local* use 'in the house,' an old fashion surviving in poetry.

l. 29. εἴπερ, 'since,' as often.

l. 30. ἀγγέλλων πρέπει, 'brightly tells,' lit. 'shines telling.' Again a picturesque phrase. (ἀγγέλων of Med. etc. is clearly an error.)

l. 31. [*Here the watchman executes a triumphal dance.*]

ll. 32–33. These two lines become clear when one sees that the metaphor is all from dicing: 'My master's luck I'll mark as prosperous, now that this fire has thrown me sixes three.' θέσθαι, 'to put it down,' as we say; somewhat as θέσθαι παρ' οὐδέν, ἐν ἀδικήματι θέσθαι, κ.τ.λ.

l. 34. δ' οὖν. The regular use of these particles is in *dismissing a subject, cutting short* a train of thought, *resuming* after a digression, and such situations. ἔστω δ' οὖν ὅπως ὑμῖν φίλον Soph. O. C. 1205, οὐκ οἶδ'.

5

AGAMEMNON.

ἐμοὶ δ' οὖν ᾖ τ' ἄγαν σιγῇ βαρύ *ib.* Ant. 1250. So Ag. 224, 255. 'Well, be it mine to grasp my lord's dear hand.'

l. 35. βαστάζω, prop. 'to bear, or lift,' so 'to feel,' 'to hold.' χέρα ἀλόχου β. Eur. Alc. 917; σῶμα β. Soph. O. C. 1105.

l. 36. The first shadow of the tragedy falls on the almost boisterous joy and playfulness of the rustic watcher, namely the dark hint of the unfaithfulness of Klytaemnestra, which is to lead to the 'worse that remains behind.' βοῦς ἐπὶ γλώσσῃ .. βέβηκε, 'a huge ox stands upon my tongue,' a pithy rustic metaphor for enforced silence; βοῦς being proverbially a *silent* animal (the idea of a reference to *bribery*—βοῦς being the ox on the old Attic coins—is less likely). βέβηκε, 'stands,' 'lies,' present sense, as is natural to perfect. So χῶρος ἐν ᾧ βεβήκαμεν, 'where we stand,' Soph. O. C. 52; ἐπὶ πώλου βεβῶσαν, 'riding,' 'seated,' *ib.* O. C. 313.

l. 38. ὡς, 'for,' gives the reason for σιγῶ. ἑκών, 'purposely,' goes with λήθομαι chiefly (as Eng., Schn., Pal., point out), the first verb, αὐδῶ, being less important. (Observe the Epic μαθοῦσι for τοῖς μ.) 'For purposely, as I speak to those who know, to those who know not—I forget.' λήθομαι is rather unexpected, and is another touch of what may be almost called his rustic playfulness. With this dark hint he goes off; and the chorus of Argive elders enter the orchestra by the side passage (πάροδος). The proper choral odes begin 104.

[PARODOS. ll. 40-103. *Enter the chorus, marching in time to the anapaestic song.* The general sense of the opening or entrance song is as follows: 'Ten years are passed since the Atreidae sailed forth with the fleet for vengeance, like vultures robbed of their young (40-54). Zeus Xenios is wroth with Paris and sends the avenging host, bringing long struggles for both sides, and the end to be as fate wills' (55-71). *Meanwhile the queen Klytaemnestra appears, and begins the preparations for sacrifice.* 'What hast thou heard, lady? See, all the altars begin to blaze! What does it mean? We waver between anxiety and hope' (72-103).]

ll. 40-42. 'This is the tenth year since Priam's great foe King Menelaos and Agamemnon.' It has been noticed as odd that μέγας ἀντίδικος should be applied only to Menelaos, and that Agamemnon, the 'king of men,' is second. It may be only accidental, as in the next two lines (ὀχυρὸν ζεῦγος) and below (109 δίθρονον κράτος) they are treated with equal honour. Or, perhaps, ἀντίδικος is used strictly, and Menelaos comes first as the wronged party, Agamemnon being his helper. ἀντίδικος, metaphor from law-courts, meaning simply 'antagonist.' ἐπεί and even ὅτε are used in this sense 'since;' the precise phrase is ἐξ οὗ.

l. 43. διθρόνου .. τιμῆς, gen. of *description* or *equivalence* as it is called, one of the numerous shades of *relation* described by genitive.

6

NOTES. LINES 35-62.

Translate, 'The mighty pair of Atreus' sons, each dowered from Zeus with rank of throne and sceptre.' (It is literally, 'pair of Atreidae, of two-throned honour,' etc., i.e. 'consisting of;' the τιμή is the abstract aspect of the kings.) Grammatically τιμῆς and Ἀτρειδᾶν are parallel, both being gen. after ζεῦγος. Διόθεν qualifies the adjectives. Ἀτρειδᾶν, Doric gen.; the choruses contain many Doric forms.

l. 47. ἦραν, 'sped;' αἴρω, prop. 'to lift,' is used commonly for 'to start,' both trans. στόλον, στρατόν, and intrans. στρατῷ, ναυσί, both of land and sea. It probably originally meant simply 'to take up' your things and be off.

l. 49. τρόπον (acc. of *apposition* to sentence, like δίκην, χάριν), 'like.'

l. 50. οἵτε, Epic form of rel. ἐκπατίοις (πάτος, 'path'), 'out of the path,' may mean either 'strange,' 'unbounded,' 'terrible,' or 'lonely;' the latter very well suits the eagles wheeling over their craggy nests; and is the meaning given by the Scholiast. παίδων, 'for their young.' Gen. of relation, common after words of feeling, as anger, grief, surprise, etc. [Blomfield's ἐκπάγλοις is very probable.]

l. 51. ὕπατοι λεχέων, 'high o'er their nest,' ὕπατος governing gen. much as ὑπέρ does, by a slight extension of usage.

l. 52. 'The oarage of their wing,' a fine phrase for the flight of large birds. Lucretius, 6. 743, imitates (*remigi oblitae pennarum*) and Vergil has followed (*remigio alarum*, Aen. 1. 301, 6. 19).

l. 53. δεμνιοτήρη πόνον ὀρταλίχων ὀλέσαντες, 'having lost the guardian-task of their brood,' i.e. 'the task of keeping the nest:' the adj. describes in what the task consists. The word occurs again 1449, in the sense of 'keeping the bed,' i.e. 'confining to bed' of sickness.

l. 55. 'Above there is one that hears, either Apollo,' etc. Observe idiomatic use of τις, where we should say 'perchance,' So Verg. Aen. 1. 182 'Anthea *si quem* iactatum vento videat.' *Apollo* protects the birds as god of augury: *Pan* as god of the forest and wild animals: *Zeus* as god of justice. (Schn.)

l. 56. Notice the loaded adjectives, in Aeschylus' weighty manner, 'the shrill lament of winged mourners who dwell in his skies :' μετοίκων being a finely imaginative word: the birds are the *sojourners* in the god's home.

l. 59. παραβᾶσιν, 'to the transgressors,' the older Epic use of the partic. without τοῖς. So μαθοῦσι 38.

l. 61. ἐπ' Ἀλεξάνδρῳ, 'against Paris;' ἐπί with dat. lit. 'on' (as we say, 'he marched on Rome'). It is an Epic use, see illustrations on 357; in Attic and prose it would be acc. ξένιος, because the crime of the rape of Helen was an offence against the sacred laws of hospitality, which were under the protection of Zeus Xenios.

l. 62. πολυάνορος, 'wooed by many a suitor.'

7

AGAMEMNON.

l. 64. Gen. abs. 'when the knee is bowed in the dust.' ἐρειδομένου, lit. 'resting.'

l. 65. προτέλεια, 'the prelude,' usually the sacrifice before marriage (τέλος, 'rite'); here the 'prelude of the battle,' but suggesting the other sense, that the fighting was a bitter *marriage-prelude* for Paris.

l. 67. ἔστι ὅπη νῦν ἔστι, 'the issue is—as it is now,' an intentionally enigmatic sentence. In the mouth of the chorus it naturally means 'there is good news; the Trojans are vanquished' (though they do not as yet know the details). But to the spectators it has a second and deeper meaning, as Agamemnon is returning to find unfaithfulness, conspiracy, and murder, and so in a terrible sense τελεῖται ἐς τὸ πεπρωμένον, 'it draws to its fated end.'

The Greek dramas are full of such double meanings, bearing only a single sense to the speaker; and the contrast between the two senses, or between the position of the speaker as he conceived it, and as it was known to the audience, often formed most effective situations, of Dramatic Irony, as it has been called.

ll. 69-71. ὑποκλαίων of the MSS. gives a tiresome repetition with δακρύων, so I have taken Casaubon's ὑποκαίων (adopted by Eng., Schn.), making a very natural antithesis of *offering* and *libation*. The sense will then be, 'Neither by secret offering, nor by secret libation, nor by tears shall one soothe their stubborn wrath (i.e. the gods' wrath) for the unburnt sacrifices.' Again a double meaning. (1) In the chorus' mouth it means, 'The Trojans cannot soothe their angry gods by any expiation;' but (2) to the spectators it has a second deeper sense, 'Agamemnon cannot by any offering assuage the anger of the gods for his sacrifice of Iphigeneia.' It is hard however to be sure what is the meaning of ἀπύρων ἱερῶν in (1), or the surface sense, it may mean 'rejected sacrifice' (offering which will not burn); or as Schn., Pal., 'unholy rite' (rite without fire, i.e. the marriage of Helen and Paris); or thirdly, as Enger, 'Shall soothe the stubborn wrath *of* the unlit sacrifice,' the wrath of the god being transferred to the sacrifice which will not burn.

l. 72. ἀτίται, 'unhonoured' is the best sense (though the termination is rare in passive sense, cp. ἀφέτης, κηροδέτης). [Others say 'not-paying,' i.e. either 'not serving' or 'not avenging;' but both are less smooth and natural.]

l. 73. ἀρωγῆς, common gen. after λείπεσθαι, ἡσσᾶσθαι, etc., like gen. after comparative, 'left out of the army that gave aid.'

l. 77. ἀνάσσων, 'leaping' (H., Dind., Schn., Eng.), better far than ἀνάσσων, 'ruling' (MSS. and Pal.). The gen. sense is, 'the strength of the old is like children's (ἰσχὺν ἰσόπαιδα); for the very young vigour is as unfit for war as the very old feebleness.' In 76-82 he simply develops the idea 'the old are no better than children.'

NOTES. LINES 64-94.

l. 78. ἰσόπρεσβυς, 'is like unto age,' i.e. the vigour of boyhood is yet no fitter for war than decrepit age. Ἄρης .. χώρᾳ, 'and Ares is not in his place,' i.e. is not *there* in his place, his place being the full-grown man. κατὰ χώραν is the prose phrase for ἐνὶ χώρᾳ.

l. 79. τό θ' ὑπέργηρων, 'and the last old age,' the neuter expressing the *class*, like τὸ νέον, τὸ καλόν; by a loose but natural construction it becomes masc. at 81, στείχει, a vivid personal verb, having prepared the way.

The MSS. are corrupt, only Fa. reads as above. We might read τί θ' ὑπέργηρως, 'what of the very old?' with Eng., but prefer to follow Fa., the question being not very idiomatic or natural.

l. 80. τρίποδας, 'the three foot ways' are of course the old men walking with a stick.

l. 82. 'He strays, a mid-day dream,' a feeble shadowy life. The day-dream being even more unreal than the night-dream.

[*While this song has been singing, the queen Klytaemnestra comes out and begins to make arrangements for the sacrificing, lighting up the altars and ordering about her train of maidens. The chorus address her directly.*]

l. 83. Τυνδάρεω, irregular gen. from Τυνδαρεύς, as though Ionic gen. of Τυνδάρης.

l. 87. πευθοῖ, 'from hearing;' most MSS. have πειθοῖ, 'from belief,' a commoner but less appropriate word. Fl. has πυθοῖ, which suggests the real reading. περίπεμπτα θυοσκεῖς, 'art sacrificing by word sent round?' i.e. 'art sending round the word to sacrifice?' περίπεμπτα being adverbial (strictly, in agreement with cogn. acc.). θυοσκεῖς, MSS. θυοσκινεῖς, probably corrupted to complete the full line. The right word, θυοσκεῖς, is restored from Hesych. (θυος, κα- καίω, 'to burn offering.')

l. 88. 'And of all the gods that guard our city, above, below, in the heavens, in the mart.' ἀστυνόμοι, the same as the commoner words πολιοῦχοι and πολισσοῦχοι. ὕπατοι were gods like Zeus, Apollo, Hera, etc. χθόνιοι were Ge, Pluto, Hermes, Eumenides, etc.

The other antithesis, 'in the heavens, in the mart,' is less obvious, but by ἀγοραῖοι he probably means those who do specially preside over the city-life; by οὐράνιοι those who do not. Ἀγοραῖος is applied to Zeus (Eum. 979), to *Hermes* (Ar. Eq. 297), to *Artemis* and *Athena* (Paus. 3. 11. 9). (In Theb. 257 τοῖς πολισσούχοις Θεοῖς Πεδιονόμοις τε κἀγορᾶς ἐπισκόποις, a different division is apparently meant, 'all our native gods, of the country and the town.')

l. 93. ἀνίσχει, 'arises,' intrans., as often from Homer onwards, esp. of the sun. See Lexicon.

l. 94. 'The pure unguent's soft and guileless spell' is a thoroughly

AGAMEMNON.

Aeschylean phrase, loaded and imaginative. It is called 'guileless' probably simply because παρηγορία, 'persuasion,' was so often guileful: the persuasion of oil to fire is genuine.

l. 96. πέλανος, 'a clot or lump' of solid or thick liquid, so here of oil. μυχόθεν, 'from the inner store,' adv. used (with the looseness of the primitive style of Aeschylus) to qualify the subs. πελάνῳ.

The MSS. reading βασιλείῳ quite good. It is needless to alter it to -ων.

l. 97. λέξασα.. παιών τε γενοῦ, the τε is not wanted, but it is a very natural anacoluthon. (Eng., Hart., Karst., etc., read λέξαις, which sets the grammar right, but is needless.)

l. 98. αἰνεῖν, in old sense. 'to tell of.'

l. 100. 'Which now is bitter, and now again hope from the altar fires bright shining drives back the relentless care of the grief that gnaws the heart.' The change in the constr. is very natural, and more effective than if he had finished the sentence strictly, 'and now again is lighter,' or something of that sort.

l. 101. I keep ἀγανὰ φαίνουσ', on the whole nearest to the MSS., φαίνουσα meaning 'shining,' common intransitive use.

l. 103. The reading is Hermann's; the only practical question is whether we should read τῆς θυμοβόρου φρένα λύπης or τὴν θυμόβορον φρένα λύπην. The latter is in apposition to φροντίδ', the former is governed by it. I follow H., Schn., Eng., in preferring the genitive; the mass of accusatives is so very clumsy. In either case φρένα is governed by the adj., a rare construction. Cp. 1090 πολλὰ συνίστορα, Pr. 904 ἄπορα πόριμος, Soph. Antig. 786 σὲ φύξιμος, where however the adjectives are more like simple verbals, and so the construction is easier.

[*Klytaemnestra has finished her preparations and has retired.*]

ll. 104-257. The general outline of the chorus' songs from here to the end 257 is as follows:

Strophe 1. (104-121.) I can tell the tale of victory, and the signs that went before—I yet am young enough for song—the omen of the two eagles, devouring a pregnant hare. (Woe, woe, but let the good prevail.)

Antistrophe 1. (122-139.) Kalchas the wise seer knew the sign, and prophesied: 'One day this host shall capture Troy. Only I pray no wrath of gods may strike it, for Artemis is angered against the eagles and pities the hare.' (Woe, woe, but let the good prevail.)

Epode (140-159). 'I pray Artemis therefore, though she loves the wild beasts, to suffer the triumph of the eagle princes. And Paean Apollo I invoke, to stay her from raising adverse gales, while she urges on a lawless sacrifice, the slaughter of a child, fraught with evils to the house.' So Kalchas spake. (Woe, woe, but let the good prevail.)

Str. β'. (160-166). Zeus—whate'er his rightful name—is the greatest of all.

Ant. β'. (167-175). Ouranos and Kronos are passed away—Zeus is the victor.

Str. γ'. (176-183). Zeus has appointed a law, that man shall learn by suffering, reluctant though he be.

Ant. γ'. (184-191). So then Agamemnon—uncomplaining, when the host was wind-bound and suffering at Aulis [*Str. δ'*, 192-204], and the delay was destroying the ships and men—but when Kalchas advised a bitter cure, the slaughter of Iphigeneia, to appease Artemis [*Ant. δ'.* 205-216], then Agamemnon spake: ''Tis evil to disobey, and evil to obey, how can I slay my child? how forsake my comrades?' [*Str. ε'.* 217-226]. So he bowed to necessity, and undertook the impious deed, misled by Madness the source of woe, and he slew his child. [*Ant. ε'.* 228-237]. Her youth and prayers they set at nought, and like a kid they raised her to the altar, in her flowing robes, and stifled her cries. [*Str. ς'.* 238-246]. She bared her breast, like a picture, striking all with pity; for often she had sung to them in her father's halls. [*Ant. ς'.* 247-257]. The rest I cannot tell; it was accomplished. For the future—let it come; what skills foreboding? Our friendly wish is that all may be well.

While the chorus sings, the day is supposed to break; and when Klytaemnestra returns (255) *it is broad day.*]

l. 104. κύριός εἰμι θροεῖν, 'I am he that shall sing,' 'I am the man to tell.' κύριος is 'the one who has the power,' 'the right one.' κυρία the *right* or *appointed* day. κράτος αἴσιον, 'the fated victory,' slightly strained but natural sense of κράτος. αἴσιος is properly used of omens, 'auspicious,' and is here transferred from the omens (ὅδιον) to the victory. ὅδιον, 'foretold by signs upon the way;' there were various kinds of omens—entrails, the flight of birds, chance cries, and *signs on the way*, ἐνοδίους τε συμβόλους Pr. 487. So in Ar. Ran. 197 the slave, being unlucky, says, τῷ συνέτυχον ἐξιών; 'what can have met me when I came out?'

l. 105. ἐκτελέων. Pal. takes this as a partic.—'accomplishing,' i.e. 'singing the accomplishment.' It is less harsh to take it as gen. of adj. ἐκτελής, 'complete,' 'consummate,' used in strained sense for 'royal,' 'high.' H., Schn., Eng., read ἐντελέων; needless, because it is equally used off its meaning, and MSS. all give ἐκτ. ἔτι γὰρ θεόθεν .. αἰών, a well-known difficulty, about which numerous conjectures have been made. Only four views are near enough. to the MSS. to be worth mentioning; the full reading of the MSS. is: ἔτι γὰρ θεόθεν καταπνείει πειθὼ μολπὰν ἀλκὰν ξύμφυτος αἰών. (1) Goodwin

AGAMEMNON.

(Amer. Phil. Ass. Trans. 1877) defends the MSS., and puts a comma at μολπάν: 'For still Persuasion from the gods breathes song upon me, still my old age (breathes) strength to sing.' It is very ingenious, but the antithesis (which the absence of 'and' emphasises) is harsh, 'age' and 'persuasion' being so unconnected, and the *point* surely is simply 'I am not too old to sing.' (2) Enger reads μολπᾶν, and makes μολπᾶν ἀλκάν an apposition to πειθώ: 'Still my age breathes from the gods upon me Persuasion, the strength of song.' (Old though I am, I am still inspired.) (3) H., Pal., Schn., etc., read μολπᾶν and ἀλκᾷ, though interpreting differently: 'Still age growing with strength (i.e. "not yet decrepit") breathes on me persuasion of song' (Pal.), or 'Still Persuasion of song breathes (intr.) upon me, namely the time commensurate with the war,' H., Schn., Kl. Paley's is good sense, though ἀλκᾷ σύμφυτος is harsh. Hermann's is very harsh and obscure and indeed impossible. (4) Prof. Campbell neatly suggests πειθοῖ μολπᾶν ἀλκάν, which he translates, 'by persuasion of song my life breathes valour.' Better take it, 'by persuasion from heaven my age yet breathes the strength of song,' the only ἀλκή I have is that of song. On the whole I prefer (2): and next best (4) or (3) with Paley's interpretation.

l. 109. ὅπως, 'how,' takes up the first clause, κύριός εἰμι θροεῖν, after the parenthesis. 'The twin sovereign power, ruling with one heart,' is a characteristic Aeschylean abstract phrase for the Atreidae.

l. 110. ξύμφρονα τάγαν, 'ruler of one heart;' the singular is strange, but due probably to κράτος. See 41, 112. [It must be τάγαν, acc. of τάγης, 'a leader,' not ταγάν, acc. of τᾰγή, 'rule.'] Keck suggests ἥβαν ξύμφρονα ταγοῖν, 'friendly might of the princes.' Ingenious.

l. 111. πράκτορι, 'avenging,' from πράσσειν in a special sense, 'to exact.' Eum. 624, τὸν πατρὸς φόνον πράξαντα. The MSS. here have σὺν δόρι δίκας πράκτορι, a plain gloss; fortunately the line is rightly quoted in Ar. Ran. 1288.

l. 112. 'The fierce bird' (θούριος, from θυ-, first 'smoke,' then 'violent movement or impulse') is said to 'send the kings to Troy,' because the sight of the eagles tearing the hare was the omen that encouraged them. θούριος ὄρνις becomes plural in the next line, but easily, by help of the adjectives.

l. 115. ὁ κελαινὸς .. ἀργᾶς, 'one black, one white of tail :' the black one is no doubt Agamemnon, the white-tail Menelaos (ἀργᾶς, alluding to Ἄργος, as often). Aristotle (Hist. Anim. 9. 32) aptly says, 'the largest eagle is the *White-tail* .. the strongest is that called the *Black Eagle* or *Hare-slayer*.' Perhaps Menelaos is intentionally hinted at as the less courageous.

l. 116. χερὸς ἐκ δοριπάλτου, i.e. 'on the right,' the lucky side for omens: the Greek augurs looking North, and the luck coming from the

East. Hence δεξιός gets a secondary meaning, 'favourable.' Notice ἐκ where we say 'on;' to the spectator the vision *comes from* right (subjective), but it *is on* the right (objective).

l. 119. φέρματα is Hartung's excellent emendation for φέρματι, the MSS. reading still retained by many. Those who retain it have to explain how γένναν can mean the *mother*, and how it can agree with βλαβέντα; a feat which they attempt. With φέρματα it is both easier and far more effective, 'rending the hare's young, an unborn brood, checked from their after-roamings;' λαγίναν γένναν will then be not the mother, but the unborn young within her. βλαβέντα, etc., neither hare nor young can roam any more, the eagles devour them.

l. 121. 'Echo the cry of wail; but let the good prevail.' In the refrain, fear and hope are mixed; the reason for the foreboding is not yet told; it occurs below.

l. 122. 'The good seer of the host' is of course Kalchas. δύο λήμασι δισσούς of the MSS. is meaningless; to say 'two differing in spirit,' as Paley takes it, is irrelevant; he is comparing 'the royal pair' to the two eagles; he calls them above ξύμφρονα τάγαν, 'princes one in heart;' and their *union* is the point wanted, not their *difference*. We had better therefore read λήμασιν ἴσους (ῐ according to the Epic scansion) with Dind., Eng.

l. 123. ἐδάη .. ἀρχάς, 'knew the hare-devourers and the leaders of the host,' i. e. 'knew that the hare-devourers *were* the leaders;' ἀρχάς, abst. for concr., like δίθρονον κράτος. Others take πομπούς ἀρχάς, 'the powers conducting,' i. e. the *birds*, whose omen led them; a much more far-fetched meaning.

l. 126. ἀγρεῖ, the prophetic present, as though the seer saw it happening. κέλευθος, lit. 'path,' i. e. 'expedition,' 'armament.' 'One day shall this host capture the city of Priam.'

l. 127. 'And all the gathered wealth of the people before the battlements Fate shall ravage with violent hand.' So the MSS. πρόσθε, which can be best taken with πύργων, and makes good sense. Others needlessly read πρὸς δὲ τὰ .., i.e. 'the wealth of the towers, and likewise the people's stores.'

l. 130. πρὸς τὸ βίαιον, like the commoner πρὸς βίαν, πρὸς ὀργήν, lit. 'towards' violence, wrath, etc., i. e. 'violently.' So Prom. 214, πρὸς τὸ καρτερόν.

l. 131. οἶον, 'only.' ἄγα, 'envy'—Hermann's certain correction for the MSS. ἄτα, which will not scan and makes a worse meaning. προτυπὲν στόμιον μέγα Τροίας στρατωθέν .. 'lower on the mighty curb of Troy (i. e. the Greek army), the embattled host, stricken before its time (i. e. before it reaches the foe).' The seer darkly foretells here the wrath of Artemis, which was to delay the host at Aulis.

AGAMEMNON.

l. 135. οἴκῳ, to say 'the pure maiden is wroth *against the house*, meaning the family of Agamemnon, is no doubt sense; but the correction οἴκτῳ makes infinitely better sense; 'for from pity Artemis the pure maiden is wroth with the winged hounds (eagles) of her sire.' In this way we are saved the harsh apposition οἴκῳ .. κυσί. Other corrections, οἴκοι, οἴω, need not be considered. οἴκτῳ is due to Scaliger.

l. 136. πτανοῖσι κυσί, 'the winged hounds,' i. e. the eagles. Cf. Prom. 1022, Διὸς δέ τοι πτηνὸς κυὼν δαφοινὸς αἰετός. The bearing of this is a little obscure, but it is of this kind: The sign of the eagles is an encouraging sign to the Greeks, boding victory; but as Artemis is offended by the eagles devouring the hare, so she is wroth with the Greeks; and her anger may do harm.

l. 137. αὐτότοκον, adj. used rather strangely = αὐτοῖς τοῖς τόκοισι, 'young and all.' So αὐτόχθονος 536, αὐτόπρεμνος Eum. 401, αὐτόκωπος Cho. 163. πρὸ λόχου, 'before the birth.'

ll. 140-145. With the ordinary readings ἁ καλά (140) and αἰτεῖ (144). This passage is taken to mean, in general sense, 'Though so gentle to all the young of beasts, the goddess asks for the accomplishment of these omens, good and evil alike.' The difficulty is, why should Artemis *ask* for the accomplishment of the cruelty which she hates (στυγεῖ δὲ δεῖπνον)? Schütz suggests τούτων, αἰτῶ, ξύμβολα κράναι, optative. 'may she accomplish.' It is much better to read, with all the MSS. but one, καλά (vocative), for ἁ καλά, and read αἴνει (imper.) for αἰτεῖ. It then will run 'Though so kindly to the tender young of mighty lions, O fair maiden, and loving the suckling brood of all the wild wood beasts, yet *consent* to the accomplishment of the signs of these things, visions of good and ill.' This makes 140-145 addressed to Artemis, as 146-155 is to Apollo.

l. 141. I take the generally adopted λεπτοῖς for the meaningless MS. ἀέπτοις: in the original uncials A and Λ were very near.

l. 145. στρουθῶν is clearly corrupt, as it lengthens α of φάσματα, and as there is nothing about 'sparrows' here at all. It has got in by some one confusing this story with the story of the sign of the sparrows in ll. 2. 311.

l. 146. Παιᾶνα, 'the healer,' well-known name of Apollo. Ἰήϊος, also name of Apollo; said to be from ἰή, and to mean 'invoked with the cry,' like εὔιος for Dionysos.

l. 148. χρονίας ἐχενῇδας ἀπλοίας, 'adverse gales, long delaying the fleet.' (ἐχενῇς from ἔχω-ναῦς, 'ship-detaining.')

l. 150. τεύξῃ, i. e. Artemis. Apollo is asked to prevail with his sister not to delay the host by adverse winds.

l. 151. θυσίαν, the 'other sacrifice, lawless, unfeasting,' is the sacrifice of his daughter Iphigeneia, which Agamemnon made to appease

NOTES. LINES 135-179.

Artemis, as told below. The δαίς being the feast on the meat of the sacrifice, this offering was clearly ἄδαιτος.

l. 152. 'A seed of strife clinging to the race (σύμφυτον) fruitful of rebellion against the lord' (lit. 'not fearing the lord' of the house), the last words being a dark hint of the murder that awaits Agamemnon from the faithless Klytaemnestra.

ll. 154, 155. A characteristic instance of Aeschylus' accumulation of phrase. Here are six adjectives and one substantive. 'For wrath abides, rising again, haunting the house with guile, unforgetting, avenging the children.'

l. 157. μόρσιμα, a euphemism for 'evils.' 'Such fated ills, yet with great blessings, sang Kalchas from omens on the way,' etc.

l. 161. 'Zeus, whoe'er he be, if by this name it please him to be called;' τόδε, i.e. Zeus alone, without other more definite title.

l. 164. οὐκ ἔχω προσεικάσαι, either 'I cannot conjecture,' i.e. 'refer it all to any but Zeus,' or better and simpler, 'I cannot compare any but Zeus (to Zeus),' i.e. 'Zeus is incomparably above all.'

l. 165. εἰ τὸ μάταν.. ἐτητύμως, 'if in good truth I must cast from me the vain load of care.' τὸ μάταν ἄχθος describes 'the vague foreboding,' 'ill-defined, shadowy care.' The sense is therefore: if I am to get rid of my vague and gloomy forebodings, I must rest on Zeus as the greatest of all. Others K., Schn., etc., take μάταν as *proleptic*; 'cast away my care so as to be vain,' which is not so good.

l. 170. οὐδὲ λέξεται πρὶν ὤν, lit. 'will not even be spoken of as having been of old,' i.e. 'his day is past, we shall not even tell of him.' The MSS. read οὐδὲν λέξαι πρὶν ὤν or οὐδέν τι λέξαι (Fa.), which will neither scan nor construe. The above correction is the slightest and the best; it is due to Ahrens, and is adopted by Eng., Schn., and later D. The allusion is to Ouranos, the father of Kronos, whom Kronos conquered and dethroned; exactly the same fate awaited Kronos himself from the hand of his own son Zeus.

l. 171. ὃς δ' ἔπειτ' ἔφυ, Kronos. τριακτῆρος, lit. 'one who throws thrice (τρία, τρεῖς) in a wrestle,' the three throws being necessary for victory. So τῶν τριῶν παλαισμάτων Eum. 589. διὰ τριῶν ἀπόλλυμαι Eur. Or. 434.

l. 174. 'Shouts the triumph-song of Zeus.' ἐπινίκια, cogn. acc.

l. 175. See Appendix II.

l. 177. τὸν πάθει μάθος.. ἔχειν, 'who has appointed *wisdom by suffering* as a sure law,' i.e. 'that wisdom shall be learnt by suffering.' MSS. read τῷ πάθει by a natural error.

l. 179. στάζει, 'trickles,' intr., the most natural meaning. (Not as Pal. 'drops wisdom,' understanding τὸ σωφρονεῖν in the acc. ἐν θ' ὕπνῳ: the θ' is odd. Schömann's ἀνθ' ὕπνου is ingenious and probable.)

l. 180. καὶ παρ' ἄκοντας, 'and wisdom comes to men in their despite,' i. e. by suffering, by ways they would not choose.

l. 182. The MSS. read δαιμόνων δέ που χάρις, βιαίως σέλμα σεμνὸν ἡμένων, usually construed, 'and surely 'tis a favour of the gods, seated in might upon their solemn thrones.' Only βιαίως cannot mean 'mightily,' it must mean 'with force or violence.' The best alteration is perhaps Turnebus' βίαιος, with comma after it: 'and the gods' favour is oft forced on men, the gods who sit on their glorious thrones.' In fact, another expression of the same truth as παρ' ἄκοντας ἦλθε σωφρονεῖν. But perhaps it is altogether corrupt.

l. 186. The poet returns to the narrative. The connection of this intervening religious ode with the story seems to be this: The seer warned Agamemnon of the mixed good and evil that was in store for him, and especially foreboded the evil results of the child's slaughter (154-5); but Agamemnon, in spite of all, did the deed, and incurred the curse. *Zeus is above all, and has ordained that man shall only be taught by suffering.* καὶ τόθ', application of the general reflections to the special case; 'so then.'

l. 187. ἐμπαίοις, literally, 'striking upon,' i. e. 'his stormy lot,' prob. the same met. as συμπνέων, 'not breathing against,' i. e. 'yielding to.' So again, 219.

l. 189. βαρύνοντ', imperf. augment omitted, as often in the choruses.

l. 190. Χαλκίδος πέραν ἔχων, 'camped on the shore that faced toward Chalkis,' i. e. at Aulis, opp. to Chalkis in Euboea. πέραν usu. taken as adv. and ἔχων intr., but it is prob. the acc. of the old word πέρα (which of course the adv. is originally), and means 'holding the other side.' We have the gen. (read by M. and Schol.) πέρας in Supp. 262 ἐκ πέρας Ναυπακτίας.

l. 191. παλιρρόχθοις, 'eddying,' 'surging back.' MSS. read παλιρρόθοις, with same meaning; altered to suit metre, βίαιος σελ-, 183.

l. 192. Στρυμόνος. The Strymon was the great river of Thrace, which flowed out past Amphipolis. The N.E. wind would bar their passage out of the strait at Aulis. Notice the piling up of adjectives here again, as in l. 154.

l. 195. βροτῶν ἄλαι, in a kind of strange apposition, lit. 'wanderings of mortals,' i. e. 'drifting men away.' βροτῶν opp. to νεῶν τε καὶ πεισμάτων.

l. 196. παλιμμήκης, as we say, 'as long again,' 'lengthening out the time twice-told.'

l. 197. τρίβῳ, 'with wasting,' rarer for τριβῇ.

l. 199. 'Another cure of the bitter tempest,' their ordinary sacrifices having been vain for long.

l. 201. προφέρων Ἄρτεμιν, 'pleading (the wrath of) Artemis.'

NOTES. LINES 180-227.

l. 202. χθόνα ἐπικρούσαντας, in rage, of course. So Achilles in Homer, ποτὶ δὲ σκῆπτρον βάλε γαίῃ Il. 1. 245.
l. 206. κήρ, 'fate,' old Epic word.
l. 210. This line in the MSS. does not correspond with the strophe (197): and both show rather a strange metre at the end: accordingly I adopt Hermann's Ἄργους and Schömann's πρὸ βωμοῦ for βωμοῦ πέλας.
l. 211. τί τῶνδ' ἄνευ κακῶν; i. e. 'whiche'er I choose is woe.'
l. 212. 'How can I (bear to) desert my fleet, and lose my comrades?' i. e. to have the whole expedition broken up, by not taking the only means. First the fleet scatters (ξυμ. ἀμ.), then the disgrace of the failure falls on Agamemnon.
l. 216. MSS. read ὀργᾷ περιόργως ἐπιθυμεῖν, 'to long, desiring with desire,' an almost Eastern fulness and repetition. The subject of ἐπιθυμεῖν is 'the comrades,' or ξύμμαχοι. This might do, but Schömann's correction, περιόργῳ σφ', improves sense and structure.
ll. 217 sqq. 'But when he had shouldered the yoke of necessity, breathing an impious veering gale of spirit, unblest, unholy—then his heart turned to thoughts of uttermost daring.' Lit. 'he changed his purpose (μετέγνω) so as to devise' (φρονεῖν, epexeg. inf.). τροπαίαν, 'veering gale,' because he gave up the struggle and went straight for the wicked deed.
l. 220. Some put comma at μετέγνω, take τόθεν relative (as it is in Epic, and may easily be in Aesch.), and ἔτλα δ' οὖν as the principal verb. So Pal. quoting Schol. as authority: the Schol. however is so wrong about the rest of the line, that it may be wrong about τόθεν; and the pointing in the text is in any case clearer and better.
l. 222. Notice the piled adjectives again, 'fell distraction, base-devising, the fountain of woe.'
l. 224. δ' οὖν, see 34. 'Well—he had the heart to be the slayer,' as though he said, 'However it may be (with the general remarks about παρακοπά) anyhow the fact was so.'
l. 225. ἀρωγάν and προτέλεια are acc. in apposition to the *action* or the *sentence*, as often in Greek, 'to aid the war .. for the fleet an expiation.' προτέλεια, 'the preliminary sacrifice' (see l. 65) before the fleet could go. Observe the significant antithesis, θυγατρὸς .. γυναικοποίνων, 'he slew a *daughter* .. to help in vengeance for a *wife*.' The daughter is a blood-relation, the wife a stranger.
ll. 227-250. The astonishing beauty of this passage has struck all readers from that day to this; it is at once melodious, imaginative, picturesque, and overpoweringly pathetic. It suggests many touches in Lucretius' fine picture of the sacrifice, 1. 87-100.

'And her prayers, and her cries of "father," and her maiden prime they set at nought, the bloodthirsty judges ...'

B

AGAMEMNON.

It is disputed whether κληδόνας means 'her appeals to the name,' or 'the name,' whether Ag. disregarded her calling him father, or his own fatherly feelings. The first is better.

l. 229. παρ' οὐδὲν ἔθεντο. Exactly the English 'set at nought,' literally used of estimating, reckoning in an account.

l. 230. βραβῆς are properly 'those who preside at a contest,' and so used here picturesquely of Agamemnon and Menelaos.

l. 231. φράσεν, no augment, 189.

ἀόζοις, 'the ministers,' 'the attendants.' (ἀ-όδ-ι-ος, 'on the road with,' 'accompanying,' like ἀ-κύλουθ-ος; the ἀ- appears in ἄ-λοχ-ος, 'bed-fellow,' ἀ-δελφύς, 'born of the same womb,' etc. Curt. 598.)

l. 233. πέπλοισι περιπετῆ, 'with her robes flowing round her.' πέπλοις, dat. respect.

l. 234. παντὶ θυμῷ προνωπῆ. It is possible, and tempting at first sight, to take these words together, 'with all her spirit drooping;' but it is more like Greek to refer παντὶ θυμῷ to the ἀόζοι; the order of the words then marks the sharp antithesis, 'he bade the ministers unfaltering raise the drooping maid.' (So ἄπαντι θυμῷ Eum. 738.) They were to be eager, she was fainting with fear and grief.

l. 235. The MSS. read φυλακάν. We might retain this and construe φυλακὰν κατασχεῖν, 'to hold guard,' i.e. 'to check,' φθόγγον being the object accusative by a loose but not uncommon construction (like Soph. O.C. 584 τὰ δ' ἐν μέσῳ .. λῆστιν ἴσχεις, 'the time between thou forgettest'), governed by the idea φυλάσσεσθαι contained in φυλακάν, 'to keep guard over her fair lips *against* the cry.' But φυλακᾷ is a very slight alteration, and makes the construction quite easy; and moreover they do not want 'to guard against' (φυλακὰν κατασχεῖν) the cry, but 'to check' (κατασχεῖν); so I have taken it, following Blomf. and Eng. 'And with the curb to stifle her sweet lips' cry, fraught with curses to her house.'

l. 237. 'With violence and the muffled might of bonds;' a fine phrase for the gag. Notice ἀναύδῳ, epithet transferred from the bound victim to the bonds. The line hangs over into the next stanza, just as in 175; but it spoils the passage not to take it with what precedes.

l. 239. κρόκου βαφάς, 'her robe of saffron,' her dyed princess' robe. So Antigone unties 'the saffron splendour of her robe,' στολίδος κροκόεσσαν τρυφάν Eur. Phoen. 1491. Stanley and Schn. understand it of blood!! Observe the unusual hiatus χέουσα .. ἔβαλλε: perhaps the text is wrong.

l. 241. 'Plain as in a picture, fain to speak.' We are often reminded in the Greek tragedians of the works of painting and sculpture which enriched Athens. So in this play, 416, 801, 1329; and Eum. 50 εἶδόν ποτ' ἤδη Φινέως γεγραμμένας δεῖπνον φερούσας, Eur. Hec. 564 στέρνα θ' ὡς

NOTES. LINES 229-250.

ἀγάλματος κάλλιστα, *ib.* 807 ὡς γραφεὺς ἀποσταθεὶς ἰδοῦ με, Ar. Ran. 537 γεγραμμένην εἰκόν' ἑστάναι. So Eur. Hipp. 1009, Troad. 682. About fifty years after this play was acted a celebrated painter at Sikyon, named Timanthes, painted this very scene, and Agamemnon standing by with his face veiled (Pliny, 35. 10). In the museum at Naples there is a fresco of this subject, taken from 'the house of the Tragic Poet.'

l. 244. ἁγνᾷ (Triclin.'s obvious correction for the awkward ἁγνά of MSS.) ἀταύρωτος αὐδᾷ, 'with virginal voice the spotless maiden.' Paley well suggests that the emphasis of this beautiful phrase is intentional; the banquet songs of later days were sung by very different people from the pure and lovely princess.

l. 245. Read εὔποτμον παιᾶνα with Hartung (Eng., K., Dav., and Pal.) for MSS. εὔποτμον αἰῶνα, which will not scan and makes bad sense, '<u>lovingly graced her loving father's chant of happy fortune, sung at the third</u> libation.' The third libation was poured to Ζεὺς Σωτήρ, and then the συμπόσιον or drinking-bout began, the δεῖπνον being ended. With the end of the libations came the παιάν, or song. So in Plato's Symposium [ἔφη] δειπνήσαντας σπονδὰς ποιήσασθαι καὶ ᾄσαντας τὸν θεόν, which last phrase clearly refers to the paean. See 1386.

l. 247. The sacrifice itself could not be more impressively told than by this terrible hint. 'The rest I saw not neither speak; but Kalchas' word (lit. 'arts') is not unfulfilled.' Others (Eng., Schn.) refer τὰ δ' ἔνθεν not to the slaughter, but to *all that is to come of it*. No doubt in 250 the Chorus are thinking of the ill to follow; but that is led up to by the thought 'Kalchas' word is not unfulfilled,' meaning first his advice to slay Iphigeneia, then (suggested by that) his prophecy of the φοβερὰ μῆνις (154). It is far more poetical and effective to take τὰ δ' ἔνθεν as euphemism for the bloody deed.

ll. 250-254. This passage is well known for its corruptness and difficulty. The true reading is, however, probably preserved in Fa., which reads:—

δίκα δὲ τοῖς μὲν παθοῦσιν μαθεῖν
ἐπιρρέπει. τὸ μέλλον
ἐπεὶ γένοιτ' ἂν κλύοις, προχαιρέτω.

The others (M., Fl., G.) read, ἐπιρρέπει τὸ μέλλον· τὸ δὲ προκλύειν ἐπεί, κ.τ.λ., which is impossible to equate with the strophe, and nearly impossible to construe. Goodwin (Trans. Amer. Phil. Ass. 1877) has however pointed out the important fact that in M. not only τὸ δὲ προκλύειν but also *the colon after* μέλλον is by a later hand; so that the original reading of M. (much the oldest) confirms Fa. We only require δέ after τὸ μέλλον to make both sense and metre. The meaning will then be: 'To them that suffer, justice brings wisdom. What is to

AGAMEMNON.

be, thou canst hear when it has come (κλύοις ἄν principal verb, ἐπεί γένοιτο optative indefinite, assimilated in mood to κλύοις as grammar requires): ere that, have none of it (πρὸ χαιρέτω, lit. 'before hand, farewell to it'); 'tis but too early sorrow.' I. e. 'hear it after the event; have nothing to do with it (hearing it) before the time; hearing before the time means lamenting before the time.' So that the subject to ἶσον (ἐστί) is τὸ προ-κλύειν, *exactly what some intelligent reader wrote on the side*, and which has crept into the text. Enger is certainly right in reading πρὸ χαιρέτω in two words; the meaning is clearer, and it would be more likely to lead to the gloss which has caused all the difficulty. πρό is then adverbial, in the Epic fashion.

l. 254. τορὸν γὰρ ἥξει σύνορθον αὐταῖς is the reading of M. and Ven. retained by Goodwin, who explains, 'for clear it will come out, in accord with them' (the τέχναι Κάλχαντος). But αὐταῖς is a very weak word, and very far from τέχναι; and the emendation σύνορθρον (Wellauer) αὐγαῖς (Herm.), 'clear it will come with the rays of the dawn,' is very near the MSS., and gives a fine sense, and is generally adopted.

l. 255. δ' οὖν, 34.

MSS. give εὔπραξις, verbal from εὖ πράσσειν: some prefer to write it in two words according to the ordinary rules, but there is doubt whether it will not stand.

τἀπὶ τούτοισι, 'as to what comes after.'

l. 256. 'This one sole defence of the Apian land, bound by close ties.' These words may mean either 'ourselves,' or 'Klytaemnestra,' who just then enters. The former is perhaps the more natural thing to say; but ἄγχιστον and μονόφρουρον look like the latter, and in that case μονόφρουρον, 'sole-guarding,' is (as Schn. remarks) full of irony to the spectators who know of her faithlessness.

'Ἀπίας, old name for Peloponnese; it is derived from AP-, Lat. *aqu*-, 'water,' and means 'the water-girt land.' Cp. Μεσσαπία, 'between the waters.'

[ll. 258-354. Scene I. *Klytaemnestra now comes out of the central door, and the leader of the Chorus turns to the stage and addresses her.* He asks the news, and is told of the capture of Troy. the tidings have come by beacon, the stages of which are then described; Klyt. imagines the scene in Troy, and expresses a hope that it will end well.]

l. 261. 'But whether thou hast heard good news, or naught heard but hast hope of good, that thus thou art busy with sacrifice,' in this sense the εὐαγγέλοισιν ἐλπίσιν only belongs to the second alternative, to the μὴ πεπυσμένη. Mr. Morshead turns it well, 'Now be it sure and certain news of good, or the fair tidings of a flattering hope, that bids thee spread the light.' etc.

NOTES. LINES 254-282.

εἴ τι κεδνόν, an old conjecture for MSS. εἴτε κεδνόν, and a necessary alteration.

l. 263. εὔφρων, 'glad,' i.e. 'gladly.' Others take it, 'being well disposed,' a clumsier sentence.

οὐδὲ σιγώσῃ φθόνος. 'Nor shall I grudge thy silence,' i.e. if thou keep silence.

l. 264. 'With happy tidings—so the proverb runs—may the dawn spring forth from her mother night.' The whole couplet is the παροιμία, with its simple and strong imagery; the use of εὐφρόνη, with the slight play on the double meaning, is of course appropriate to the proverb. The 'good-hearted' night would naturally bring forth a 'dawn of good news.'

l. 271. εὖ φρονοῦντος is predicative. 'Ay, for thine eyes show forth thy heart as loyal.'

l. 272. This line is best read as two questions, with Pal., Ken. If it is read as one question, the answer is not to the point.

l. 274. εὐπειθῆ, 'persuasive.' (No need to alter to εὐπιθῆ with Blomf., H., etc.)

l. 275. οὐ δόξαν ἂν λάβοιμι, 'I would not accept (i.e. 'believe') the fancy.'

l. 276. 'What? has some wingless rumour puffed thee up?'

ἀλλ' ἦ, of surprised or excited inquiry usually (Phil. 414; El. 879; Hipp. 932); here the surprise is scornful. 'Art thou so foolish?'

πιαίνω, prop. 'to fatten,' one of Aeschylus' bold metaphors.

ἄπτερος φάτις is difficult. The only plausible interpretation (Pal., K.), 'rumour sped by no bird,' i.e. spontaneously arising, is a little far-fetched. Perhaps, in view of the common Homeric ἔπεα πτερόεντα, and the strange phrase, τῇ δ' ἄπτερος ἔπλετο μῦθος Od. 17. 57, which probably means, 'and her word was unwinged,' i.e. unspoken (Facsi), we may construe here, 'an unspoken rumour,' i.e. as K., 'a strange presentiment.' [H. and others say 'wingless,' i.e. 'unfledged,' 'immature.' Obscure.]

l. 278. ποίου χρόνου, comprehensive gen., like νυκτός, ὑπάγεσθαι τῆς ὁδοῦ, θέων πεδίοιο, etc., 'within what time?'

καί emphasises the verb, '... has the city been sacked?'

l. 279. νῦν, 'but now.' See note on 104.

εὐφρόνης, the *case* is kept to answer to χρόνου.

l. 280. καὶ τίς, incredulous, just as in English, '*and what* messenger could come so quick?' (So, e.g. Soph. O. C. 73, 606, 1173.)

τάχος, adverbial acc., a kind of quasi-cognate or internal acc.

l. 282. 'Beacon sped beacon on with courier-flame.' ἄγγαρος, a Persian word; the system is fully described by Herodotus, 8. 98, in his inimitable style. 'Now no mortal thing arrives quicker than these messengers; such is the system the Persians have invented. A number of men and horses are posted at intervals, equal to the number of days required for the despatch, each man and horse being a day's journey from the next. These neither snow nor rain, nor heat nor night, stops from accomplishing their appointed stage at full speed. The first gives the despatch to the second, and the second to the third, and so forth. This they call ἀγγαρήϊον.' [The MSS. read ἀγγέλου, but the line is quoted with ἀγγάρου in various old gramm.]

The stations for the beacons are: Ida in the Troad; Mt. Hermaios in Lemnos; Mt. Athos, S. E. promontory of Chalkidike; Mt. Makistos in S. Euboea; Mt. Messapios and Kithairon, in Boeotia; Mt. Aigiplanktos in the Megarid; Mt. Arachnaios in Argolis.

ll. 286–289. This passage is a well-known crux. The words, as they stand, mean: 'And soaring so as to overpass the sea the might of the marching torch all joyfully —— the golden gleam like some sun, to the heights of Makistos passing the tidings on ;' where the dash (—) stands in the place of πευκή. It is highly probable that πευκή, a gloss upon ἰσχὺς πορευτοῦ λαμπάδος, has ousted the verb from its place; if some word like 'sent' be put into the blank, the sense is complete. Eng. reads πέμπει, which may be right. Kennedy's προὔκειτο will hardly do, it is an unnatural word in spite of its ingenuity. All the MSS. agree in reading σκοπάς; the acc. may be right if the lost verb was a transitive verb of motion, 'sent the golden gleam *to* the heights . . . :' but on the whole, especially considering the position of παραγγείλασα, the dative is more likely.

The alternative is to keep πευκή, read ἰσχύν, and suppose that πρὸς ἡδονήν is a corruption of the verb: either προήνυσεν, Camp. or προσήνυσεν, Elmsl., Hart.

πορευτοῦ, not from πορευτύς (which has three terminations), but probably from πορευτής, 'traveller;' agreement, like σωτὴρ τύχη, Soph. O. T. 80; Ag. 664. So also θέλκτωρ πειθώ, Suppl. 1040, καρανιστῆρες δίκαι, Eum. 186. πρὸς ἡδονήν might be taken of the joy in those who saw it; but if so, there would have been a dative of the person. It is quite good of the fire. παραγγέλλω has a special fitness; its proper use is military, 'to pass the word down the line.' So 294, 316.

l. 291. παρῆκεν ἀγγέλου μέρος, 'neglected not the herald's part.' the negatives going on from οὔτι μέλλων οὐδ', κ.τ.λ. This is the common way of taking it, and it is quite possible; but I rather incline to prefer Paley's, 'passed on his share of the message.' Not that ἄγγελος means 'message ;' it means 'messenger,' and the phrase literally is 'his messenger's share,' quite a possible expression.

l. 292. Euripos, the narrow strait between Euboea and Boeotia.

l. 297. Ἀσωποῦ, the river of Boeotia, north of Plataeae.

l. 299. 'Awoke a new relay of missive flame.' *Ken.*

l. 300. οὐκ ἠναίνετο, 'did not disown,' poetic understatement, he means 'welcomed,' 'recognised and attended to.'

l. 301. **φρουρά,** 'the guard,' who were on the look-out on Kithairon.

πλέον καίουσα τῶν εἰρημένων, 'lighting a fiercer fire than those I have told of,' seems a very flat line, though the MSS. are agreed upon it. But one cannot help being strongly tempted (with D., Schn.) to believe that a half line, found in Hesychius (Alexandrine lexicographer and grammarian, 4th century A.D., who has preserved many scraps of the ancient writers), **προσαιθρίζουσα πύμπιμον φλόγα,** belongs to this place. The line means, 'raising to the skies the missive flame;' a thoroughly Aeschylean expression, exactly suiting the place, and clearly describing a beacon. The words in the text may then have been a dull gloss on **προσαιθρίζουσα** ; though, as they appear in all the MSS., I have not ventured to make a change.

l. 302. **λίμνη Γοργῶπις,** a little inlet in the N.E. corner of the Corinthian gulf.

l. 304. **μὴ χαρίζεσθαι** is the MSS. reading, which makes no sense. Various conjectures have been made, **μηχαρίζεσθαι** (a word which does not exist), 'to devise,' (?) Well., K. **μὴ χρονίζεσθαι,** 'not to linger,' Pal., **μὴ χατίζεσθαι,** 'not to fail,' lit. 'not to be missed,' Heath, H., D., Eng., Schn. The last seems the best. 'Urged on the fiery ordinance not to fail,' a fine phrase ; the personification of the two fires being quite in Aeschylus' imaginative style. Better still **μηχανήσασθαι** Marg.

l. 305. **ἀν-δαίω.** Epic syncope of **ἀνά,** like the Homeric **ἄμ φυτά, ἀγκαλέω, ἀγξηραίνω, ἀλλέξαι,** etc. So **ἐπαντείλασαν** 27 ; cf. 1021, 1599.

l. 306. 'A mighty beard of fire,' a bold and picturesque image for a blaze streaming in the wind.

καὶ Σαρωνικοῦ, etc. 'Even to overpass the headland that looks down on the Saronic gulf.' **κάτοπτον** (for the meaningless MSS. **κάτοπτρον**), adj., the **κατά** governing gen. The 'headland' is evidently Mount Geraneia.

ll. 306-8. Probably corrupt, the MSS. reading in 308 **εἶτ' ἔσκηψεν εἶτ' ἀφίκετο,** which is certainly wrong ; and **φλέγουσαν** after **φλογὸς μέγαν πώγωνα** is at least suspicious. The best way in such a case is to make the least needful alteration, which is done by correcting one or both of the **εἶτας:** either **εἶτα .. ἔστε,** (D.); **εἶτ' .. εὖτ',** (Pal.); or **ἔστ' .. εὖτ',** (H., Eng., Schn.), which is perhaps on the whole the best, and has been adopted. The sense will then run, 'Then kindling with unstinted might they send a mighty beard of flame, even to surmount the headland overlooking the Saronic bay, blazing onward, till it alighted, when it reached the Arachnaian steep, our city's neighbouring beacon height.' **ὑπερβάλλειν** will be epexegetic inf. quite natural after **πέμπουσι. φλέγουσαν** will be **κατὰ σύνεσιν** (constructed according to *sense,* not *grammar*) with **φλογὸς πώγωνα,** fem. because the *thought* is ' bearded flame,' and *flame* is fem.

l. 311. **οὐκ ἄπαππον Ἰδαίου πυρός,** 'true scion of Idaian fire.' *Siv.* The gen. is common after these neg. adjectives; it is a gen. of reference,

AGAMEMNON.

combined perhaps with the gen. of *emptiness*. So Soph. ἀψόφητος κωκυμάτων Aj. 321, ἄσκευον ἀσπίδων El. 36, ἡμερῶν ἀνήριθμον Tr. 247, etc.; and Ag. 649 ἀμήνιτον θεῶν.

l. 312. τοιοίδε τοί μοι, 'such I ween;' μοι, Ethical dative. Others divide not so well, τοιοίδ' ἕτοιμοι, 'such means of communication the queen has at her disposal,' says Pal., not very poetically.

The next passage has some difficulties. 'Such the ordinances of our torch-racers one from another by succession accomplished,' i.e. Klyt. compares the series of beacons to the torch-race or λαμπαδηφορία at Athens. What this was is not quite clear, but apparently there was a *number* or *chain* of runners engaged, each of whom carried the torch a certain distance and then handed it on to the next. The torch had to be brought in alight. The competition was probably between rival chains of runners. The only point of resemblance here is the *quick succession* and the *fire*, and it is curious that Herodotus, in the passage quoted above (282) on ἄγγαρος, compares the Persian courier system (which Aesch. likens to the beacons) to this very λαμπαδηφορία, in respect of the succession of carriers. The next line is variously taken:—(1) 'And first and last alike they win the race,' (Eng., Schn., Klaus., etc.), i.e. just as the victory in the torch-race belongs to all the *chain*, so here the triumph is won by first and last alike. The omission of the article (χὠ τελευταῖος) is not surprising in the looser style of Aeschylus; so 324 we have καὶ τῶν ἁλόντων καὶ κρατησάντων. Perhaps we should rather have expected some word for 'equally,' 'alike.' (2) 'And the first wins, last also in the race' (Peile), i.e. and the victory is with the one who *arrived* first, having been lighted last. The victory, because it brought the news; the resemblance to the torch-race being dropped. (3) 'And he who ran first and last wins,' the same sense as (2) but grammatically different, or (4) '*though* he ran last,' Ken. καί for καίπερ. It is impossible to decide confidently; but (1) is rather simpler and better than the others.

l. 317. αὖθις, 'later.'

l. 319. ὡς λέγοις πάλιν, the optative is given by two out of the three MSS. here (Fl., Fa.), and is probably right. It is the *assimilated* optative, not uncommon in the dependent clause where the principal verb is opt.; it is due to the feeling of the principal verb *being continued* on into the dependent. 'I would fain hear at length .. according as thou wouldst tell it again.' So Plat. Men. 92 C πῶς ἂν εἰδείης περὶ τούτου οὗ ἄπειρος εἴης; Soph. O. C. 560 δεινὴν .. ἂν πρᾶξιν τύχοις λέξας ὁποίας ἐξαφισταίμην ἐγώ; Plat. Phaed. 65 ἐκεῖνος ἂν ποιήσειε .. ὅστις ἴοι.

ὡς λέγεις, 'as thou dost tell it,' the reading of B., is easy enough, but not quite such good sense. He wants more details, not a repetition of the story as told.

NOTES. LINES 312-347.

l. 321. ἄμικτον, 'discordant,' not blending; as her simile shortly makes clear.

l. 323. φίλως (the MSS. reading) is much better than φίλω, a common correction. 'Unfriendly sundered wouldst thou call them.'

l. 324. καί answers to τ' after ὄξος. We should say, 'as .. so ..' δίχα, 'apart,' i. e. 'distinct' from each other.

l. 326. οἱ μέν, 'the captives,' largely women, as we see from ἀνδρῶν, etc.

l. 327. φυταλμίων γερόντων, 'fostering sires.' There is no need to alter this to φυτάλμιοι παίδων γέροντες with Weil., Eng.; 'the old men' need not have been too old to fight.

l. 330. ἐκ μάχης, 'after,' so τυφλὸς ἐκ δεδορκότος, ἐξ εἰρήνης πολεμεῖν, etc.

νυκτίπλαγκτος, etc., 'night-roaming toil sets them hungry down to such fare as the city has;' the meaning is clear, but the expression is fanciful and picturesque, after his manner.

l. 332. 'According to no token in order due,' a grim kind of irony; the banquet in the sacked town was no well-ordered festival, where each received his *token* and took his appointed seat (ἐν μέρει); but just as it chanced (333) he took what he got (331).

l. 333. This line goes better with what precedes, so with Eng., K., Dav., I put a stop after it; and read ἐν δ' next line, as Eng.

l. 336. MSS. ὡς δυσδαίμονες, unconnected and nonsense. ὡς δ' εὐδαίμονες (Stanl., Eng, Schn., K.) is the best alteration. 'And like happy men shall sleep all night without watch to keep' (ὡς δὲ δαίμονες is too strong a phrase for merely getting a good night's rest).

l. 340. A good example of *certain* emendation: the MSS. read ἄν γ' ἑλόντες or ἀνελόντες, and αὖ θάνοιεν or ἂν θάνοιεν.

l. 341. μὴ ἐμπίπτῃ. The subjunctive expresses a misgiving, 'only beware lest,' common in Homer: ὦ μοι ἐγώ, μή τίς μοι ὑφαίνῃσιν δόλον αὖτε Od. 5. 356, also in Attic μὴ ἀγροικότερον ᾖ τὸ ἀληθὲς εἰπεῖν Plat. Gorg. 462 E.

l. 342. This caution 'not to sack holy things' they neglected; cp. 527 βωμοὶ δ' ἄϊστοι, etc.

l. 344. δίαυλος, 'the double course,' where the runners went round a post and back to the start; a good metaphor for the double voyage.

ll. 345-7. The meaning of these lines is simpler than has been supposed. Taking the MSS. reading ἀναμπλάκητος, which Goodwin has shown (Trans. Am. Phil. Ass. 1877) to be read in Fl. as well as the others, we shall construe: 'but if the army returned without such offence to the gods, the woe of the dead might yet wake, if sudden ills did not befall.' The second 'if' is a repetition of the first in other words; the whole drift is, 'let no impious desires assail the army; (that might bring judgment and peril on them, for) they have to return home;

AGAMEMNON.

but if they kept free of such offence, (and accordingly) if no such sudden judgment befell, there still might wake the woe of the dead,' which makes good sense, and there is no reason to read ἐναμπλάκητος. The last words contain a *double entendre*; to the chorus they mean, 'the army might suffer for *Trojans* slain, if they escaped storm (649) or other judgment;' but the hidden meaning is, '*Agamemnon*, if he escaped shipwreck, might pay the penalty for Iphigeneia,' as he does.

l. 349. τὸ δ' εὖ κρατοίη. She takes up the refrain of the chorus (121, 139), and seems still more sanguine: for instead of οἴλινον, 'the mixed woe and joy,' she wishes 'no doubtful good.' But again there is the grim second meaning, 'let us have complete triumph' over Agamemnon.

l. 350. πολλῶν γὰρ ἐσθλῶν τήνδ' ὄνησιν εἱλόμην, 'for this have I chosen, as the enjoyment of many blessings,' i. e. counting it as equal to the enjoyment of many other blessings: namely, 'that all should return safe;' or, as she really means, 'that I should have my revenge.' τήνδε is attracted to ὄνησιν as usual. The MSS. read τήν, and Hermann corrected it.

l. 354. 'For joy is wrought not unworthy of our toils' is the best meaning: both χάρις and ἄτιμος being used in slightly strained senses: cp. 1443 ἄτιμα δ' οὐκ ἐπραξάτην, 'they have fared *as they deserve*.'

[ll. 355-487. STASIMON I.
Klytaemnestra goes in, and the chorus sing the first stasimon.
The general sense is:—

'Zeus it is who has cast the inevitable net on Troy; the late but sure vengeance on Paris.' (Introductory anapaests 355-366.)

Str. a'. (367-384). "'Tis the stroke of Zeus; the impious deny the interference of the gods, but it has been shown here in punishing the proud and over-wealthy. Moderate wealth is better; riches cannot protect the unjust.

Ant. a'. (385-401). 'The wicked man is lured to his ruin by Delusion; and then his true black heart appears; the wicked pursues vanity, like a child a bird; his prayers are vain. Such was Paris.

Str. β'. (402-419). 'The Faithless one left her home, leaving War to her kin, bringing Ruin to Troy. The seers sang Woe! Woe! the scorned lord is silent and stricken; in dreams he sees the lost one; his joy is departed.

Ant. β'. (420-435). 'Sorrowful visions haunt him, fleeting and mocking; the people are filled with mourning for those who go forth, but naught returns save ashes in the urn.

Str. γ'. (436-455). 'War the cruel arbiter sends back from Ilion dust for men; the people praise the dead and curse their rulers; the conquerors hold their graves only.

Ant. γ'. (456-474). 'Grievous the wrath of the city; I forbode some evil. The gods forget not, the unjust are laid low, and none can aid. 'Tis best to be neither cruel conqueror nor wretched captive.

Epod. (475-487). 'The beacons glad tidings spread; but who knows whether it is true, or a delusion? Women are too credulous; their joyful news turns out often short-lived joy.']

l. 356. κτεάτειρα (Epic form, fem. of κτε-ατήρ, from κτά-ομαι), 'winner.'

l. 357. ἐπὶ πύργοις. Epic use of dat. after verb of motion, cp. βαλλόμενα προτὶ γαίῃ for γαῖαν (II. 22. 64), νηυσὶν ἔπι γλαφυρῇσι νεώμεθα for νῆας Il. 22. 392. See 60.

l. 358. στεγανόν, 'close drawn,' from στέγω, 'to cover,' and is used often of that which *keeps out* (like *hair* which keeps off wet, armour against arrows, shed against rain, etc.) or, as here, *keeps in*.

ὡς for ὥστε. Epic usage common in poets.

l. 359. μήτ' οὖν: οὖν is used in *second* half of alternatives often: εἴτε .. εἴτ' οὖν Soph. Phil. 345, οὔτε .. οὔτ' οὖν O. T. 90. μήτε .. μήτ' οὖν .. *ib.* 271. ὑπερτελέσαι, 'to overleap,' cp. ὑπερτελής, 286.

l. 360. 'The mighty snare of slavery, destruction sweeping all away,' the capture bringing ruin on all. Eng. supposes μέγα δουλείας a gloss, as it wants a vaguer word to include *death* as well as *slavery*, which ἄτη πανάλωτος does. But the poet is here thinking of the *capture* chiefly, the sack, and the slavery, and the misery.

l. 362. αἰδοῦμαι, 'venerate,' more choice and forcible word for 'pray.'

l. 363. ἐπ' Ἀλεξάνδρῳ, 'against Paris;' for dative compare 357.

l. 364. 'That so neither before the time nor beyond the stars the bolt might vainly fall,' i.e. that the vengeance might duly fall, and at the due time, and with due effect. πρὸ καιροῦ is usually taken 'short of the mark,' which makes a good antithesis with ὑπὲρ ἄστρων; but though καιρός might perhaps be used in this sense (see 786), still the point of the sentence is the long delay of justice, till the *time should be ripe*. Moreover, 'at the proper time and proper place,' is just as good an antithesis as 'neither too short nor too far.' See note on 786.

l. 365. ὑπὲρ ἄστρων (perhaps proverbial expression, as Schn.), an obvious hyperbole for 'too far,' 'shot into the sky.'

Observe ὅπως ἄν with final opt. σκήψειεν, a Homeric usage not allowed in Attic final sentences. Od. 8. 21 ὥς κεν Φαιήκεσσι γένοιτο, 24. 334 ὄφρ' ἄν ἐλοίμην δῶρα. In Attic the ἄν would be dispensed with. That the sentence is final is clear both from the sense and from the μή.

l. 367. Lit. 'they have the blow of Zeus to tell of,' i.e. ''tis the stroke of Zeus, they know it.'

l. 368. πάρεστιν not πάρεστι (Enger); then the line is in metre like 367, and in antistrophe 386 we can read προβούλου, which makes better sense.

AGAMEMNON.

l. 369. ἔπραξαν (Franz) ὡς ἔκρανεν is best reading. 'They suffered as he willed.' The MSS. have the plainly false ὡς ἔπραξεν ὡς ἔκρανεν.

l. 370. ἀξιοῦσθαι, 'deign' (rarely Med., but quite good Greek). μέλειν, personal and active, 'to care for' = ἐπιμελεῖσθαι. This is rare, but is found: μέλειν ἡμῶν Soph. Aj. 689, τῆς τικτούσης μέλειν El. 342, τῶν ἀδίκων μέλουσι Eur. II. F. 773.

l. 371. ὅσοις, dat. agent, not uncommon after perf. and aor. passive, rarer with pres., 'by whomsoe'er the glory of their holy things was trampled down.'

l. 372. πατοῖθ', opt. indef. It is past, because of ἔφα.

ll. 374-376. The MSS. give πέφανται δ' ἐγγόνους ἀτολμήτων ᾽Άρη πνεόντων μεῖζον᾽ ἢ δικαίως, which is not a sentence at all, and has no construction. We can see that the poet said, 'it has been shown,' and then something about 'too proud warriors;' from which the drift can be inferred 'that the proud at last fall.' The ordinary correction ἐκγόνοις ἀτολμήτως, 'it has been shown (that gods do care) to the offspring of those who breathe out war insufferably' is very unlikely; the subject of πέφανται is wanting, and ἀτολμήτως does not really mean 'insufferably,' but 'in a manner not be ventured.' On the whole I much prefer Hartung's ἐκτίνουσα τόλμᾱ τῶν ᾽Άρη, etc., quite as near the MSS., and much better sense; also the article τῶν is happy. 'We have seen it paying penalty, the wickedness (τόλμα, 'criminal daring') of those who breathed out war more fiercely (μεῖζον) than was just.' i.e. Paris and the Trojans have suffered vengeance. Observe τόλμα with a long; this is the Doric quantity, and is common in Pindar.

l. 377. φλεόντων, 'overflows,' with riches.

l. 378. ἔστω, 'let there be what brings no woe, yet suffices for him whose heart is wise' (lit. 'so that he who is well gifted in respect of mind should be content'). The meaning is, 'a humble competence, sufficient, but not entailing trouble, is best.' This is the best sense that can be got out of a difficult and rather doubtful passage.

l. 379. ἀπαρκεῖν is used personally, 'I am content,' instead of the ordinary impersonal ἀρκεῖ, 'it suffices;' just as δίκαιός εἰμι, ἄξιός εἰμι, etc. (τοσοῦτον ἀρκῶ σοι Prom. 621 is something like it). Schütz's conj. λαχόντι would make an easier constr., but is not necessary.

l. 380. πραπίδων, gen. of reference after εὖ ; cf. ὡς εἶχε ποδῶν, etc.

l. 381. 'For there is no defence in wealth to a man who insolently spurns the great altar of Justice out of sight.' πρὸς κόρον, like πρὸς βίαν, πρὸς ὀργήν, etc., adverbially. (Others, as Eng., Schn., H., take εἰς ἀφάνειαν with ἔπαλξις, 'protection against destruction;' but it is too far off; and ἀφάνεια is not a good word ; and εἰς is the wrong preposition. Pal. formerly so took it, but now takes it as above.)

l. 385. βιᾶται, 'forces him on.' The sense is, 'the wicked man is led on by Temptation (πειθώ), which is sent him by the Ruin or Curse he has roused, which plots his destruction.'

l. 386. Read with Hartung προβούλου παῖς ἀφ. ἄτ., 'the fatal child of scheming Ruin,' instead of the MSS. προβουλόπαις, a very unlikely compound in that sense; it would mean 'with scheming children,' and would in any case be adj. D. quotes αἰνοπάτηρ Cho. 315; but that *is* adj., and so is no parallel. [Others, as Karst., Dav., K., read πρόβουλος, which is ingenious and simple, but hardly so effective.]

l. 387. 'The evil is not hidden; but shines, a baleful glare.' The evil being his wickedness. The sentence is a little harsh, and perhaps there is some corruption.

l. 391. 'By rubbing and by blows' of the touchstone to try the metal; he is found 'black smutched' like bad copper (instead of being bright like gold) when tested, δικαιωθείς, a bold use of the word.

l. 394. I. e. '*he is as* a boy chasing a winged bird.' Paris, in his vain expectation of success in his crime, is like a boy chasing a bird, a proverb for vanity. The omission of 'as' is both Lat. and Greek usage in comparisons.

l. 395. προστρίμμα, not 'brand' (L. S.), but 'an infliction,' 'a woe;' we have προστρίβειν used with ζημία Prom. 329, πληγάς Ar. Eq. 5, συμφοράν Dem. 786. 6.

l. 397. τῶν, demonstrative, 'these things;' an Epic usage. This correction of MSS. τῶνδε is Klausen's, to suit ὥστ᾽ ἀπαρκεῖν in 379, which is better rhythm.

ἐπίστροφον, 'conversant with,' a Homeric word: ἐπίστροφος ἦν ἀνθρώπων Od. 1. 177.

l. 398. καθαιρεῖ, sc. ὁ θεός, easily understood from οὔτις θεῶν. Cf. the well-known passage in Hor. Sat. 1. 1. 1, 'Qui fit Maecenas ut nemo .. contentus vivat, *laudet* diversa sequentes?' i. e. omnes laudent.

l. 405. 'The din of shield and spear and naval armaments.' MSS. read κλόνους λογχίμους τε καί, etc.; bad position of τε, and not suitable to πάρεισι δόξαι of antistr. 421. Read with H. τε καὶ κλόνους .. ναυβάτας θ᾽.

l. 406. ἀντίφερνον, 'in place of dowry;' Aesch. is fond of these strange compounds, where the ἀντί *governs* (so to speak) the subst. with which it is compounded, ἀντήνωρ 443, ἀντίπαις Eum. 38, ἀντίδουλος Cho. 135, ἀντίκεντρον Eum. 131.

l. 409. 'The seers of the house,' taken by some of Greek seers wailing, by others of the Trojan seers warning. It reads more like the former; but perhaps refers to a story in the Κύπρια of the prophecies of Helenos and Kassandra about Paris' marriage.

l. 411. στίβοι φιλάνορες, lit. 'husband-loving tracks,' i. e. 'print of her loving form,' 'loving' as she was once; φιλάνωρ so used 856.

AGAMEMNON.

l. 412. The MSS. reading is hopeless. I have taken Hermann's, who is followed by Eng., Schn., and is the least violent; it also leaves the metre its cretic character; ἰδεῖν πάρεστι then go together. 'Behold the silence, scorned yet unrebuking, of those so shamefully deserted;' a very fine picture of Menelaos' misery. The plural σιγάς of an abstract word is unusual, but may be supported by ἀχηνίαις 419, μανίας 1575.

l. 416. 'And the loveliness of fair-limbed statues becomes to him a loathing; he has lost the light of her eyes and all love is departed.' Besides the astonishing beauty of the mere words, there is almost a modern depth and tenderness in the thought. Some have strangely referred ὀμμάτων ἀχηνίαις to the 'blank eyes' of the statues; others take it 'in the loss of his eyes,' i. e. loss sustained by his eyes (subject. gen.); but this does not seem so good.

l. 422. ὁρᾷ (Eng., Dav., K.) is probably right; it might easily have got corrupted after δοκῶν into inf., especially as the sense is, 'for vainly, when one sees in fancy delights, the vision is gone,' etc. Literally, 'when a man sees fancying he sees delights,' ὁρᾶν being easily supplied in thought from ὁρᾷ.

l. 426. 'On wings that follow the ways of sleep.' Another wonderful line. Perhaps ὑπαδοῦσ' is right: an easier construction.

l. 428. There is no need for Hermann's τὰ δ' ἐστί, which would rather require τὸ πᾶν γάρ in the next line. 'The woes in the house, in the hearth, are these, and yet more bitter than these; but for all who sailed,' etc. (Lit. 'on the whole, for those who sailed.') Ἕλλανος, as adj. with a fem. word, occurs again 1254.

l. 430. τλησικάρδιος, 'suffering.' by a bold transference applied, not to the afflicted man, but to the affliction.

l. 435. Notice the beautiful effect in this pathetic line of the implied antithesis to οἶδεν; instead of the familiar and loved face comes back the *unknown* urn and ashes.

l. 436. The 'dust in the urn' suggests a bold figure to the poet. 'War is a gold-merchant dealing in bodies; he has his balance (holding the scales of fight, a Homeric idea from Il. 8. 69, where Zeus weighs fates); he sends back ψῆγμα, 'dust,' πυρωθέν and βαρύ, *burnt* and *heavy*, like gold-dust, but in another sense; he fills the jar with ashes in place of men.'

l. 441. βαρύ, 'grievous,' a pathetic *double entendre.*

l. 444. εὐθέτους, for MSS. εὐθέτου; it is a more natural phrase, and better applied to λέβης. It means 'well-ordered,' and is used by Aesch. of σάκος, and ἀρβύλαι elsewhere. If we keep εὐθέτου, it must mean 'easily stored,' and there is no trace of such a usage. Moreover, the order of the words favours the change.

l. 449. διαί, Epic form, restored by Herm. for sake of metre.

NOTES. LINES 412–481.

βαΰζει, properly, 'barks;' so, 'mutters,' 'grumbles.'
l. 450. ὑπ'.. ἕρπει (Epic tmesis for ὑφέρπει), 'steals over' the citizens. Ἀτρείδαις is dat. after φθονερόν.
πρόδικος seems to mean properly an 'advocate;' 'champion' will do here.
l. 455. There is a pathetic irony in κατέχουσι, .. ἔχοντας, words naturally used of conquerors who *occupy* land. 'Many stalwart heroes possess graves of Trojan earth; the earth of their foes has covered the possessor.' The Greek custom seems to have allowed burial as well as cremation. Socrates speaks of his body ἢ καιόμενον ἢ κατορυττόμενον (Plat. Phaed. 115 E.).
l. 457. 'Of a public curse it pays the debt,' i.e. 'does the part.' (Eng. translates, 'he pays the debt,' i.e. the hated ruler; good sense, but such a change of subject is scarcely possible.)
l. 460. 'My boding thought awaits tidings from the dark:' imaginative way of saying, 'I anxiously forebode some hidden mischief, soon to be revealed.'
l. 464. παλιντυχεῖ τριβᾷ βίου, 'with sad reversal of life's lot.' |
l. 465. ἐν δ' ἀΐστοις .. ἀλκά, 'he lies among the unseen, with none to aid;' ἀΐστοις may include any kind of destruction, even death, cp. Ἀΐδης.
l. 466. ὑπερκόπως, 'overmuch,' necessary correction for MSS. ὑπερκότως, 'wrathfully.'
l. 470. ὄσσοις, 'upon his eyes.' Pal., K. say, 'by the eyes of Zeus;' surely that would be *from* the eyes, ἀπ' ὄσσων. Possibly it is corrupt.
l. 471. κρίνω, 'I judge best,' used somewhat as δοκεῖ is. ἄφθονον, 'unenvied,' not its usual sense, which is 'plentiful.'
l. 474. βίον, 'the life,' i.e. of a captive, readily understood from ἁλούς; the phrase is varied from its natural form.
Notice the gradual way in which the chorus hint forebodings of ill against Agamemnon. The triumphant opening leads them to speak of Paris' sin and punishment ; then the sorrow and loss of Menelaos; that leads to the suffering and slaughter of the Greeks who fought for the Atreidae; then the murmurings, caused by that, against the kings; the danger of too great success, especially if wrought by much bloodshed. 'The conqueror's lot is not one to be wished any more than that of the conquered.'
l. 478. MSS. ἥ τοι θεῶν ἐστι μὴ ψῦθος, a possible but very strange position of μή. There are various emendations, of which I have given Ahrens' as the simplest and best.
l. 479. φρενῶν κεκομμένος, 'stricken in mind,' gen. of ref.
l. 481. πυρωθέντα, 'fired.' The construction is acc. and inf. *consecutive*, with the usual ὥστε wanting.

AGAMEMNON.

l. 483. "Tis like a woman's temper to welcome joy before the truth be known.' αἰχμᾷ, an obscure word, taken by most edd. (H., Schn., Eng., Well., etc.) to mean 'rule' here and Cho. 630. But there seems reason for believing, with Blomf. and Pal., that the word means 'spirit,' 'temper.' 592 confirms this view. [Hart. suggests αὐχᾷ.]

l. 485. Again an obscure passage, the clue to which lies (as Pal. shows) in the proper meaning of ἐπινέμω, 'to graze flocks over the border.' 'Too credulous, the bounds of her belief suffer a swift encroachment; but by swift fate perishes the rumour spread by her tongue,' i.e. she believes too readily, and her false reports are soon exposed. The assonance of ταχύπορος, ταχύμορος, is of course intentional, to point the rebuke.

l. 488. These lines are given to Klytaemnestra in MSS. They clearly belong to the chorus and are always printed so now.

[ll. 488-680. SCENE II.

The herald is now seen coming on the left side of the stage crowned with olive. The leader of the chorus speaks from the Thymele. 'Now we shall know all.' The herald prays to all the gods; then describes the sufferings before Troy. Klytaemnestra comes forward, and sends a welcome to her coming lord. The chorus ask news of Menelaos: the herald tells the story of the storm which scattered the fleet. Still Menelaos may come.]

l. 490. παραλλαγάς, 'changes,' i.e. 'successions.'

l. 494. κάσις πηλοῦ ξύνουρος. Observe the quaint and almost grotesque expression 'thirsty dust, neighbour brother of the clay.' Schn. sees in this speech a parody of Klytaemnestra's picturesque style; but there is no need to invent such refinements. Aeschylus' style, when applied to homely things, is liable to border on the grotesque.

ll. 496-7. Means simply that the tidings will be conveyed by voice, no longer by fire. σοι is rather a strange Ethic dative. as the chorus are not exactly addressing anyone, 'lighting thee the flame of wood;' Herm. suspects it.

l. 498. 'Either he will utter joy,'—or the reverse, he means; but stops short (aposiopesis) to avoid ill omen.

l. 500. 'To good already come may good be added' (lit. 'may addition be well').

l. 501. The want of a connection is so strange that several editors suggest τάδ' ὅστις. Those who give 488 to Klyt. give this to chorus.

l. 504. φέγγει ἔτους, merely picturesque-poetic for ἔτει, 'tenth-year's light.' Observe that the herald arrives from Troy, announcing the landing of Agamemnon, immediately after the beacon fires, on the morning after the capture. Such violations of possibility were held quite allowable by the licence of dramatic poetry.

NOTES. LINES 483-532.

l. 507. μέρος is usually omitted after μετέχω, the verb itself (with the partitive gen.) giving the idea sufficiently.

l. 509. The statues of these gods stood probably on the stage, according to the custom, in front of the palace.

l. 510. For Apollo was also the god of Pestilence and had shot his shafts at the Greeks 'for nine days long; and the pyres of the dead burnt thick.' Il. 1. 52-3. (μηκέτι of course after imperative χαῖρε.)

l. 511. ἦσθ' (Askew, K., D., Eng.) is the simplest and best reading. ΗΣΘ became ΗΛΘ by an easy corruption, which was then altered to ἦλθες by somebody who knew that it ought to be 2nd pers. but did not know the metre. (H.'s ᾖσθ' for ᾔεισθα is ingenious but unlikely, the phrase is so harsh.)

l. 513. ἀγωνίους, the best sense to give to this disputed word is derived from the old Homeric meaning of ἀγών, 'gathering' (like ἀγορά). Iliad 15. 428, 16. 500 νεῶν ἐν ἀγῶνι, 24. 1 λῦτο δ' ἀγών ; cp. ἀγῶνας θέντες 835. So ἀγώνιοι will be the same as ἀγοραῖοι, 'gods of the gathering,' i.e. of the city life, see note on 88. (The Schol. on Hom. 24. 1 expressly says that Aeschylus calls ἀγοραῖοι ἀγώνιοι.)

l. 514. τιμάορος [τιμα- Ϝορ-, cp. πυλωρός, οἰκοῦρος, φροῦρος, etc.], lit. 'honour-guarder,' so 'champion,' 'protector.' The meaning 'avenger' was secondary, though naturally following from the primary one.

l. 517. δορός, gen. of separation, as after words of 'freeing,' 'emptying,' etc. ; 'those whom the spear hath spared.'

l. 519. 'Royal seats,' the marble throne of the king at the door of the palace, where he sat to do justice, or on any state occasion.

ἀντήλιοι (Ionic form for ἀνθ.), 'sunward-facing,' the statues being placed to look east.

l. 521. κόσμῳ, 'duly.' Observe three datives of instr., manner, and time.

l. 524. καὶ γὰρ οὖν, 'for indeed it is fitting;' the οὖν adds earnestness or emphasis. So καὶ γὰρ οὖν κείνην ἴσον ἐπαιτιῶμαι Soph. Ant. 489, εὖ γὰρ οὖν λέγεις ib. 771, οὐ γὰρ οὖν σιγήσομαι O. C. 980.

l. 526. τῇ κατείργασται πέδον, 'wherewith the soil has been ploughed up,' a kind of grim irony; 'the mattock of avenging Zeus' having in a terrible sense 'ploughed up' the soil of Troy. (τῇ, Epic rel. for ᾗ.)

l. 527. This line is like Pers. 811 and some suspect it.

l. 532. 'For neither Paris nor the city, sharer of his ruin, can boast that their deeds surpassed their sufferings.' One οὔτε is omitted. So Soph. Phil. 771 ἑκόντα μήτ' ἄκοντα: and Shakespeare has it, 'but my five wits *nor* my five senses can dissuade one foolish heart from serving thee' Sonn. 141.

συντελής means, 'one who pays taxes with,' 'is rated with;' hence many take it to mean simply 'city connected with Paris:' but the idea of 'payment' must have been present to the poet in choosing the word ; so the version given above is better.

AGAMEMNON.

l. 534. Paris is compared to a man convicted of 'theft and plunder.' If one so convicted refused to pay, the claimant seized property of his in pledge for his claim; and the thing seized was ῥύσιον. Helen is here the ῥύσιον, which does not therefore mean 'spoil,' as L. S., Pal., though it might be so construed in default of a word to express the associations of ῥύσιον more precisely.

l. 536. αὐτόχθονον, 'land and all,' 137; but the reading is suspect.

l. 537. θἀμάρτια, τὰ ἀμάρτια, 'the penalty for sins,' they have paid twice over. The word is formed like εὐαγγέλια, 'reward for good tidings.' (Schol. so takes it.)

l. 538. τῶν ἀπὸ στρατοῦ, the common pregnant construction.

l. 539. Enger's emendation for χαίρω· τεθνάναι is good; there is no such word as τεθνάναι; and the syllable which has fallen out is so like the next one: ΓΕΤΕΘΝ. [Karsten's τὸ τεθνάναι is also good.]

l. 542. τερπνῆς, pred., 'a sweet disease this that ye were affected with.'

l. 543. I.e. 'Tell me, and I shall understand.'

l. 546. ὡς for ὥστε, as often. See 358.

l. 547. στρατῷ, the MSS. reading, is plainly vicious, having come from 545. Hermann's φρενῶν is as good as any conjecture, the phrase occurring Ag. 1307, Cho. 80. 'Whence came this bitter gloom of heart upon thee?' [Or take φράσον with Weil: very simple.]

l. 550. νῦν, 'just now,' as we say.

τὸ σόν, 'thy words,' referring to 539. 'As thou saidst but now, 'twere joy to die.'

l. 552. MSS. read εὖ λέξειεν, which Paley retains. But not merely is ἄν required (Paley's instances being all either corrupt or not conditional, see below, 620); εὖ is plainly bad with εὐπετῶς, from which indeed it has arisen.

ll. 555-7. 'For were I to tell of our troubles and ill lodgment, scant deckways, and hard bivouacs—what hour of the day did we not groan, and [suffer]?' There is no apodosis to εἰ λέγοιμι—the break in the construction is more effective. παρήξεις is doubtful. It is commonly taken 'landings,' but παρήκω means 'to pass along,' and παρῆξις should mean 'passages;' probably (as Pal., Br.) on board ship, because it is opposed to τὰ χέρσῳ. The Schol. takes it so. In the last line λαχόντες is plainly corrupt. Pal. says, 'what did we not *receive as our daily portion*?' but ἤματος μέρος cannot surely mean this. We want some word like πάσχοντες or κλαίοντες.

l. 558. 'And again on land we had still worse to bear.' τὰ δ' αὖτε χέρσῳ. lit., 'and other things again on land.' χέρσῳ, dat. local.; it is prop. adj., 'dry,' but in Hom. is always used as subst. without art. ἐπὶ χέρσον, προτὶ χέρσον, ἐν χέρσῳ.

l. 562. τιθέντες ἔνθηρον τρίχα, 'matting our locks like beasts.' The masc. τιθέντες is strange; Schn. suggests he had ὄμβροι in his head; he must have meant to include rain, which would be far worse than mere dew. [Perhaps there is some corruption.]

l. 566. Notice this beautiful line: the poetic feeling for beauty of nature is so rare among the Greeks. 'When on his midday couch windless and waveless ocean sank to sleep,' as Conington finely turns it.

l. 567. Again the construction is effectively broken; εἰ λέγοι has no apodosis.

l. 568. τοῖσι μέν. The natural antithesis, 'the living,' is practically given 571.

l. 569. Consecutive constr. again, just as in 15.

l. 570. ἐν ψήφῳ λέγειν, lit. 'reckon by the pebble;' i.e..'count up accurately.'

l. 571. τύχης, gen. of reference, common after emotion verbs, μηνίσας φόνου, οὗ χολωθείς, δείσας φίλου, θαυμάζω τινός, etc.

l. 572. 'Nay, I bid a long farewell to our sufferings.' καταξιῶ is used in a strange sense, εἰπεῖν or λέγειν being the common word; but this must be the meaning; πολλὰ χαίρειν is always so used. Somewhat similar is ἀξιῶ, 'I hail,' 903. [Perhaps ξυμφοράς (Bl. Dav.) is right.]

l. 575. 'So that it is fit we (the survivors) should make boast before this beam of the sun.' ὡς for ὥστε.

l. 578. 'To the gods of Greece have nailed up these spoils in their shrines a glory for all time.' Notice the double dative, θεοῖς recipient, δόμοις probably local. ἀρχαῖον, unusually but effectively used for 'to be ancient' (proleptic), 'lasting;' see however App. V.

l. 580. κλύοντας, 'anyone' hearing such things; yourselves and future generations.

l. 581. Observe *passive* future τιμήσεται of the older form; in the *pure* verbs this form is common, as ἀγορεύσομαι, ἀδικήσομαι, ἀνιάσομαι, ἀξιώσομαι, ἀπατήσομαι, etc. See Veitch, Greek Irregular Verbs.

l. 584. Lit. 'learning well is ever young for the old;' i.e. 'the old are ever young enough to learn.' εὖ μαθεῖν is really the subj. of ἥβᾳ. There is therefore no need for Enger's ingenious νοῦς γέρουσιν, which indeed makes the expression duller. [Still better ἥβῃ Marg.]

[*At this point Klytaemnestra advances from the palace by the middle door; the chorus-leader continues with a look towards her.*]

l. 586. σὺν δὲ πλουτίζειν ἐμέ, 'but should gladden me likewise;' the subject of πλουτίζειν being surely ταῦτα, 'the tidings;' not Klytaemnestra, as H., nor σέ, as Pal.

l. 590. καὶ τίς μ' ἐνίπτων clearly refers to the incredulity of the chorus, 483. How would K. know of this, it is asked, as she was not there? The answer is that the chorus only express the general feeling of the citizens which she can naturally be supposed to learn.

AGAMEMNON.

l. 593. Observe the imperfect ἐφαινόμην. 'They strove to show me deluded.'

l. 594. γυναικείῳ νόμῳ, 'with womanly strain.' This may mean only that the women began, but the men (ἄλλος ἄλλοθεν) joined in; but perhaps she is still keeping up her satire against the chorus: 'like women (as you would say) the whole city joined in the cry.'

l. 597. κοιμῶντες, 'lulling to rest,' causing it to burn low and die out: with incense and perhaps wine.

l. 598. τὰ μάσσω, 'the further tale.'

l. 599. These lines are full of tragic irony to the audience who know her plot.

l. 600. It is best to take ὅπως final. 'In order that I may best welcome—(then the parenthesis)—take this message,' etc. If we construe ὅπως ἄριστα together, 'as well as I may,' and put a stop at δέξασθαι (as H., D., Eng., Schn., etc.), ταῦτ' ἀπάγγειλον is very abrupt.

l. 606. εὗροι. Observe the terrible irony of this wish, sent as a loving message to Agamemnon.

l. 607. οἷάνπερ οὖν ἔλειπε, 'ay, even as he left her.' οὖν is used something like English 'in short;' the second phrase being substituted for πιστήν, as more expressive. Cp. Plat. Prot. ad init. καὶ γὰρ πολλὰ ὑπὲρ ἐμοῦ εἶπε, καὶ οὖν καὶ ἄρτι ἀπ' ἐκείνου ἔρχομαι, 'he said many kind things for me, and *in short*, I have only just left him.'

l. 612. χαλκοῦ βαφάς. Perhaps the best way of taking this difficult expression is to suppose a *double entendre*. 'I know no more of dalliance or rumour of shame from other man than—how to dip the brass;' i.e. than I do of the manufacture of tempered swords, clearly not a woman's province. But in her heart she knows well 'how to dip the brass' in Agamemnon's blood, and means to do it.

l. 613. τῆς ἀληθείας γέμων is effective, considering the cynical falseness of Klytaemnestra's speech.

ll. 615, 16. A difficult couplet. τοροῖσιν ἑρμηνεῦσιν can be taken (dat. inst.) with μανθάνοντι or with εὐπρεπῶς. The latter is perhaps most likely, as ἑρμηνεύς is naturally a person, and the instrumental use unlikely. 'Thus hath she spoken to thy listening ears her word—to clear interpreters fair seeming;' a very delicate way of hinting that she has said rather too much of her own virtues.

l. 617. πεύθομαι, other form of πυνθάνομαι. Similar pairs are λείπω λιμπάνω, φεύγω φυγγάνω, λήθω λανθάνω.

l. 620. 'I could not tell false tidings to seem fair;' καλά being predicative. ὅπως λέξαιμι is the remote deliberative optative; see Appendix I.

l. 621. 'For friends to reap delight therefrom for long;' i.e. the pleasure of good news if false is shortlived. καρποῦσθαι, epexegetic inf.

NOTES. LINES 593–650.

l. 622. The chorus reply, imitating the form of the herald's sentence: 'Would that then thou couldst speak truth to seem good;' κεδνά being predicative, like καλά. So Klaus., Ken. [It is usually taken (e.g. Herm., Eng., Schn., etc.), 'How then couldst thou, speaking good news, chance to speak truth?' understanding εἰπών again. This is possible, but not so neat as the other.]

l. 626. 'Setting sail in sight of all' (did he perish?); i.e. was he parted from you by his own act or by a storm?

l. 630. The important words are ζῶντος ἢ τεθνηκότος, which are predicative. 'Did rumour speak of him as alive or dead?' is the sense. αὐτοῦ, obj. gen. after φάτις; see 1367.

l. 635. 'How rose, how sank the storm?' *Mors.*

l. 637. χωρὶς ἡ τιμὴ θεῶν, 'the honours of the gods are apart (from evil tidings);' i.e. 'it beseems not the service of the gods.' He goes on to explain that if news of disaster were brought, instead of triumph, then a paean to the Erinyes (as opp. to θεοί) would be the right thing; as the news is good, and there is thanksgiving, it must not be spoiled.

l. 640. τυχεῖν is perhaps best taken as epexegetic inf.; and then ἕλκος and πολλούς are both accusatives in apposition to πήματα 638. Otherwise ἕλκος τυχεῖν is acc. inf., and then we have the awkwardness of the construction being changed to participle in 641. The sense is, 'to the *city* one woe, the public loss, to suffer, and many *men*,' etc.; i.e. the public loss and the private sufferings. [τυχόν, H.: neat but needless.]

l. 641. ἐξαγισθέντας, an expressive word; 'victims cast out,' 'cast out and consecrate to death.' *Mors.*

ll. 642, 3. 'With the two-thonged scourge, that Ares loves, a double-pointed curse, a bloody pair;' imaginative and high sounding phrases for the twofold suffering to state and individual already given 640.

Notice τήν, Epic relative. The accusatives in 643 are best taken as in agreement (by a kind of natural attraction or loose apposition) with the relative τήν.

l. 644. μέντοι, 'indeed,' ''tis true;' 'with such woes indeed laden one should sing this paean of the Furies.' μέντοι concessive, as often.

l. 645. τόνδε, i.e. such a one as suits these woes.

l. 648. Again the construction broken; he springs from the general statement (which expects πῶς πρέπει τοῦτον συμμίξαι; or something of the kind) to the first person.

l. 649. Taking the corrected reading Ἀχαιοῖς..θεῶν. Construe: 'storm sent by wrathful gods upon the Achaioi.' For ἀμήνιτον θεῶν see 311.

l. 650. Paley aptly quotes Milton, Par. Reg. 4. 412 'Water with fire in ruin reconciled;' and Schn. no less aptly Shakesp. Troilus and Cressida, 2. 2 'The winds and waves, old wranglers, took a truce.'

37

AGAMEMNON.

l. 651. τὰ πίστ' ἐδειξάτην, 'proved their bond.'
l. 653. Some put the stop at νυκτί; but it is better as it is.
l. 654. Θρήκιαι, 'north winds;' cp. 192.
l. 656. 'With violent storm and splash of beating rain.' Only in Epic style he couples the dat. of circumstances (χειμῶνι) to the dat. after σύν. The cases really describe the same relation, the preposition only making it more precise. Some propose to take τυφῶ as gen. after ζάλῃ; but it is better and simpler to take it, as above, with χειμῶνι.

l. 657. 'With the whirling gust of the evil shepherd;' a sudden bold metaphor flashing out in Aeschylus' style. The hurricane is 'an evil shepherd;' the fleet are his sheep which he drives hither and thither to their ruin.

l. 659. ἀνθοῦν νεκροῖς, 'flowering with dead,' another audacious metaphor; though ἀνθέω is more familiarly used in Greek metaphorically than 'flower' with us.

l. 661. γε μὲν δή, 'however;' γε μήν, γε μέντοι, γε μὲν δή, all used in this corrective or qualifying sense. Soph. Tr. 484 ἐπεί γε μὲν δὴ πάντ' ἐπίστασαι. ἀκήρατον σκάφος, best taken as apposition; not as Pal., 'unharmed in hull.' [Auratus' νεώς τ' is possible.]

l. 662. 'Stole us away or begged us off' from destruction; a bold but quite characteristic phrase, requiring no emendation.

l. 664. Paley prosaically thinks that this splendidly imaginative line describes an electric phenomenon! 'And on the bark sat Fortune the saviour, a willing passenger.'

l. 665. ὡς for ὥστε.

κύματος ζάλην ἔχειν, 'wave-tossed;' the subject is ἡμᾶς, or 'the ship,' readily understood from 661.

l. 666. ἐξοκεῖλαι, intr. 'run aground.'

l. 669. ἐβουκολοῦμεν, a metaphor quite different from, but as strange and picturesque as, the English 'brooded over.' So βουκολούμενος πόνον, Eumen. 78.

l. 670. σποδουμένου, lit. 'dusted;' i.e. 'beaten,' 'buffeted.'

l. 672. τί μή, 'why should they not?' the verb understood being the deliberative subjunctive, as μή shows. This is possible, though the phrase is unusual [it occurs Soph. Aj. 668], but perhaps τί μήν is right.

l. 674. γὰρ οὖν, justifying his good wish: 'May it turn out well; [and I mean it], for indeed Menelaos you may expect, first and most of all.' See 524.

l. 676. δ' οὖν, 'anyhow;' hastening to practical conclusion, cf. 34. ἱστορεῖ, 'finds.' The word is from Ϝιδ-, and properly means, 'to get knowledge,' hence is used (like πυνθάνομαι) to mean both *inquire* and *learn*.

[*After* 680 *the Herald goes off, and the Second Scene ends.*
The Chorus then sing the Second Stasimon, as follows:—

NOTES. LINES 651–695.

Str. a'. (681-698). 'Who was it so fitly named Helena, the ἑλέ-ναυς? forth she sailed, with the armed huntsmen after her, to Simois' shores. *Ant. a'.* (699-716). The marriage-κῆδος (bond) proved indeed a κῆδος (care); Zeus exacted after-vengeance from those who triumphantly sang the marriage song, changing the note to bitter wailing.

Str. β'. (717-725). 'As a man rears a lion's whelp, gentle and a plaything at first; *Ant. β'.* (726-735) but soon its savage temper shows, and it ravages the flocks, filling the house with blood; so (*Str. γ'.* 737) Helena came, fair and lovely, to Troy; but she proved a curse.

Ant. γ'. (750-762). 'The old saying makes sorrow born of prosperity; this I do not hold with; it is impiety, not wealth, that begets evil offspring.

Str. δ'. Ant. δ'. (736-781). 'The old wickedness brings forth new wickedness when the appointed day comes, and fatal daring. But justice burns brightly in the cottage, flying from the guilty palace; she guides all to the goal.'

For the bearing of the Chorus on the drama, see Introduction, p xviii.]

l. 684. μή τις. 'Was it some one?' μή, interrogative; originally, no doubt, *banishing the thought* (μή not οὐ). 'Surely not one who ...!')

l. 685. ἐν τύχᾳ, 'by good hap,' it was a chance name, yet guided by secret foresight (πρόνοια) of what was to follow.

l. 686. δορίγαμβρον ἀμφινεικῆ θ', 'the sword-won bride, the source of strife.'

l. 687. The MSS. both give ἑλένας, which form points the wordplay much better than ἑλέναυς the ordinary reading, if it is a possible form. It may be a Doric form from ἐλε-ναϝ-ς, as Μενέλας is from Μενε-λαϝ-ς (Salmasius, Eng.) 'Ship's hell, Man's hell, City's hell,' says Browning, though the English is stronger than the Greek. To the Greek mind there was something mysterious about the suitability of names to fates of men; it had a deep significance, and was not trivial or accidental. Compare Soph. Aj. 430; Theb. 658.

l. 690. ἀβροτίμων, 'delicate-costly,' a bold but not unlikely compound. [No need to accept Salmasius's ingenious emendation ἀβροπήνων, 'delicate-woven:' though Aesch. may have written it.]

l. 692. γίγαντος, 'mighty;' γίγας is redupl. from γα-, 'grow,' and means, 'the big-grown one,' 'the monster.'

l. 695. 'The host of shielded huntsmen' are of course the Greek pursuers.

MSS. κατ' ἴχνος πλάταν ἄφαντον κελσάντων, which will construe, 'on the track of those who drove ashore on Simois' leafy coast the vanishing oar,' but the emendation πλατᾶν makes the sense so vastly richer and better, '... huntsmen on the oarblades' unseen track not a visible trail like other hunters] of those who,' etc.; a splendid phrase.

AGAMEMNON.

l. 699. 'Wrath, its end accomplishing, sped to Ilion this marriage bond, a trouble indeed,' a play on the two meanings of κῆδος.

l. 700. ἀτίμωσιν πρασσομένα, 'exacting requital for the wrong;' τίοντας, 'from those who honoured,' the regular construction of πράσσεσθαι in this sense. Cf. Εὐρυμέδοντα χρήματα ἐπράξαντο Thuc. 4. 65.

l. 705. 'Those who honoured over-much the bridal strain' were the γαμβροί, or 'marriage kin' of Helena, i. e. the children of Priam, who sang triumphantly the marriage song, glorying in Paris' deed. ἐκφάτως is a doubtful word, either 'unspeakably,' or better perhaps 'loudly' (lit. 'outspokenly.') τίοντας, they *honoured* the violent deed; they *dishonoured* hospitality and Zeus protector of friendship. The article is omitted with the participle, as 59.

l. 706. τότ', 'at the time,' significantly; afterwards they 'sang another tune,' 709.

l. 707. ὑμέναιον is in apposition to μέλος.

l. 709. 'The note is changed, the city wails with bitter lament.' Literally, 'learning a new song of bitter lament (πολύθρηνον, predicative) the city groans.'

l. 711. Mr. Verrall, in the Journal of Philology, 9. 140, ingeniously explains αἰν-όλεκ-τρον as a play on 'Αλέξ-αν-δρον with inverted syllables, 'calling Paris (no longer the man-repeller, but) the man of the fatal bridal.' But we can hardly accept this as more than a brilliant guess. It would, no doubt, suit excellently with the temper which dwells on the significance of 'Ελένα and κῆδος; but the real objection is not the play on the words, but the remoteness of the resemblance.

ll. 714-16. Corrupt, but not so as to obscure the sense. πολίταν of the MSS. must be πολιτᾶν, gen. plur., and the first word must be an adv. 'utterly,' or an adj. 'miserable.' I have taken provisionally παμπερθῆ (Seidler., Herm.) πολύθρηνον αἰῶνα διαὶ πολιτᾶν μέλεον αἷμ' ἀνατλᾶσα, 'having borne a ruined life of lament for the piteous blood of her sons.'

διαί (Davies) for sake of metre, instead of ἀμφί; which might be a gloss on it.

l. 717. λέοντος ἶνιν, 'lion's whelp,' Conington's splendid and certain emendation of λέοντα σίνιν, which spoils the sense; in the strophe the lion is young and a delight, it is only in the antistrophe that it is grown up and become a pest. ἶνις, old poetic word, from ἴς, 'strength,' meaning the 'vigorous young' thing, occurs Eum. 323, Suppl. 43.

ἔθρεψεν, habitual aorist, used from Homer down, e. g. κοτύλην τις τυτθὸν ἐπέσχε Il. 22. 494; so the verbs below, ἔσχε, ἀπέδειξε, ἔτευξε, ἐφύρθη. Construe it by the present, 'rears.'

l. 718. δόμοις, local (Epic use).

40

NOTES. LINES 699-762.

ἀγάλακτον, 'robbed of his mother's milk,' antithesis to φιλόμαστον, 'desiring the breast.' [Others take ἀγάλακτον οἴκοις, 'fed with the same milk as the house' (ἀ-γαλ, like ἄ-λοχος, ἀ-δελφός), and Hesych. so explains the word; but the other sense seems better.]

l. 720. προτελείοις, 65.

l. 723. MSS. ἔσχ', intrans. 'lay,' but as ἔχω is only used with adverbs intransitive, probably ἔσκε (Homeric frequentative for ἦν), which occurs Persae 656, is the right reading.

l. 725. σαίνων γαστρὸς ἀνάγκαις, 'taught to fawn by its hunger-pangs.'

l. 728. ἦθος (for MSS. ἔθος), Conington's emendation, again improves the sense, and suits the strophe.

l. 730. MSS. μηλοφόνοισιν ἄταις or ἄταισι. The best correction is μηλοφόνοισι σὺν ἄταις, Ahrens (Eng., Schn.), the syllables -σι συν having run into -σιν.

[Other attempts, ἄγαισι, ἄγαισι, H., ἄσαισι, Con., θανάτοισι, K., are less suitable.]

'For, in requital to those who reared him, with fell destruction among the flocks he makes a feast unbidden.'

l. 735. ἱερεύς τις ἄτας, 'a priest of ruin,' fine imaginative phrase, suggesting that Ἄτη, or Destruction, sends the lion to sacrifice to her.

l. 737. '(So) I should say there came at the first a spirit of windless calm,' etc.

παρ' αὐτά, 'at first,' opposed to what happened afterwards, παρακλίνασ' ἐπέκρανεν. So Eur. πάραυτα δ' ἡσθεὶς ὕστερον στένει. The point of the comparison is the contrast between the softness and sweetness *at first*, and the bloody and bitter end.

Observe the passion and the splendour of these wonderful lines.

[Others take πάραυτα, 'in like manner.' Kl., K., Eng. So L.S., who however, mistranslate it in Demosthenes, l. c. Moreover Hesych. says παραχρῆμα.]

l. 745. 'Yet turning aside [from the first sweetness and softness] she brought to pass a fatal fulfilment of marriage: she came an evil neighbour, an evil guest, to the sons of Priam, at the bidding of Zeus, god of friendship, a Fury, a woe of brides.'

l. 750. Observe γέρων used as adj., 'old.' It is a poetical use from Homer down (γέρον σάκος, Od. 22. 184).

l. 751. μέγαν τελεσθέντα ὄλβον. 'Prosperity when grown to full estate.' Aeschylus is rejecting the old Greek superstition that Prosperity of Wealth brings woe; it is not wealth, he says, but always Sin. See Introduction, pp. xiii, xviii.

l. 760. μέτα, 'afterwards,' adverbially.

l. 762. καλλίπαις, 'is blessed in the children,' i.e. is good and prosperous in succeeding generations.

ll. 763–771. For the lesser corruptions of the MSS., which have been corrected, see critical notes. The only important corruption is νεαρὰ φάους κύτον, which is desperate. I have adopted Ahrens' φάος τόκου as the best sense and least violent change. (νεαρά comes from a gloss.)

[Paley's correction, νέα δ' ἔφυσε κύρον, gets a good sense and antithesis to παλαιὰ μέν: but the real antithesis to παλαιὰ μέν is given in νεάζουσαν ὕβριν, and κόρον is too bold, introducing as it does an altogether new idea.]

l. 764. 'At this time or at that, whene'er the appointed day of birth arrive.'

l. 770. To take θράσος μελαίνας μ. ἄτας together, 'the boldness of a black Curse' (with H., Kl., Eng., Schn., Weil, etc.,) is very harsh; it is far better that the two births should be 'Young Violence,' 763, and Θράσος, 'Recklessness,' 'black curses to the house, like to their parents,' reading εἰδομένας.

l. 775. To omit βίον suits the metre and improves the sense; 'honours the just man.'

l. 776. τὰ χρυσόπαστα δ' ἔδεθλα, 'the gold-bespangled dwellings.' ἔδελθα, a certain and beautiful emendation by Auratus of the meaningless MSS. ἐσθλά.

l. 779. ὅσια προσέμολε, sc. ἔδεθλα, 'she visits the pure dwellings.' προσέμολε, gnomic aor. 717.

l. 780. παράσημον αἴνῳ, met., as often in Greek, from coining, 'with its counterfeit glory' (lit. 'stamped amiss with praise').

l. 781. 'And she guides all to the goal.'
Ostensibly the meaning of all this reflection (750–781) is that the sin of Paris and Helena has brought the misery on themselves and Troy; but the underlying meaning to the audience is that the past sins of Agamemnon and his house must bear other sins and ruin in the end. So there is a terrible sense concealed in πᾶν δ' ἐπὶ τέρμα νωμᾷ, namely, the shadow of the coming tragedy, which is effectively pointed by the entry of *the king*.

[*Agamemnon now approaches in a triumphal car, with his attendants and prisoners, and in another chariot Kassandra as prisoner; the Chorus address him.*]

ll. 782–809. 'Conqueror, my king, how shall I fitly address thee? It is easy to profess joy; show of sympathy in woe or weal is common, where there is no true feeling. Yet, a wise king can detect false flattery. When thou didst go forth we did not think well of thy wisdom; but now we greet heartily the victors. And thou shalt discern who of the citizens has been true guardian of thy state.']

l. 786. 'Neither overshooting nor running short of the due mark of praise,' where the English renders exactly the mixed metaphors of ὑπεράρας ('the bow'), and ὑποκάμψας ('with the chariot'), in the Greek.

l. 788. τὸ δοκεῖν εἶναι, 'Seeming to be,' they prefer [to being really].

l. 791. 'While no stab of pain reaches the heart,' i.e. without any sincere grief.

l. 793. ὁμοιοπρεπεῖς, 'in seeming sympathy.'

l. 794. 'Constraining their grave looks' to a false smile.

l. 795. προβατογνώμων, 'wise to discern his flock,' an obvious metaphor.

ll. 796-8. 'The eyes of no man can escape him, which, as though from a kindly heart, with a watery love are fawning,' i.e. he can discern the 'watery' love with its pretence of good will. ὑδαρής, a most expressive word.

l. 801. 'No graceful portrait had I drawn of thee (μοι, dat. agent after pf. pass.), nor as one well wielding,' etc.

l. 803. MSS. read θράσος ἑκούσιον, no metre or sense. Some read ἀκούσιον, 'bringing to dying men courage against their will,' forcing the reluctant and suffering army to persevere. This is surely impossible. Franz ingeniously suggested ἐκ θυσιῶν, 'bringing to dying men courage from sacrifices,' 'encouraging the afflicted army by sacrificing Iphigeneia.' This is scarcely more satisfactory; but provisionally I adopt it.

ll. 805, 6. With the MSS. reading πόνος we can only construe, 'but now from the depths of a friendly heart (lit. 'not from the top of the heart, nor unlovingly') the toil is welcome to those who have accomplished it,' which can only mean, 'the army no longer complain;' but the point is that 'we the *citizens* have changed our unfavourable opinion;' so the ordinary reading makes irrelevant sense. Weil suggests πνόος (= πνοή, Hesych.) and Eng. adopts it; the sense is then satisfactory: 'but now from the depths of a friendly heart a breeze of good-will is wafted to the victors.' Intrinsically the word is quite possible, it is exactly like ῥύος, ῥοῦς, πλύος, πλοῦς. [Karst. suggests πόνον; but that makes the construction of εὔφρων harsh: 'I am friendly.']

l. 808. ἀκαίρως, 'amiss,' a euphemism; he means of course to hint at the plotting and faithlessness of the queen and her lover.

[ll. 810-974. SCENE III. *The chariots stop; Klytaemnestra comes out of the palace to welcome the king, who speaks from the chariot.* First he gives thanks; speaks to Chorus about false friends; promises to see well to the state. Klytaemnestra describes her wretchedness while her lord was away, and her joy at seeing him again; she then calls her attendants to lay down purple carpeting for him to enter the palace. After some reluctance he agrees, and descends, bidding her be kind to Kassandra. The queen says she scorns the waste of wealth in comparison with joy at his return, and ends with a cry to Zeus to accomplish *her prayers.*]

l. 811. τοὺς ἐμοὶ μεταιτίους, might mean 'who helped to win *for me*'

AGAMEMNON.

(K.), but it better suits the pride of the speech to take it, 'helpers with me in our return.'

l. 812. ὧν, attracted relative for ἅ, since πράσσεσθαι has double acc. (700).

l. 813. δίκας..κλύοντες, 'not hearing pleadings from the tongue,' but with divine insight and justice.

l. 816. ψήφους ἔθεντο, 'voted,' only the word which ought to be a transitive verb governing φθοράς is expanded at the last moment into the more vivid ψήφους ἔθεντο. Grammar is sacrificed to picturesqueness. So exactly Soph. El. 709 στάντες δ' ὅθ' αὐτοὺς οἱ βραβῆς κλήρους ἔπηλαν, i. e. *stationed* them by lot.

l. 817. The MSS. reading requires no alteration here: 'but to the opposite urn hope of the hand came nigh, yet it was not filled,' a quaint and fanciful but quite characteristic way of saying 'the other urn expected votes but did not get them.' The two urns (called in Attic κάδισκοι) were one for condemnation, one for acquittal; 'the bloody vessel' is of course the former. This was only one among various methods of balloting at Athens. [Others take χειρός, less naturally, as gen. after πληρουμένῳ. Paley's χεῖλος spoils the sense.]

l. 818. 'The smoke yet plainly shows the captured city;' ἁλοῦσα attributive, not part of the predicate.

l. 819. Ἄτης θύελλαι ζῶσι, 'the gusts of Destruction yet live; and dying with them the ash sends forth rich incense of wealth.' There is no need to alter with Herm. to θυηλαί, 'sacrifices;' the strong bold imagery of Aeschylus might easily call the Fire of Troy 'the storms of Destruction.'

l. 823. I adopt Hermann's and Paley's ἐφραξάμεσθα for the MSS. (inappropriate) ἔπραξ. 'We set our wrathful snares close round the city.' The same word, φράσσω (properly 'to hedge in,' or 'fence close'), is used of a net, 1376.

l. 824. 'The wild beast of Argos' is the armed troop concealed in the wooden horse.

l. 826. 'Springing its leap, what time the Pleiads set,' i. e. in early November. The common story that Troy was taken in spring Aeschylus deserts; probably tradition varied.

l. 828. αἵματος, gen. after ἄδην; cf. *satis, c. gen.* in Lat.

l. 830. μέμνημαι κλύων, not 'I remember hearing,' which is flat, but 'I heard and remember.'

l. 833. φίλον τὸν εὐτυχοῦντ', 'the prosperous friend;' φίλον substantival, as often.

l. 834. 'The poison of illwill seated at the heart.' καρδίαν, acc. after verb of sitting, cf. σέλμα ἡμένων 184. ναῦν ἐφέζετο 664.

l. 836. αὐτός, displaced to get next to αὐτοῦ, a common tendency; so ἐπ' αὐτὸς αὐτῷ Pr. 921; and similarly πρὸς ἄλλοτ' ἄλλον ib. 276.

ll. 838-40. These words are variously taken according to the punctuation. The following seems simplest and most natural. 'I know and can tell (for well have I learnt) of that ghost of friendship, that phantom of a shade, men seeming to wish me truly well.' I. e. κάτοπτρον, εἴδωλον, δοκοῦντας, all in apposition. and acc. after λέγοιμ' ἄν. κάτοπτρον, a bold word for 'image;' it properly means 'mirror.'

l. 841. οὐχ ἱκών, so (Odyssey 24. 117) Agamemnon says: 'And it was a full month ere we had sailed all across the wide sea, for scarce could we win to our cause Odysseus' (Butcher and Lang, p. 392).

l. 842. σειραφόρος, 'trace-horse,' who helped the yoke horses (the Atreidae) to draw the chariot.

l. 843. 'Whether indeed he be dead or living of whom I speak.'

l. 844. τὰ ἄλλα πρός, 'the other things which concern,' the article goes on to the πρός.

l. 845. ἀγῶνας, 'gathering,' see note on 513.

l. 848. ὅτῳ, best taken neuter and general.

l. 850. πῆμ' ἀποστρέψαι νόσου. Porson's beautiful and convincing emendation of MSS. πήματος τρέψαι νύσον: which Hermann strangely defends, though τρέψαι is an unnatural word, and νύσον πήματος much harsher than πῆμα νύσου.

l. 852. δεξιώσομαι, 'I will give greeting;' but the construction is usually transitive, with acc. What he did do when he reached the μέλαθρα and δόμους ἐφεστίους was very different from thanksgiving!

l. 856. Observe her cynical shamelessness: she adopts the tone of a chaste and modest matron who scarcely likes to speak of her wifely love before others.

l. 857. A deadly double meaning here; in a terrible sense 'fear was waning' for her, but to Agamemnon the meaning was natural and simple, 'the elders and I have grown familiar in the king's long absence.'

l. 862. Note the dramatic irony again of ἔρημον in the mouth of the adulteress.

ll. 864, 5. Order a little loose, but meaning clear; 'and that when one had come with one woe another should bring a worse thereafter, announcing them to the house.'

l. 867. ὠχετεύετο, rumour 'came pouring in.'

l. 868. Ahrens' τέτρηται is a great improvement on MSS. τέτρωται, which is dull after τραυμάτων, 'no network were as full of holes as he' (Mors.). The cold-blooded phrase suits Klytaemnestra.

l. 871. Certainly interpolated. πολλὴν ἄνωθεν has got in from 875, and the rest was written by some dull copyist. (H. has an elaborate and astonishing defence of it.) Without the line the sense is, 'a second

45

AGAMEMNON.

Geryon, with triple body, a triple vest of earth he might have boasted, dying once with each shape.' Geryon, the three-headed (or as here three-bodied, *forma tricorporis umbrae*,) monster whose oxen Herakles drove away from Spain.

l. 872. ἐξηύχει λαβών, the MSS. reading is possible, 'he might have boasted it, having received it;' but λαβεῖν is perhaps more likely.

l. 875. 'Ofttimes have others loosed the high-hung halters from my neck, caught violently in the noose.' Others construe, 'seized me by violence and loosed;' but that would be ληφθείσης, the *act*, not λελημ- μένης, the *state*. [See however App. V.]

l. 878. 'In whom lie the pledges of our love.' κύριος, 'the owner,' 'the lord.' MSS. πιστευμάτων; but πιστωμάτων, the regular word, is surely right.

l. 880. Strophios, king of Phokis, friend (and according to one story brother-in-law) of Agamemnon, received Orestes, and brought him up with his own son Pylades. The details are given very variously.

l. 881. ἀμφίλεκτα (like Lat. *anceps*) here means simply 'double;' 1585 it means 'disputed:' literally, it is 'spoken both ways,' which covers both meanings.

l. 884. βουλήν, 'the council,' the πρέσβος Ἀργείων who have helped the queen to rule.

ὥστε for ὡς, 'as it is men's wont.'

l. 885. πεσόντα is Agamemnon, whose fall before Troy would have been 'doubly' woeful; to himself, and to his kingdom and family at home.

l. 886. μέντοι, confirmative, 'verily,' 'assuredly;' so Plato, Phaed. 65 D φαμέν τι εἶναι δίκαιον; φαμὲν μέντοι νὴ Δία, 'assuredly we do.'

l. 887. ἔμοιγε μὲν δή, 'for myself however,' 661.

l. 888. κατεσβήκασι (intr. perf.), 'are dried up;' so of the sea, 959. So Hesiod. Op. 588, speaks of αἶγες σβεννύμεναι, 'goats which will not yield milk.' The common use is 'to quench,' of fire, etc.; but probably the earliest meaning was vaguer, suiting both fire and liquids.

l. 890. 'Weeping that the watch-fires lit for thee were ever un- regarded,' i.e. the fires we lit night after night awaiting thee, who never camest. This is better than supposing λαμπτηρουχίαι to refer to *beacons of victory*. which would give a very strained sense to ἀτη- μελήτους, viz. 'unlit.' [Enger takes it as above, only reads needlessly καίουσα.]

l. 892. ὑπαί, best taken as governing ῥιπαῖς, 'beneath the light hum of the singing gnat.'

l. 893. θωύσσω, word of obscure origin, usually 'to call, shout, cry.'

l. 894. 'More woes than the time of my sleep,' an abridged (but quite intelligible) expression; she means 'more woes than could be

suffered in the time I was asleep.' Observe also the picturesque συνεύ-
δοντος, the time 'is sleeping with her' that passes while she sleeps.
The *personifying* instinct pervades the language of Aeschylus. Somewhat similarly in Soph. χρόνος συνὼν διδάσκει O. C. 7, ὁ προστατῶν
χρόνος διῆγέ μ᾽ El. 781, and σύμφυτος αἰών above, 107.
  l. 896. σταθμῶν, in the old Homeric sense, 'stalls,' or 'folds.'
  l. 897. 'The saviour fore-stay of the ship,' *Br.*, πρότονος being the
ropes from the top of the mast to the bows, which kept the mast from
falling back.
  l. 899. καί has offended many editors, as the other nouns are unconnected; but Kl. and Schn. are no doubt right in saying that it connects
896-899, which describes the *protection and security* afforded by the
master, with 899-901, which describes the *delight* of his unhoped-for
return. The transition from one set to the other set is marked by καί.
  l. 902. τἀναγκαῖον, 'the stress of need.'
  l. 903. ἀξιῶ, 'I greet him,' see 572.
  l. 904. 'Let none envy me' my luck; 'let no (god or man) grudge my
joy and triumph at my lord's return:' she acts the ordinary feeling of a
pious Greek in moments of great delight. which increases the irony of
the situation to those who know her purpose.
  [*Here Klytaemnestra kneels to him.*]
  l. 908. τέλος, 'task.'
  l. 912. Observe the splendid irony again of this terrible line, 'That
justice lead him to a home unlooked for.'
  l. 913. 'All else my care. not overcome by sleep, shall order justly
with God's aid, as fated.' εἱμαρμένα. 'being fated,' really causal use of
participle. The dark irony is carried through these lines also. They
seem to mean, 'We will be careful with God's aid to order things as is
fit;' they do mean, 'What justice and fate require (the murder) I will
by God's aid accomplish.'
  l. 914. Leda, wife of Tyndareus. visited by Zeus in the form of a
swan, laid two eggs; out of one came Helena and Klyt., out of the other
Castor and Pollux. This was one common form of a variously told tale.
  l. 915. εἰκότως governs the datives; 'as befits my absence.'
  l. 920. A contemptuous line; 'pour thy low-grovelling clamour in
my ears.' Note χαμαιπετές transferred from her to the cry.
  l. 924. ἐμοὶ μέν, 'to me at least;' the antithesis being suppressed,
μέν gets this meaning naturally.
  l. 925. λέγω, 'I bid,' as often.
  l. 926. ποδοψήστρων, 'foot-rugs' [ψα-, 'rub'], contemptuous again.
  l. 927. κληδὼν αὔτει, 'fame's voice is loud.'
  l. 929. 'Count a man happy when he has ended his life in prosperity,'
the well-known Greek thought, cf. Soph. O. T. 1530. The rapidity of

AGAMEMNON.

Agamemnon's thoughts make the language a little obscure. 'Fame does not require such gauds; prudence is God's best gift; no man can be called happy till his death;' i. e. they are needless, these splendours, and perhaps dangerous; who knows what may happen even to me?

l. 930. MSS. read εἰ πάντα δ' ὣς πράσσοιμ' ἄν, which is quite possible Greek, but only as a *double* conditional sentence, where πράσσοιμ' ἄν is the verb, not only of the protasis to εὐθαρσὴς ἐγώ, but also strictly of the *apodosis* to some other protasis understood. E. g. Dem. Meid. 582 fin. εἰ οὗτοι χρήματα ἔχοντες μὴ προοῖντ' ἄν, if these men *would not spend money if they had it*; Isocr. Archid. 120 εἰ δὲ μηδεὶς ἂν ἀξιώσειε ζῆν ἀποστερούμενος τῆς πατρίδος, ' if no one *would care to live if deprived* of his country.' And without second protasis expressed, εἰ μὴ ποιήσαιτ' ἂν τοῦτο Dem. Phil. 1. § 18. So here the MSS. reading means, 'if in all things so [not *I were to prosper*, which is πράσσοιμι, but] I *might* prosper' ('should chance so befal' or something of the kind). Putting it otherwise, εἰ πράσσοιμι means, 'if I *were to* prosper,' εἰ πράσσοιμ' ἄν, 'if I *have a chance* of prospering,' and this latter makes quite good sense. In fact πράσσοιμ' ἄν is a variation, not for πράσσοιμι, but for πράξω, less confidently expressed. I see therefore no need to take πράσσοιμεν (H., D.), though doubtless this also would make perfectly good sense: 'If so I fared in all things then I need not fear,' if everything were to turn out as this has, my luck would indeed be good. Nor is there any need of Weil's ingenious conjecture εἶπον τάδ' ὣς ...

l. 931. 'Yet order this not counter to my purpose.' Observe aor. imper. with μή, contrary to rule; but readily explained by the order, the verb coming first. γνώμη, like γνῶναι, can be used for 'resolve.'

l. 932. 'I too, be assured, shall not break my purpose;' ἐμέ is emphatic as well as γνώμην; as though he said, 'Purpose! I too have one as well as thou.'

l. 933. 'Perchance *in fear* thou mad'st this vow?' Having failed to get him to comply as a favour, she tries a taunt of cowardice. ἄν of course goes with ηὔξω; she *means*, 'you *did* vow,' but the conditional form of the sentence ('you may have done' = '*perhaps* you did') points the sneer better, with its ironical moderation. So Soph. O. T. 523 ἦλθε τοὔνειδος τάχ' ἄν, 'perchance this reproach came.' So παρεκόπης ἄν 1252.

l. 934. The answer is that of a dignified and unyielding king: 'If e'er man did, with knowledge I spake my resolve.' τέλος, 'the final decision.' Agamemnon replies in effect that it was not a cowardly vow but a deliberate purpose.

l. 935. τί ἂν δοκεῖ, one of those short phrases like ἵνα τί, where one would not say the verb is understood, but rather that τί stands for the omitted clause. So Plat. Phaedr. 234 C τί σοι φαίνεται ὁ λόγος; οὐχ ὑπερφυῶς εἰρῆσθαι (see Riddell, Dig. of Gr. Id. 121).

NOTES. LINES 930–957.

l. 938. The very sentiment of the chorus, 456.

l. 939. 'Who stirs no hatred, is not envied either.' You must risk φθόνος, the evil envy, if you wish to have ζῆλος, the desirable envy. So (Menex. 242 A) Socrates, describing Athens after the war, says, ἦλθεν ἐπ' αὐτὴν ὕπερ φιλεῖ τοῖς εὖ πράττουσι προσπίπτειν, πρῶτον μὲν ζῆλος ἀπὸ ζήλου δὲ φθόνος. Arist. Rhet. 2. 11 defines the two, ἐπιεικές ἐστιν ὁ ζῆλος καὶ ἐπιεικῶν, τὸ δὲ φθονεῖν φαῦλον καὶ φαύλων.

l. 940. Agamemnon, already yielding, tries a last appeal to her womanly dignity. 'A woman should not be contentious;' but she skilfully appeals to his generosity as victor. 'It becomes the fortunate to be vanquished too,' to yield in their turn.

l. 942. 'Dost thou too esteem this victory in the strife?' νίκην τήνδε, this victory of which you speak, taking up νικᾶσθαι. [Goodwin, who has discussed with great subtlety all this passage (Trans. Amer. Phil. Ass. 1877), translates, 'is *this* the kind of victory ..?' i.e. τὸ νικᾶσθαι, ironically. But καὶ σύ is the really emphatic part, not τήνδε, and the meaning given above is simpler.] Observe δήριος, Ionic gen.

l. 943. 'Yield: yet the victory grant me willingly;' i.e. give way, but with good grace. For μέντοι γε, cf. Dem. Phil. 1. § 49 οὐ μέντοι γε μὰ Δία προαιρεῖσθαι, 'not however by Zeus that his intention is.' The line seems to have no caesura; but μέντοι is perhaps slightly felt to be a divisible word, being a compound of two particles.

l. 944. ὑπαί .. λύοι, tmesis, 450.

l. 945. 'These sandals, slaves beneath my feet' (*idors*.) renders the expression very aptly. For πρό-δουλος, cf. ἀντί and its use in comp., see 406. Aesch. uses ἀντίδουλος Frag. 180.

l. 946. The reading of Fa. σὺν ταῖσδε (i.e. ἀρβύλαις) makes good sense, but the μή is then too late in the sentence, since it means 'lest;' with καὶ τοῖσδε, μή is 'not,' and its position natural.

ἀλουργές (used as subst. from adj. ἀλουργής, 'sea-wrought,' i.e. made from sea-purple), 'sea-purple cloths.'

l. 948. MSS. σωματοφθορεῖν, corrupt; best reading is δωματοφθορεῖν (Schütz, Herm., Eng., Schn.), 'to waste the house's wealth,' which she answers 961.

l. 950. τούτων. gen. of reference, lit. 'as regards these things.' 'Thus much for this.' Cf. τοῦ κασιγνήτου τί φής; Soph. El. 317.

l. 954. ἐξαίρετον, the regular word for the choice prizes *taken out* of the booty for kings or heroes: ἐξαίρετον δώρημα Eum. 402, ἐξεῖλεθ' αὐτῷ κτῆμα Soph. Tr. 245.

l. 956. 'But since I am subdued, to hearken to thee in this.' ἀκούειν consec. or epexegetic inf.

[*After* 957 *Agamemnon's sandals are untied by an attendant while the queen is speaking; she then, probably yet speaking, escorts him slowly*

AGAMEMNON.

to the central door: after 972 he enters with his train, and she utters her short prayer, 973. 4, then follows him. Kassandra remains seated and silent in the chariot.]

l. 959. A fine answer to his scruples: the sea is boundless (κατασβέσει 888), we can get more purple; the house is royal and wealthy.

l. 960. 'The juice ever fresh, precious as silver, of plenteous purple,' very Aeschylean accumulated phrase. Schn. quotes Theopompus (150 years later than Aesch.) as saying, 'the sea-purple (among the Kolophonians) fetched its weight in silver.'

l. 961. 'We have a house, to supply store of these things.' No reason to alter οἶκος of MSS. to οἴκοις. ἔχειν, epexegetic. τῶνδε, partitive, 'some of.' Cf. Ar. Ach. 184 ξυνελέγοντο τῶν λίθων, 'they began to collect stones.' [Perhaps ἅλις for ἄναξ (Karst.) is right.]

l. 964. προύνεχθέντος, 'had it been ordered,' to me .. when devising, etc., gen. abs. conditional.

l. 965. MSS. μηχανωμένης; possible Greek ('when I was devising'), but very unlikely with the other fem. genitives. The dative is the best correction, governed by προύνεχθέντος. κόμιστρα, 'price for thy return.' Lit. 'for bringing thee back,' κομίζω.

l. 966. ἵκετ', gnomic aor.

l. 967. σκιὰν σειρίου κυνός, 'shadow *against* the Scorching Hound,' loose use of the gen.

σειρίου κυνός: Seirios was 'the dog of Orion,' constellation near Orion (the brightest star usually being called Scirios): it rose about mid-July, the hot, unhealthy time of year. Hence Hom. Il. 22. 30 says of it κακὸν δέ τε σῆμα τέτυκται. Cf. Verg. G. 4. 285 '*rapidus torrens Sirius Indos.*'

ll. 968-72. An expansion of two metaphors: 'the return of the master brings as it were warmth in winter and coolness in summer.'

l. 972. τελείου, 'the rightful lord,' the man whose will is law in the house, who has the τέλος or final authority. This suggests to her τέλειος Ζεύς, in a different sense, 'Zeus the fulfiller.'

[*Agamemnon goes in: she stops and prays with lifted hands.*]

l. 974. τῶνπερ, Epic for ὧνπερ.

[*Klytaemnestra goes in, and the Third Scene ends. The Chorus sing the Third Stasimon.*]

Strophe 1 (975-86). 'Whence come these obstinate forebodings? My heart is fearful. It is long since they sailed to Troy.' (*Ant.* 987-1000). 'I have seen them safe-returned; yet still within comes misgiving; may it be false!'

Strophe 2 (1001-17). 'In health, disease is near; in prosperity, a hidden reef. But wealth may be saved by timely sacrifice; famine averted by timely harvest.'

50

NOTES. LINES 959–1006.

Ant. 2 (1018–34). 'Only blood once spilt no charm can recall; for did Zeus not slay Asklepios? But for the uncertainty of the future I should have poured out these misgivings; as it is, I hide them in gloomy silence.'

l. 976. Several edd. prefer δεῖγμα (Fl.), construing 'a spectre,' but there is no evidence of any such meaning, and δεῖμα (Fa.) is more impressive and natural. προστατήριον, 'stationed before,' describes the *haunting* of the misgiving, 'why flits thus obstinately this fear, haunting my heart prophetic?'

l. 979. Notice the imaginative language: the fear is now called 'a prophetic song.'

l. 980. οὐδ' ἀποπτύσαι is much the easiest reading, and being a MS. reading, should be preferred to conjecture ἀποπτύσαν. 'Nor to spurn it away like dark dreams does ready confidence sit at my heart's dear throne;' the inf. depending on θάρσος.

l. 983. The reading of MS. Farnese, with alteration of ξυνεμβόλοις (unknown word) to ξυνεμβολαῖς, will construe: 'Time has grown old since the cables were fastened (on the fastenings of the cables) of the vessel on the sand.' But there is probably some corruption: ἐπί is odd, so is συνεμβολαῖς, so is ἀκάτας sing.

l. 990. The 'dirge,' or θρῆνος, was sung with only flute, no lyre. So Eum. 331 ὕμνος ἐξ Ἐρινύων ἀφόρμικτος.

l. 992. τὸ πᾶν, see Appendix II.

l. 995. 'Not vainly bodes my thought, my heart beating with eddies against my true prophetic breast' (or τελεσφόροις δίναις, 'with eddies of fulfilment').

σπλάγχνα and κέαρ are in apposition. The sense is, 'my boding heart is not vain; my bosom's foresight is true, and will be fulfilled.'

l. 998. I have taken Kennedy's τοιαῦτ' for the corrupt τοι of Farnese MS. as nearer than Hermann's τὸ πᾶν. The Fl. MS. has no metre. The meaning then is, 'But I pray that such things may turn out lies, far from my expectation, and be not accomplished.'

l. 1001. MSS. are corrupt here: see notes on text. The metre is probably ⏑⏑–⏑⏑– three times repeated: and I have taken Paley's μάλα γέ τοι | τὸ μεγάλας | ὑγιείας (only spelling this last word as usual, and supposing –ει– short with Klausen, compare δείλαιος, γεραιός, τοιοῦτος, etc., see 1256). The sense is, 'Of lusty health at least the bounds are insatiable,' i.e. no man is ever satisfied with the greatest prosperity: (*forebodings are therefore just*) 'for disease the neighbour presses hard behind the wall.' The words in italics show the connection.

l. 1005. Perhaps a line omitted here, see 1022.

l. 1006. ἔπαισεν, gnomic aorist, 'strikes ofttimes a hidden reef;' so ἔδυ, ἐπόντισε below.

AGAMEMNON.

l. 1008. 'And of gathered wealth if fear casts out a part with well-measured throw,—the whole house doth not founder, with sorrow overladen, nor does it sink the hull.' The construction is broken: ὄκνος βαλών is nom. pendens, and the subject is changed. It is true (as K. observes) that ὄκνῳ would set the construction right ('the house if it cast out in fear'). But it is more in Aeschylus' manner to personify fear; and the anacoluthon is of a natural kind. Cf. Soph. O. C. 1150 λόγος δ' ὃς ἐμπέπτωκε.. συμβαλοῦ γνώμην, 'the tale that has reached my ears, advise me.'

πρὸ χρημάτων may go together, 'part *to save* the wealth,' i. e. part to save the whole; but it is better to take πρὸ .. βαλών as tmesis. (Perhaps indeed Enger's πρὸ μέν τι is right.)

l. 1015. 'A bounteous gift of plenty from Zeus,' etc. The adjectives accumulated, as often. The connection is abrupt: perhaps τοι is corrupt.

l. 1018. Sense: (a labouring boat may be saved, a famine averted,) 'but blood once shed is irrevocable.' The terrible words τὸ δ' ἐπὶ γᾶν, etc., at once raise the thought of the bloody past of the Pelopidae, of the slaughter of Iphigeneia not yet avenged,—and of the coming vengeance which the chorus suspect and would fain avert.

ll. 1022–24. I have taken Hartung's ἀπέπαυσεν as the nearest to the MSS. αὗτ' ἔπαυσε, and read it as a question. 'And did not Zeus slay, for a warning, him that was skilled to bring back from the dead?' Zeus killed Asklepios, son of Apollo, the healer, with lightning for bringing the dead to life. But these lines do not correspond to the strophe; and either a line is (as I have marked it) there omitted, or here is something superfluous. If the latter, Hermann's reading Ζεὺς δὲ τὸν ὀρθοδαῆ τῶν φθιμένων ἀνάγειν ἔπαυσεν (omitting αὗτε, οὐδέ and ἐπ' εὐλαβείᾳ) is as likely as any other; but it is perhaps best to leave it.

l. 1025. 'But were it not that one lot by divine decree hinders another from winning overmuch, my heart, outstripping my tongue, had poured out these bodings;' as it is, I brood in secret. I. e. I take refuge in the thought that sometimes fate interferes with fate (and so there may be an unseen counter-fate to check the evil destiny of Agamemnon's house).

l. 1026. ἐκ θεῶν with εἶργε, really repeating more precisely the notion of τεταγμένα. The above is substantially Prof. Goodwin's rendering, and it is the clearest sense proposed for these difficult lines.

l. 1031. 'In grief of soul without a hope to unravel aught profitable 'mid the stirrings of my heart.' τολυπεύω is a Homeric metaphor for 'contrive,' 'accomplish,' lit. to 'wind off wool.' The rapid change of metaphor, from 'winding wool,' to 'stirring fire,' is not unlike the poet, see 786.

NOTES. LINES 1008–1053.

[ll. 1035–1071. SCENE IV. (first part), *Klytaemnestra comes out and sees Kassandra still seated in the chariot. She speaks to her imperiously.*
 'Go within, and take your lot humbly; our royal house will treat you more kindly than others might.' Then, as she gets no answer, she becomes more impatient, and finally departs.]

l. 1036. ἀμηνίτως, 'graciously;' with cold scorn Klytaemnestra treats the fate of Kassandra as a favour of the gods.

l. 1037. 'A partner in the lustral bowl;' i. e. a member of the household; for all, even slaves, shared in the household religious rites.

l. 1038. κτησίου βωμοῦ, 'the altar of Zeus Ktesios,' or guardian of wealth, which included slaves.

l. 1041. I have kept the reading of Fa. But perhaps the right reading is Fl. emended thus: δουλίας μάζης βίον, 'the life of slavish fare.' Blomf.

l. 1042. δ' οὖν, coming to practical conclusion, 'be that as it may,' 'anyhow.' Cf. 676. 'Should this hard lot oppress one,' the opt. generalising the statement by removing it from this case. But the Farn. reading ἐπιρρέπει may be right.

l. 1044. ἤμησαν καλῶς, 'have reaped good harvest,' i. e. got rich. The general sense is ' old-established wealthy houses are kinder to slaves than *nouveaux riches.*' It suits Klytaemnestra's royal pride to say so: but the remark savours more of democratic Athens, with her commercial wealth, than the heroic times.

l. 1046. I. e. 'thou hearest how we are wont to deal with slaves.'

l. 1047. λέγουσα παύεται, 'she has spoken.' The chorus can only call Klytaemnestra's speech ' clear,' σαφῆ; they feel its cold cruelty.

l. 1048. 'Thou art caught within the toils of fate: obey if thou canst, but perhaps thou wilt not.' (ἁλοῦσα, great improvement on MSS. ἂν οὖσα; ἄν is not wanted in advance, the sentence being only formally conditional.)

πείθοι' ἂν εἰ πείθοιο is the mildest way possible of advising; lit. it is 'thou would'st hearken if thou would'st.' So 1394 χαίροιτ' ἂν εἰ χαίροιτ', 'joy if ye will.' The ἄν is carried on to ἀπειθοίης; so Soph. O. T. 937 ἥδοιο μέν, πῶς δ' οὐκ ἄν; ἀσχάλλοις δ' ἴσως. So also Ar. Eq. 1054.

l. 1050. The 'swallow' was a recognised simile in Greek for 'foreign speech;' the non-Hellenic languages they despised, and compared to the twittering of birds. So Ar. Ran. 681, when the poet satirises Kleophon for his foreign birth, he says, ' on his lips screeches Θρῃκία χελιδών.' So Av. 1681.

l. 1052. | ' My words must reach her mind and so prevail.'

l. 1053. τὰ λῷστα τῶν παρεστώτων, 'the best as things are.' The chorus are sympathetic, but see the hopelessness of resistance. They treat Kassandra simply as a dazed captive, too timid to move or speak.

l. 1055. MSS. θυραίαν τήνδ', which is no sense. θυραίαν τῇδε (D.) is no use, for the constr. σχολὴ ἐμοὶ τρίβειν θυραίαν, possible in itself, is impossible if θυραίαν comes first. Read θυραίᾳ τῇδ', 'I have no time to loiter here without.' (Some suppose τήνδε = τήνδε τὴν τριβήν, after τρίβειν: sufficiently improbable.)

l. 1056. τὰ μὲν .. μῆλα, article separated from subst., really a usage from Epic poetry, where the article is still a demonstrative or pronoun: 'they, the sheep.' Cp. τὰ δ' ἐπῴχετο κῆλα θεοῖο Il. 1. 383, 'they came flying, (the) shafts of the god.' So here, 'they stand already by the central hearth, the sheep ready for the fiery sacrifice.' The 'central hearth' was the altar of the Ζεὺς ἑρκεῖος, or 'god of the household enclosure,' the representative family deity: Ζηνὸς ἑρκείου (Soph. Antig. 487) means 'the family.' Observe the loose local gen. ἑστίας μεσομφάλου, vaguely indicating the *region*, again an epic usage, e.g. Il. 9. 219 ἷζεν τοίχου τοῦ ἑτέρωιο, Od. 1. 23 ἔσχατοι ἀνδρῶν, οἱ μὲν δυσομένου Ὑπερίονος, *ib.* 12. 27 ἢ ἁλὸς ἢ ἐπὶ γῆς.

l. 1058. ἐλπίσασι, sc. ἡμῖν, ' for ne'er we hoped,' etc. There is however something to be said for K.'s reading ἡμῖν for ἤδη: ἐλπίσασι is harsh with no preceding dative.

l. 1061. σὺ δ' ἀντὶ φωνῆς φράζε καρβάνῳ χερί, 'then show me with barbarous hand instead of voice;' the apparent stupidity of such a suggestion is removed on the stage by Klytaemnestra's meaning gestures. Notice δέ superfluous in apodosis: an Epic use.

l. 1064. κακῶν κλύει φρενῶν, 'obeys her foolish thoughts.'

l. 1067. 'Foam out her spirit in blood,' splendidly continuing the metaphor begun in χαλινόν of a wild colt.

l. 1068. 'I will not waste more words and be thus scorned.'
[*She goes out resentfully.*]

l. 1071. καίνισον ζυγόν, 'handsel thy yoke,' i.e. 'submit.'

[SCENE IV. (second part), ll. 1072-1177. *Kassandra steps out of the chariot and advances to the front of the stage.*]

In this astonishing scene Aeschylus seems to have touched the limit of what speech can do to excite pity and terror. The cries come forth to Apollo, repeated louder and more wildly as the inspiration grows upon her; she smells the 'rust of murder on the walls' of the bloody house to which she comes a prisoner, and visions rise, first of the past wickedness, then of the present; and lastly she bewails, in songs of 'searching and melting beauty,' her own piteous fate. The chorus sustain the part of the Argive citizen, sympathetic and horror-struck, and finally bewildered and overpowered by her clearer and clearer prophecies of the bloody deeds that are imminent.

NOTES. LINES 1055–1099.

l. 1072. 'Woe, woe, alas! O Earth! O Apollo, Apollo!' She is looking no doubt at the god's image.
πόποι is simply an interjection like παπαῖ, τοτοῖ, etc.; the old scholiastic note which translated it 'gods' is now generally rejected.
δᾶ is Doric form of γᾶ or γῆ.

l. 1074. ὀτοτύζω, like φεύζω 1308, αἰώζω, οἰμώζω, etc., is a verb formed from an interjection.
Λοξίας, name of Apollo, as the 'utterer' of oracles, cf. Eum. 19 Διὸς προφήτης ἐστὶ Λοξίας πατρός.

l. 1075. 'He is not one to need a mourner' (lit. *to have*). Apollo is the god of light (φοῖβος) and joy and healing (παιᾶν), and has nothing to do with groans and laments, which belong to the Chthonian gods, Hades, and the Furies, etc.

l. 1079. προσήκοντ' (observe the *personal* construction, like δίκαιός εἰμι, see 16), 'it beseems him not to be at hand in lamentation.'

l. 1081. ἀγυιάτης, collat. form of ἀγυιεύς, 'god of the ways,' a title of Apollo as presiding over the out-door life. There was no doubt a statue in front of the palace, cf. 1072.
ἀπόλλων, 'my destroyer,' see note on 687. Apollo had loved her, and been deceived, and in revenge he made all disbelieve her. See 1203 sqq.

l. 1082. οὐ μόλις, lit. 'not scantily,' i.e. 'utterly.'

l. 1084. δουλίᾳ περ ἐν φρενί, 'even in a slave's heart,' the strict meaning of περ.

l. 1091. Read κακὰ καὶ ἀρτάνας, as the Farnese MS. has it (only καὶ ἀρτ. for κάρτ.) instead of the nom. as the other MSS. read it; for it is far better to construe συνίστορα transitive; it is the *house* which σύνοιδε, not the *crimes*; and the nom. of the MSS. is due to not seeing this. For adj. governing acc. cp. θυμοβόρου φρένα 103. 'Nay, a god-accursed house, that knoweth many a murder of kindred, and many a strangling; a human slaughter-house, a dripping floor.' αὐτοφόνα: for αὐτός, used in compounds for describing murder of kin, compare Soph. Antig. 57, 1175; Theb. 805; inf. 1573.
'ῥαντήριος cannot be passive,' says Paley, objecting to the MS. reading; but it need not be passive; it means 'a dripping' floor, not 'a besprinkled floor.' Perhaps πέδου ῥαντ.' 'splashing the floor.' (Karst.)

l. 1096. She sees a vision of the children of Thyestes (father of Aegisthos) whom his brother Atreus (father of Agamemnon) served up to him at a banquet. The quarrel is mentioned below (1583).
κλαιόμενα σφαγάς, 'bewailing their own slaughter.'

ll. 1098–9. The MSS. mostly read ἦμεν at the beginning of both lines, though M. (acc. Hermann) has ἦ μήν in 1098. This will construe: 'Verily we had heard thy prophetic fame, but we seek no

55

AGAMEMNON.

prophets;' which is very dull sense, and very bad sound. I believe with Weil and Enger that ἦμεν has been erroneously repeated, and has ousted τούτων from the second line. The sense is then 'we had heard (ἦμεν πεπυσμένοι) thy prophetic fame; but of these things we seek no prophets;' i.e. it does not require inspiration to tell *past* evils. Kassandra's vision immediately leaps forward to the future. [If the Med. really reads ἦ μήν in 1098, it is a correction to avoid ἦμεν twice; but in Merkel's facsimile edition it is given in both lines as ἦμεν.]

l. 1100. A new vision comes on, of the murder of Agamemnon in his bath, by means of a cloak thrown round him and two blows of a dagger. The murder does not happen till 1343; this is the prophetic foresight.

μήδεται, 'she plots,' Klytaemnestra of course; the audience understand, but not the chorus.

l. 1109. πῶς φράσω τέλος; the sentence ought to end with κτενεῖς; but it is broken, and these words substituted.

l. 1111. ὀρέγματα, this neat emendation is no doubt right: the acc. is cognate. Lit. 'hand after hand reaches forth a-stretch;' i.e. blow on blow comes. (The MSS. προτείνει ὀρεγομένα will construe 'stretches, reaching forth;' but προτείνει is never intrans.)

l. 1112. The prophecy is clearer; but it has only changed from 'riddles' without a clue (the vision of line 1096) to a 'dim prophecy' with details but no names (the vision of 1100); so they 'do not yet understand.'

l. 1113. ἐπαργέμοις, 'dim;' properly of a *white* film *over* (ἐπ'.. ἀργ...) the eye, probably cataract.

l. 1115. 'A net of Death' is a fine name for the cloak which made him helpless. 'But *she* is the snare, who shares his bed, who shares the deed of blood.'

συναιτία, 'sharing the guilt' with the δίκτυον; of Aegisthos there is no thought yet. [Notice the rare hiatus τι Ἅιδου. So Soph. Trach. 1203.]

l. 1117. στάσις, some comm. (Schn., Pal., K.) construe 'a troop,' and suppose it to mean the Furies, alleging ποίαν Ἐρινύν as confirmatory. It is true that Aesch. does use στάσις in this sense, but always with something to make it clear, as τῇδε στάσει Cho. 114, στάσις ἁμά ('*our* company') Eum. 311, στάσις πάγκοινος ἅδε Cho. 458. To use στάσις absolutely, without article or defining gen., for the 'band of Furies' would be very harsh.

It is better (with Eng., Kl., D.) to take it as meaning 'Strife' personified; this is quite as Aeschylean a usage (Pr. 200, 1088; Pers. 188, 715, 738; Eum. 977) and the answer ποίαν Ἐρινύν quite as appropriate; indeed, being singular, more so. 'Let Strife, insatiable against the Race, raise cry of triumph o'er the stoning-sacrifice.'

NOTES. LINES 1100–1137.

Still an obscure passage. If λευσίμου is right, Kassandra must mean: 'Let the people arise and stone the accursed murderers; let that "Strife" which besets the bloodstained family sing triumph over her death.' But if so we must suppose that the prophetess' vision as yet only foresees Agamemnon's death, not Klytaemnestra's, who died by Orestes' hand; this is reserved for a later vision, 1280. (λεύσιμος cannot mean '*deserving* stoning,' as Pal., K., L. S., etc.)

l. 1120. φαιδρύνει, 'cheers.'

l. 1121. A very difficult and corrupt passage. It is best to take Dindorf's καιρία for the varied unintelligibilities of the MSS. Translate: 'To my heart has run the blood-drop saffron-hued (i.e. pale with terror) which at the last hour (lit. *at the time appointed, the mortal moment*) falls and ends with the beams of setting life;' i.e. 'my blood is pale, like a man fainting and failing at the point of death.' The general sense is plain: the chorus are in sudden and deep alarm.

l. 1125. The murder now comes upon her in a vision of unspeakable power and terror. 'Behold, behold! Keep off from his mate the bull! in the robe she has caught him, and smites with the treacherous thrust of her black horn!' lit. 'with blackhorned device.'

l. 1127. μελαγκέρῳ, though apparently not the reading of any MS. (for Prof. Goodwin, who has reexamined M., asserts that the original reading was μελάγκερων as in most of the others), is yet plainly right; both the accusative alone and the dative μηχανήματι alone would be very harsh, while μελαγκέρῳ μηχανήματι is thoroughly Aeschylean.

l. 1128. κύτος and λέβης, the 'vessel' and 'cauldron' are varied words for the bath. κύτει, for metre's sake, for MSS. τεύχει. τύπτει does not answer to φόνου of strophe; and one is possibly corrupt.

l. 1130. The chorus are more and more uneasy; and in their restlessness break out into complaint that prophecy is always terrifying men, and bringing evil. The same complaint was made by Ahab (1 Kings 22. 8), and by Agamemnon of Kalchas (Il. 1. 108).

l. 1133. Hermann alters στέλλεται and θεσπιῳδόν into τέλλεται and θεσπιῳδοί, both needlessly. στέλλεται, 'is sent forth,' has more meaning than τέλλεται, 'comes:' and the phrase 'by woes the wordy arts bring men prophetic terror to learn' is quite Aeschylean. The scornful phrase for prophecy, πολυεπεῖς τέχναι, suits their present resentment born of fear.

l. 1137. θροῶ .. ἐπεγχέασα is the reading of all the MSS., which is a syllable too much. Herm. reads θροεῖς .. ἐπεγχέας, 'thou speakst of my woe, mingling it with his;' and most edd. follow him. But the difficulty is that the chorus had not alluded to Kassandra. The best correction is ἐπεγχέαι, given by Prof. Campbell (which had also oc-

AGAMEMNON.

curred independently to me). It is epexegetic infinitive: 'for my own woe I bewail, to mingle it with his.'

l. 1138. ἤγαγες (so MSS., no alteration needed), a sudden appeal to Apollo, as in 1087.

l. 1141. αὑτᾶς for σεαυτῆς, not uncommon in poetry, as e. g. 1297.

l. 1142. νόμον ἄνομον, 'a wild tuneless measure.' ξουθός is an obscure word, but its commonest application is to the nightingale, as here; and such phrases as ξουθοὶ ἄνεμοι, ξουθὰ λαλῶν, seem to point to its meaning 'clear-voiced.'

l. 1145. Ἴτυς son of Philomela and Tereus; the mother slew him and served him up to his father, in rage at finding a rival in her sister Prokne. The two sisters then fled from Tereus' wrath, and were changed into birds. Philomela as the nightingale never ceases to lament Itys. (Others change the names Prokne and Philomela, making the former mother of Itys.)

ἀμφιθαλῆ κακοῖς βίον, 'all her life rich only in sorrow;' a beautiful expression. The acc. is best taken as acc. of duration.

l. 1147. περιβάλον γάρ, Blomfield's satisfactory correction. 'For the gods set round her a feathery form, and a sweet life, without tears.' The difficulty is, how can the sorrow-laden nightingale be said to have 'a sweet life without tears?' The most ingenious solution is to take (with Eng.) κλαυμάτων ἄτερ with περιβάλον, 'they changed her without pain, for me remains the sharp sword.' And this is at first sight tempting. But the order is strained and really the same difficulty remains with γλυκύν. The truth no doubt is this: that the chorus say, 'You are like the nightingale, a ceaseless singer of sad song;' to which beautiful comparison Kassandra replies in effect: 'Yes, but how unlike in fate; her song is plaintive, but she has no real sorrow; she flees on free wings and has nought to mar her sweet life; I am doomed to a cruel death.'

l. 1150. 'Whence hast thou these inspired throes of vain grief, and framest in song these terrors with ill-omened cry, and likewise with loud-voiced measures?' ὄρθιοι νόμοι are the sustained lyric songs as opposed to the δύσφατος κλαγγά or meaningless cries which accompany them.

l. 1155. 'Whence the bounds of thy prophetic path, boding but ill?' i.e. who guides you on the path of prophecy? The answer to this comes really 1202.

l. 1159. ἠνυτόμαν τροφαῖς, 'I throve with nurture.'

l. 1163. MSS. read νεογνὸς ἀνθρώπων μάθοι. The sense is plain: 'a new born child could understand;' and doubtless the first syllable of ἀν-θρώπων contains the necessary particle ἄν. I have taken Karsten's guess in default of better.

58

l. 1164. δάκει for δήγματι (II.) to suit antistr.; though, as δήγματι makes a proper dochmiac, it may be right.

l. 1165. θρευμένας, i. e. σοῦ, 'when thou wailest aloud o'er thy bitter woe.' The dialectic form θρευμένας for θρεομένας is Enger's reading to suit θανατήφορα of the antistrophe.

θραύματ' is the best supported reading. lit. 'shatterings' for me to hear; i.e. 'it breaks my heart to hear.' Many adopt θαύματ' the reading of Fa., but it seems too weak a word for such a climax, and the other is not too bold for Aeschylus.

l. 1170. 'They brought no cure to save the city from suffering as indeed she suffers.'

ἄκος, a kind of cogn. after ἐπηρκέσαν: what is now called 'internal' accusative, lit. 'they aided no cure;' a perfectly natural use.

l. 1172. MSS. θερμόνους τάχ' ἐμπέδῳ. H. reads θερμὸν οὖς τάχ' ἐν πέδῳ, 'shall lay on the ground a hot ear'! Others try and construe it as it stands 'I thus passionate shall cast myself on the earth' where the adj. is awkward, the sense unsatisfactory, and βαλῶ hardly possible. Various other suggestions have been made, but I believe the best is the one given in the text, which I owe to my friend Mr. T. Miller (writing θερμὴν for θερμόν), 'and shall not I let fall a hot drop on the ground.' στάξ does not occur for ' a drop,' but στάγες does, Ap. Rh. 4.626, which may very likely therefore be an old word, an earlier form of σταγών. Schneid. had already suggested it, only he read θερμόχουν. The word is formed straight from the verb-stem, like ῥάξ (ῥαγ-) and πτάξ (πτακ-). Mr. Munro, who has discussed this passage [Phil. Journ. xi.], has pointed out that the dictionaries are probably wrong in giving θερμός as ever of two terminations: in that case we should read θερμήν, which I have accordingly done.

The chorus have expressed sympathy with Cassandra, and surprise and emotion at her wild laments, and she replies: 'Alas for our city's ruin! alas for all the sacrifices of my father! they could not aid the city: she lies low: *and shall not my blood be shed?*' [I formerly took it 'and shall not I *weep?*' and the chorus' remarks on her wailing μινυρὰ θρεομένας, 1165, and μελίζειν πάθη γοερά, 1176, make this at least possible: but I rather incline to Mr. Munro's view that 'shall not I *die?*' makes better sense on the whole.]

l. 1175. τίθησι μελίζειν, 'moves thee to sing,' 'makes thee to sing,' thy piteous deadly woes.

[ll. 1178-1330. SCENE IV. (third part). Kassandra's fit of wild visions is past, and she speaks of the past more calmly (1178-1200); then tells the chorus of how Apollo's wrath fell on her (1198-1214); then rising with new inspiration darkly and terribly announces the murder of the king (1215-1255). Next follows a marvellous speech, in which she foresees her own death, and strips off her crown; and prophesies the vengeance of Orestes (1256-1294). She then goes sadly into the house of blood.]

l. 1178. καὶ μήν, 'and now;' a new mood and resolve have come. Observe how richly and boldly the metaphors and similes come; a bride, a strong wind, a hound, a chorus, a revel-rout.

l. 1180. 'But clear and fresh it shall come blowing toward the sunrise, to dash wave-like to the light a woe far greater than mine.' λαμπρός is hard to render; the Greeks called a *strong* wind 'bright;' so here in any other language two words are required, one to be antithesis to ἐκ καλυμμάτων, the other to suit the new metaphor of wind. Cp. λαμπρὸς καὶ μέγας καθιεὶς Ar. Eq. 430 λαμπρὸς ἄνεμος Hdt. 2. 96.

l. 1184. συνδρόμως best with ῥινηλατούσῃ, 'close following I scent out the trail.'

l. 1187. σύμφθογγος οὐκ εὔφωνος, 'of harshest harmony,' an oxymoron suggested by χορός; she means the Furies. οὐ γὰρ εὖ λέγει, a meiosis, 'for its words are not well.'

l. 1188. καὶ μήν, graphic, she sees it almost; 'and lo!' (ὡς for ὥστε).

l. 1190. 'A revel-rout of sister Furies, that none can cast out!' Another bold metaphor.

l. 1192. 'The primal curse' is the first blood shedding of the bloody race; see Introduction, p. xii.

l. 1193. δυσμενεῖς can be nom. or acc., but it is better nom., being (as Eng. and Schn. observe) a grim allusion to their name εὐμενίδες. 'And in turn they loathe the brother's bed (Thyestes' adultery with Aerope), pitiless to him who defiled it.'

l. 1195. 'A babbler, knocking at doors,' a vivid vernacular phrase for 'a lying impostor' such as she was considered, she tells us.

l. 1197. H. reads τὸ μὴ εἰδέναι λόγῳ, 'that not by hearsay do I know;' i.e. 'that I know well.' So Pal., K., and others. And Prof. Goodwin points out that Ven has this reading. But the words cannot mean that, without any pronoun to mark the change of subject; as they stand they must mean 'swear that *you* do not know.' It is better to fall back on the best supported reading τὸ μ' εἰδέναι, and take λόγῳ παλαιᾶς together (so D., Well.); the rhythm is also in favour of it: 'bear witness to me with an oath, that I know the sins of this house, old in story.' It really is nothing against this int. that λόγῳ παλαιά occurs in Soph. O. T. (1395), where they do *not* go together.

l. 1198. 'And how could the noble compact of an oath become a cure?' i.e. what good would an oath do? I read παιώνιος as one MS. has it, but it is quite possible the poet wrote παιώνιον, the neuter, though not grammatically right, being due to πῆγμα .. παγέν.

NOTES. LINES 1178–1228.

l. 1201. κυρεῖν λέγουσαν, 'tell aright of.' So λέγων κυρήσαις Supp. 587: and τυγχάνω 1232.
l. 1205. ἀβρύνεται, 'grows over nice.' *Swan.*
l. 1206. παλαιστής, 'a suitor,' lit. 'a wrestler;' one of Aesch.'s picturesque and bold words.
l. 1207. 'Came ye to rite of union in due course?' [νόμῳ is however odd: perhaps γάμῳ, Schöm. or ὁμοῦ, Butl.]
l. 1211. ἄνατος, certain emendation of Canter for the natural MS. corruption ἄνακτος. κότῳ (instead of the more usual gen. after such adj.), to avoid the awkward sound of two genitives together.
l. 1212. ὡς, 'since,' 'after that.'
l. 1214. γε μὲν δή, 661.
l. 1215. The frenzy comes upon her again 'whirling and distracting' (στροβεῖ ταράσσων), as she says.
l. 1216. The MSS. read ἐφημένους at the end, which has clearly come from the next line, displacing the word, which is therefore irrecoverable. Hermann's δυσφροιμίοις is very ingenious, as it supplies a reason for the gap (filled with ἐφημένους), viz. that δυσφροιμίοις was lost through resemblance to φροιμίοις. But it remains a conjecture.
l. 1217. The vision of Thyestes' children rises again.
l. 1219. ὡσπερεί with the whole sentence, 'Children they seem, slaughtered by their own kin.'
l. 1222. πρέπουσ' ἔχοντες, 'I see them hold;' compare, for this use of πρέπω, 241, 389.
l. 1224. The 'recreant lion wallowing in the couch' is of course Aegisthos. She calls him below 'a wolf,' 1259.
l. 1225. 'Guarding the house, ah, me! for my lord returned;' the δεσπότῃ is dative after οἰκουρόν, as the order requires; and the force consists in the irony of the word οἰκουρός, which also prompts the cry οἴμοι. Aegisthos 'watched the house,' strangely indeed; dishonouring the queen and plotting with her the murder of the king.
l. 1226. φέρειν γάρ, etc. is suggested by δεσπότῃ ἐμῷ.
l. 1228. 'Knows not what things the tongue of the vile she-hound, with long-drawn smiling welcome ... shall accomplish by evil fate.' This is the best sense that can be made out of the text as it stands; but οἷα is a long way off from its verb, and φαιδρόνους is a very strange adjective, and the use of adj. for adv. is harsh with ἐκτείνασα: and we can scarcely resist the conviction that the text is corrupt. On the whole Madvig's alteration (following Tyrrwhitt) is the most probable, and is certainly highly ingenious; he reads:

οὐκ οἶδεν οἷα γλῶσσα μισητῆς κυνὸς
λείξασα κἀκτείνασα φαιδρὸν οὖς, δίκην
Ἄτης λαθραίου, δήξεται κακῇ τύχῃ.

AGAMEMNON.

...'knows not what a tongue of the vile she-hound has licked (his hand) and stretched out a joyful ear, and now like a stealthy curse shall bite him by evil chance.' The violent stretches of language making the tongue (instead of the dog) stretch out a joyful ear and bite, are hardly too strong for Aeschylus. Still they are strong, and δήξεται for τεύξεται is a considerable alteration; so I have not ventured to put the conjecture into the text. [See Appendix III.]

l. 1231. MSS. give τοιάδε τολμᾷ or τοιαῦτα. The reading in the text is the best, as all others leave θῆλυς unconnected.

l. 1232. Observe the weak ἐστιν in strong place. See on 14. καλοῦσα τύχοιμ' ἄν, 'call aright;' cp. 1201.

l. 1233. ἀμφίσβαιναν, 'a dragon,' or 'basilisk;' it is a fabulous monster that goes either way, perhaps like Sir John Mandeville's snakes with a head at each end.

l. 1235. 'Raging Dam of Death,' a bold imaginative name which it suits the frenzied mood of Kassandra to use. θύω is an Epic word, φρεσὶ θύει Il. 1. 342, ἔγχεϊ θύει ib. 11. 180. For Ἄρη MSS. read ἀράν: but ἄσπονδος almost requires Ἄρης, 'implacable war.' Perhaps Aesch. used the other form Ἄρην, which would readily account for the error. Ἄρης again 1511, in the sense of family strife.

l. 1236. 'And how she raised a cry of triumph, the murderess, as in the battle's rout, though seeming to rejoice at his safe return.' This clearly refers to her exaggerated and insincere welcome 896 sqq. δοκεῖ is present, because it means 'they think,' 'the people think;' the impression was still there.

l. 1239. ὅμοιον, 'I care not' (lit. 'it is the same,' *es ist gleich*).

l. 1243. ξυνῆκα, 'I understood,' it was past a few moments aga. πέφρικα, 'I shudder,' the horror still present.

l. 1244. ἀληθῶς οὐδὲν ἐξηκασμένα, 'no image but the very truth.'

l. 1245. ἐκ δρόμου πεσὼν τρέχω, 'I run out of the track;' i.e. 'I am astray,' as we say. The racecourse supplies the most frequent metaphors in Greek. So of madness, Pr. 883 ἔξω δὲ δρόμου φέρομαι λύσσης πνεύματι: and like this, Cho. 1022 ὥσπερ σὺν ἵπποις ἡνιοστροφῶ δρόμου ἐξωτέρω.

l. 1247. 'Peace, wretched woman, from such impious words;' lit. 'lull thy mouth to be well omened,' εὔφημον being proleptic. But as silence is the safest way of avoiding ill-omened speech, εὐφήμει practically comes to mean 'be silent,' e.g. Ar. Ach. 237; Ran. 352. So *favete linguis* in Latin.

l. 1248. 'There is no god of healing for this tidings;' εὐφημία might help, as long as there was hope of divine aid to avert ill; this case is hopeless.

l. 1249. εἴπερ ἔσται γ', 'if it is to be;' (πάρεσται the MS. reading can hardly mean this. The correction is due to Schütz.)

NOTES. LINES 1231–1270.

l. 1251. 'Is this woe brought to pass?' ἄχος is quite possible, though ἄγος (Aurat.) is not unlikely.

l. 1252. MSS. give ἦ κάρτ' ἄρ' ἂν παρεσκόπης (with -ει written over). Most edd. read παρεσκόπεις, and many alter ἄν to αὖ; Pal., K., rightly retain ἄν and construe, 'You must have missed the purport of my oracles.' This makes good sense, and may be right. Compare ηὔξω ἄν 933. Hartung however suggests ἦ κάρτα τἄρα παρεκόπης, 'Surely thou wentest astray from my oracles.' The emendation is very ingenious, being so near the MSS. (TATAP for TAP), and I have adopted it, merely keeping ἄν, which improves the sense. 'Surely thou must have gone far astray from my oracles,' παρακόπτεσθαι meaning 'to be deluded;' lit. 'to be knocked aside from.'

l. 1253. 'The murderer's plot I do not understand;' neither who is to do it, nor how. [Heimsoeth's τοὺς γὰρ τελοῦντας is possible.]

l. 1254. καὶ μήν, 'and yet,' as often, e.g. Prom. 981; Soph. Antig. 1054; Eur. Alc. 653. The sense is, 'And yet I know the Greek tongue all too well.' The answer in effect is, 'The oracles are also Greek, but not the easier to understand.'

l. 1256. Kassandra has another seizure of the prophetic fire. Observe οἷον short. See 1001.

l. 1260. It is best to follow the MSS. here, as Hermann does, only reading ἐνθήσειν with Fa. instead of ἐνθήσει, clearly altered to suit κτενεῖ. κότῳ is a bold metaphor, but there is no need to alter it (with Casaub., D., Eng., etc.) to ποτῷ. 'And like one brewing a drug, she boasts that my recompence too she will mix in her vengeance, whetting her sword against her lord, to pay back blood for that he hath brought me hither.'

l. 1263. ἀντιτίσασθαι, consec. or epexegetic inf. 'so as to.'

l. 1267. Hermann's emendation ἐγὼ δ' ἅμ' ἕψομαι, 'and I shall follow soon,' makes good sense: but the correction in the text makes even better, and is nearer the MSS. (ΟΝΤΑΓΑΘΩ for ΟΝΤΑΘΩ), 'Go to destruction: and as ye fall, thus will I avenge myself on you' (*as she speaks she throws down the staff and crown and tramples on them*). This correction is given by Mr. A. W. Verrall, in his Medea, 1881. [Appendix IV.]

l. 1268. 'Enrich another with woe instead of me,' a forcible oxymoron. (So reading ἄτης with H. for ἄτην, 'another curse,' not a very appropriate expression.)

l. 1270. The MSS. reading can be construed, if with H., Eng., Schn., etc., we read μέγα for μετά, thus: 'and having looked down on me, even in these robes scouted utterly, by friends turned foes, consenting, yet in error:—[then the parenthesis describing *how* they mocked her]—and now the seer having ruined me, the prophetess, has brought me,' etc. We find μετά for μέγα also in MSS. Choeph. 37.

AGAMEMNON.

φίλων ὑπ' ἐχθρῶν, by her people, who ought to have been friends, but scorned her; in the old days before the capture.

οὐ διχορρόπως μάτην, they all agreed to scout her, and they were all wrong. After the parenthesis the sense is taken up again, and the deferred verb ἀπήγαγεν at last comes. The above is substantially Enger's int. and it is the best that can be got without more alteration.

l. 1273. 'And like a wandering cheat I bore hard names, beggar, and wretch, and starveling.' Others include φοιτάς among the nicknames; but the line does not run so well.

l. 1275. ἐκπράξας, 'having destroyed, ruined.' Like κεραυνὸς ἐξέπραξε Soph. O. C. 1659, πῶς καί νιν ἐξεπράξατ'; Eur. Hec. 515. [The other sense given, 'having made me,' is weaker.]

l. 1277. ἐπίξηνον, 'a block' for beheading. So in Ar. Ach. 318.

l. 1278. κοπείσης, 'when I am struck.' The gen. abs. is always possible, and there is no need for κοπείσῃ or κοπεῖσαν. (Schütz's θερμόν is neat, and may be right.)

l. 1279. οὐ μήν .. γε (like οὐ μέντοι .. γε), 'not however;' Soph. O.T. 810 οὐ μὴν ἴσην γ' ἔτισεν. τεθνήξομεν, fut. formed from τέθνηκα, like ἑστήξω, 'not unregarded shall I be in death.'

l. 1283. κάτεισιν, in its strict sense, 'shall come back' from exile.

l. 1284. Restored by Hermann to its right place, from being after 1290, where it made no sense.

l. 1285. 'That his sire's fallen corse shall bring him home,' but a harsh phrase. Schöm. proposes πράξειν, 'that he shall exact vengeance for.'

l. 1288. πράξασαν ὡς ἔπραξεν, 'faring as it fared,' a euphemism. So Soph. O. T. 1376 βλαστοῦσ' ὅπως ἔβλαστε, Eur. Hec. 873 πάσχοντος οἷα πείσεται.

I take εἶλον, Musgrave's correction. εἶχον would mean the Trojans ('who *were holding*'). ἔσχον might do, but εἶλον is nearer.

l. 1289. οὕτως ἀπαλλάσσουσι, 'come to such an end.'

l. 1290. ἰοῦσα πράξω, 'I shall go to my fate;' πράσσειν seems to mean 'to do what lies before you,' to 'meet what is in store;' not an impossible meaning, but the reading is not certain.

l. 1292. καιρία, 'mortal,' lit. 'reaching the right place.'

l. 1297. αὐτῆς for σεαυτῆς, as often in Trag., Agam. 1141; Eur. Alc. 461; Soph. O. C. 930; and for ἐμαυτ. *ib.* O.T. 138.

l. 1300. 'Yet last is first in respect of time,' i. e. 'to be last is to be best off in time,' 'to lose time is to gain time,' as we might say with a similar epigram.

ll. 1302–4. Taking these lines as they are read in MSS., the sense is—
Cho. Yet know that thou art patient with a brave heart (τλήμων, 'enduring').
Ka. None that is happy is thus spoken of.

NOTES. LINES 1273–1324.

Cho. But yet an honourable death is sweet!

The chorus are compassionate and consoling; Kassandra is resigned but gloomy. The sense is good, and Pal., Con., K., Dav. seem right in keeping it. On the other hand H., following Heath, has inverted the order of the last two lines, and the German edd. have generally followed suit. It makes a good, but quite different sense :—

Cho. Yet know that bravery brings thee to misery (τλήμων, 'miserable ').

Ka. But yet an honourable death is sweet.

Cho. None that is happy hears such consolation!

But on the whole this is less likely; ἀκούει ταῦτα is much less appropriate; εὐκλεῶς κατθανεῖν is not what Kass. is thinking of; and her attitude is all through more a *miserable* than a *courageous* one.

l. 1305. εὐκλεῶς κατθανεῖν reminds her of her kindred, slain before Troy; and a new burst of grief overpowers her.

[*She advances to enter the palace; at the door she starts and stops short, as though a new horror had struck her.*]

l. 1308. ἔφευξας, from φεύζω.

l. 1310. τόδ' ὄζει, 'this scent comes from,' 'this is the scent of.' τόδε, acc. pron. in apposition to the sentence; literally, 'it smells *this*,' like ἡδὺ ὄζει, 'it smells *sweet*.'

l. 1311. 'No Syrian perfume for the house is this,' ἀγλάισμα, lit. 'splendour,' 'luxury.'

l. 1316. δυσοίζω, 'I shrink from;' properly, 'I am uneasy at.'

l. 1317. ἄλλως, 'for nought;' my fear is not vain. A necessary correction for the meaningless ἀλλ' ὡς of the MSS.

'Bear witness of this [that my fear is not vain; that I have prophesied truly] to me after my death, when a woman dies for me a woman, and a man falls for this man with evil wife' (δυσδάμαρτος gen. of δυσδάμαρ). Prophet-fashion she confirms her prophecy with another. The woman is of course Klytaemnestra; the man Aegisthos.

l. 1320. ξενόω, 'to treat as ξένος :' ἐπιξενοῦμαι (middle) 'to claim a friendly service,' lit. 'to call in a friend to yourself for a thing.' The word is usually passive, 'to be friendly entreated.'

l. 1322. οὐ θρῆνον (Hermann's correction) is a quiet and dignified rejection of the chorus' pity; see 1330. [The line is however perhaps corrupt: ῥῆσιν is an unlikely word.]

l. 1323. Read ἡλίου with Karsten; the dat. has come from the proximity of ἐπεύχομαι, but with πρὸς ὕστατον φῶς, and the succeeding datives, is unlikely.

l. 1324. An obscure and probably corrupt passage. Taking the words as they stand, we can give two possible meanings, owing to the intrinsic ambiguity of τίνω; for the murderer τίνει δίκην when he is slain, 'pays the penalty;' and also the avenger τίνει δίκην, 'pays back justice' to the guilty. So it may mean (1) 'I pray for my avengers to requite my hateful murderers.' (2) 'For my hateful murderers to pay the penalty to my avengers.' The order is in favour of (1); the commoner use of τίνω in favour of (2). But the passage for many reasons must be regarded as corrupt. τοῖς ἐμοῖς is needlessly repeated; the datives are very clumsy; τίνειν wants an object; and Kassandra could hardly speak of *her* avengers, *her* murderers only. Her real drift seems to be, 'I pray that the avengers (of Agamemnon) may requite the murderers at the same time (ὁμοῦ) for *my* death.' [Karst. proposes ἐμοῦ δούλης for ὁμοῦ, δούλης: a probable suggestion.]

l. 1326. εὐμαροῦς χειρώματος, 'an easy prey.'

l. 1328. I take Conington's correction σκιᾷ τις ἂν πρέψειεν, 'one might liken them to a sketch.' (Photius says Aesch. used πρέψαι for ὁμοιῶσαι). σκιά, 'an outline,' cf. σκιαγραφεῖν. [Others take σκιά, 'they might seem a sketch;' but τις and the aorist are rather in favour of the former.] εἰ δὲ δυστυχῇ, Epic. subj. with εἰ.

l. 1329. 'The touch of the wet sponge blots out the drawing.' ὤλεσεν, gnomic aor.

l. 1330. This line is explained by οὐ θρῆνον εἰπεῖν θέλω (1322) and the chorus' pity (1321). Kassandra gives a wonderfully imaginative and pathetic sketch of human fortunes; then adds, 'this I count far more pitiable than that' (which you pity); the general sadness is sadder than one hapless lot.

[*She goes in sadly to her death.*]

[ll. 1331–42. This short chorus fills the interval while Kassandra is going in, till the blows are struck. The drift is, 'All men desire joy without end; even princes never have enough: now if Agamemnon after all his triumph is to die, who can ever hope to be scatheless?']

l. 1332. δακτυλοδείκτων, 'envied,' i.e. wealthy, royal. Cf. Horace's *Monstrari digito*.

l. 1333. εἴργει, keeps *it* off, i.e. τὸ εὖ πράσσειν, prosperity.

l. 1334. Perhaps, in view of Cho. 313, τάδε is better taken with φωνῶν.

l. 1339. 'And dying for the dead brings to pass requital for other deaths,' i.e. dying in revenge for the dead (Iphigeneia) causes a new requital in the deaths of others (Klyt. and Aegisth.). Others take θανάτων to mean those whom Ag. has slain, i.e. the same as θανοῦσι. But the first rendering is much better sense; the chorus are saddened by Kassandra's prophecy (1280 and 1325) of yet other deaths to follow hers and the king's. [Perhaps ἐπιπράξει (Weil) is right for ἐπικρανεῖ.]

l. 1341. 'Who could boast to be born with scatheless fate?'

[SCENE V. (1343–1447).

The dying cry of Agamemnon is heard within once and again: the

NOTES. LINES 1326-1371.

chorus take counsel in helpless embarrassment: the door of the palace then opens (1371) and the queen is seen with bloody axe standing over the murdered bodies. She glories in the deed and scouts all warnings or threats of the chorus.]

l. 1343. ἔσω, 'within me,' offers no difficulty though K. suspects it.

l. 1344. The chorus become a helpless and hesitating mob of elders, each giving his own opinion. For this interlude see Introd., p. xii.

l. 1347. ἀλλὰ κοινωσώμεθ' ἥν πως ἀσφαλῆ βουλεύματ' ᾗ is the best correction. ἥν is due to Goodwin (Am. Phil. Soc. 1877), ᾗ to Enger. Hermann's ἄν πως is unlikely; πως suggests ἥν. 'But let us confer, if perchance we can find safe counsel.'

l. 1349. κηρύσσειν βοήν, 'to proclaim the call,' i. e. to summon to rescue or fight. The βοή was the 'cry' for help. Cf. εἰ βραδύνοιμεν βοῇ Supp. 730; καί εἴποι λαοῖσι βοὴ δ' ὤκιστα γένοιτο Od. 22. 133; the common Homeric βοὴν ἀγαθός means 'good at calling on' the men to fight.

l. 1351. νεορρύτῳ (υ short, from ῥέω, 'new-flowing,' not ῥύω, 'new-drawn'), 'while the sword yet drips,' i. e. *flagrante delicto*.

l. 1355. πράσσοντες, 'devising,' 'preparing.' The sentiment is a curious anachronism. The Argive elders talk of 'tyranny' as if they were members of a free Greek republic.

l. 1356. 'Spurning the credit of delay,' not caring to be deliberate in action. Observe the sententious incompetence of these elders.

l. 1359. ''Tis the doer's part also to counsel about (the deed).' Apparently a sententious shuffling off responsibility. 'I had no part in the act, and why should I be troubled to advise?'

l. 1362. 'What, to prolong our lives, shall we yield to the sway of these defilers of the house?' βίον τείνοντες, 'in trying to lengthen our lives.' ἡγουμένοις, predicate, 'as rulers.'

l. 1365. 'For 'tis a milder lot than tyranny.'

l. 1367. 'Shall we divine the man has perished?' The gen. is the Epic gen. of *intelligence about a person*: one form of the gen. of reference. Compare ὡς γνῶ χωομένοιο Il. 4. 357, εἰ δέ κε τεθνηῶτος ἀκούσω Od. 2. 220.

l. 1368. Emphasis on εἰδότας; knowledge should come before anger.

l. 1370. παντόθεν πληθύνομαι. Lit. 'I am multiplied from all sides:' i. e. 'from all sides I find support' to approve this vote. Somewhat similar, though less strained, is the use Suppl. 604 δήμου κρατοῦσα χείρ ὅπῃ πληθύνεται, 'which way the decisive show of hands prevails.' [L. S. are unsatisfactory on this word.]

l. 1371. Observe the attraction κυροῦνθ' ὅπως for ὅπως κυρεῖ; the natural construction of εἰδέναι being with a participle.

AGAMEMNON.

l. 1372. [*Here the doors are rolled open by the* ἐκκύκλημα.] For the ἐκκύκλημα, or machine for showing the interior, see Arist. Ach. 407. καιρίως, 'to serve the time.'

l. 1375. MSS. πημονὴν ἀρκύστατον, which Paley retains, might mean 'a snare-set woe.' i. e. destruction by snares; and we have ἀρκυστάταν (? -ον) μηχανάν Eur. Or. 1420, used as adj. But this would require us to explain the optat. as remote deliberative, see 620 and appendix; and further ἀρκύστατα is used as subst. Pers. 98; Eum. 112; Soph. El. 1426; therefore it seems better to follow Hermann and read πημονῆς ἀρκύστατ' ἄν. This would easily become πημονῆς ἀρκυστάταν, then πημονήν, then ἀρκύστατον. 'For how (else) could one, devising ill for foes who seem friends, fence the snares of woe too high to leap over?' i. e. how else than by deceit? ὕψος is a kind of cognate acc. *describing* the *result* of action (internal acc.).

l. 1378. νείκης (necessary correction for νίκης, meaningless) παλαιᾶς ἀγών, 'this struggle of an ancient feud;' the feud was old; the ἀγών or crisis was just come. σὺν χρόνῳ γε μήν, 'though long delayed.' γε μήν, 661. Literally, 'in course of time however.'

l. 1381. ὡς for ὥστε. 'So that he could neither flee,' etc.

l. 1383. πλοῦτον εἵματος κακόν, 'fatal splendour of garb;' it was a large fine-wrought robe.

l. 1385. μεθῆκεν αὐτοῦ κῶλα, 'relaxed at once his limbs;' αὐτοῦ, 'on the spot.' This is the most natural way of taking it. (Others αὑτοῦ; weaker. Others μεθῆκεν, intrans., possible.)

l. 1387. 'A votive gift to Hades Saviour of the dead,' a grim and ghastly piece of irony; 'just as the third libation is paid to Ζεὺς Σωτήρ (see note on 245) so I paid a third *stab* to Hades, Σωτήρ of the dead!' Enger reads Διός, which would improve τοῦ κατὰ χθονός, rather needless with Αἵδου; improve the irony; and is probable, as it would be easily supplanted by the gloss Αἵδου. But it is safer to follow the MSS.

l. 1388. ὁρμαίνει, lit. 'speeds forth,' i. e. 'gasps out his life.' H. reads ὀρυγάνει, 'belches out,' which would do, but is not necessary: the root-meaning of ὁρμαίνω is 'quick movement.' So Pindar has θυμὸς ὥρμαινέ νιν Ol. 3. 145; and Aesch. uses it intrans. Theb. 324 of a horse.

l. 1389. αἵματος σφαγήν, a bold stretch of language; we should say 'his life-blood' by an opposite metaphor.

l. 1390. 'Smites me with black splash of the murderous dew,' a fine unsparing phrase.

l. 1392. 'Rejoicing no less than doth in heaven's sweet rain the cornland at the birthpang of the buds.' Splendid lines, restored by Porson's insight from desperate corruption. For the return to nom. σπορητύς, compare πόλιν δημοκρατουμένην ὥσπερ καὶ αὐτοί Thuc. 5. 44.

NOTES. LINES 1372–1421.

l. 1394. χαίροιτ' ἄν εἰ χαίροιτ', 'joy if ye can,' see 1049 note.

l. 1395. εἰ δ' ἦν πρεπόντων, 'had it been a fitting thing,' for τῶν πρεπόντων, as above, 323. Perhaps however πρέπον τόδ' (Karst.) is right.

l. 1396. μὲν οὖν, corrective as usual, 'nay more than just.'

l. 1397. The comparison must not be pressed too far; it suffices for Klytaemnestra's grim irony, and is powerfully expressive of her horrible cold-blooded triumphant mood. 'Had it been fitting,' she says (what a time to talk of decorum!), 'to pour libations over the corpse, over him it had been just—nay more than just.' (Here one begins to see that the libation is metaphorical, in some bitter sense; then out it comes.) 'So full of curses did he fill his bowl in his house, then comes and drinks it to the dregs himself!' i. e. a libation would suit this reveller: he drank deep—*of curses!* κακῶν ἀραίων certainly go together; 'ills accursed,' 'ills curse-bringing.'

ll. 1403–6. The relentless gloating of Kl. over her deed is very finely given by these bare and bald details. ὅμοιον, 1239.

l. 1407. Observe the skill with which the chorus take to the lyric dochmiacs, when the tragedy is beyond the common speech of iambics. The general sense is, 'what drug hast thou eaten or drunk from land or sea, that thus thou hast brought on thy head the curse of the people? Thou hast slain, and shalt be outcast.'

l. 1408. πάσαμένα from πατέομαι, 'to taste' (not πᾶσαμένα from πάομαι, 'to acquire').

l. 1409. τόδ' ἐπέθου θύος, 'hast thou brought upon thyself this sacrifice?'

θύος is a euphemism for the murder. (Pal. and others construe 'incense,' explaining it to mean 'the wrath' of the people; but this is farfetched, and the common sense of θύος in Epic and Aesch. is 'sacrifice.')

l. 1410. The emphasis is on the oft-repeated preposition: 'away thou hast hurled, away thou hast cleft, and away thou shalt be cast.'

l. 1414. 'Though formerly thou didst not withstand him at all;' in the days of old when *his* crime was done.

τότε is better than MS. τόδ'.

l. 1415. 'Who caring not, as 'twere a beast that died.' μόρον is governed however by προτιμῶν.

l. 1417. 'His own daughter, sweetest pain of travailing to me;' the apposition of ὠδῖνα to παῖδα is a fine stretch of language.

l. 1420. ἐπήκοος, equivalent to a partic. 'when thou hearest.'

l. 1421. There is no occasion to alter the MSS. reading: 'I bid thee threaten and welcome, for I am prepared that likewise, if thou conquer me by force, thou shalt rule.' She shows the same contemptuous force as ever, 'I scorn your threats; let us try conclusions, and let the strongest win.' The construction of the acc. inf. after παρεσκευασμένης is not

AGAMEMNON.

unnatural considering the freedom of poetry and the great flexibility of Greek. [Perhaps however παρεσκευασμένον (Madv.) is right.]

l. 1425. 'I'll teach thee to know, though late, the ways of prudence.' γνώσει, naturally often used in threats, Soph. Ant. 779, O. C. 852, and *infra*, 1619.

l. 1426. Rather a difficult passage: the MS. is corrupt in 1428; and the proper stopping is doubtful. It seems to make the best sense with the least alteration if we read ἐμπρέπει, ἀτίετον for εὖ πρέπει ἀτίετον, the reading of Fa.: 'High is thy spirit, and haughty thy word, as indeed thy mind is frenzied by the deed of blood; the blood-stain over thine eyes is plain to see: [but yet] one day dishonoured, reft of friends, thou shalt pay for blow with blow!' [Others read ἐμπρέπειν (Pal., II., K.) after ἔλακες, 'thou didst boast that the stain,' etc., referring to 1390. But περίφρονα refers to her whole attitude, not to one phrase thirty-five lines back. Others read ἄτιτον with what precedes, 'a blood-stain unavenged.']

l. 1431. θέμις, properly (from θε-) 'ordinance,' 'that which is laid down,' 'law;' used here in a strained sense to mean something like 'sanctity,' or 'solemnity.' Construe, 'This too thou hearest, this my solemn oath.'

l. 1434. The MS. reading here means, 'Hope doth not tread for me the halls of Fear.' A fine picturesque phrase, surely not too imaginative or metaphorical for Aeschylus. She means, 'My hope does not approach fear,' 'my confidence is dashed with no misgivings.'

[Others construe, 'Expectation of fear does not tread my halls,' a much poorer sense. Others read ἐμπατεῖν, 'I have no expectation that fear (φόβον) will tread my halls,' or 'to tread the halls of fear' (φόβου). None are as fine as the MS. reading, in the sense given above.]

l. 1435. Observe the lavish imagery: Aegisthos is 'a fire' and 'a shield.'

l. 1439. 'Minion of each Chryseis before Troy.' Chryseis, daughter of the priest Chryses: the Iliad opens with her as Agamemnon's slave and concubine. This use of the plural is natural in all languages. So Plat. Theaet. 169 B οἱ Θησέες τε καὶ Ἡρακλέες.

l. 1442. ναυτίλων δὲ σελμάτων ἰσοτριβής, 'sharing alike with him the mariners' bench.' Quite good sense, and not requiring the further change of ναυτίλοις, which some edd. give.

l. 1443. ἄτιμα δ' οὐκ ἐπραξάτην, 'ay, they deserved their fate.'

l. 1446. φιλήτωρ τῷδ', 'dear to his heart.' φιλήτωρ, not verbal from φιλέω, which would be a masculine word, but from φίλος-ήτορ, adj. Hence we must change MS. τοῦδ' to τῷδ', with H. τοῦδε has easily come from misunderstanding the form φιλήτωρ.

l. 1447. 'And to me has brought a new delight for my luxurious couch.' Lit. 'a new couch-relish of my luxury.' She means she has

NOTES. LINES 1425–1461.

added to her lawless love the new delight of a doubly satisfied jealousy and vengeance. But the genitives are doubtless awkward and may be corrupt, and one is tempted to take Schöm.'s ἐμῇ .. εὐνῇ.
 [ll. 1449-1576. *Kommos, or lamentation, with answers from the stage.*
 Chorus. (1449–61). 'Oh for some speedy and painless death! Oh fatal Helena!'
 Klyt. (1461–67). 'Pray not for death nor blame Helena for all!'
 Chor. (1468–74). 'Oh fate so hard on our house! oh fatal women!'
 Klyt. (1475–80). 'You are right to call on our Fate: he is the source of bloodshed.'
 Chor. (1481–96). 'A grievous fate, from Zeus the almighty. Oh king how bewail thee, slain by evil craft?'
 Klyt. (1497–1504). 'I am not Klytaemnestra, but the Race-Avenger in woman's shape.'
 Chor. (1505–20). 'Say not you are innocent: perhaps the Avenger is your helper.'
 Klyt. (1521–29). 'He too was guilty: he slew Iphigeneia.'
 Chor. (1530–50). 'I am bewildered amid this bloodshed. Oh that I had died first! Who will bury him? wilt thou, the murderess?'
 Klyt. (1551–59). 'I will bury him: and his daughter dear shall meet him as he crosses the dark river, and welcome him.'
 Chor. (1560-66). 'Another reviling! It is hard to see clear: the spoiler is spoiled: 'tis the gods' will.'
 Klyt. (1567–78). 'Henceforth I will make truce with the family Fate: he shall go and plague others: I shall be at peace: I want but little.']

l. 1450. **φέρουσ'** ἐν ἡμῖν, 'bringing amongst us:' the use of ἐν (and other preps. which take dat. see 357) with verb of motion is Epic. Cf. ἐνὶ στήθεσσιν ὀρούσας Il. 22. 182: so προτὶ οἷ εἷλε, 'took her to him,' *ib.* 507. Hence we need not change to ἐφ' with H.

l. 1451. **δαμέντος**, 'laid low;' Epic word for 'slain.'

l. 1453. The simplest and best emendation is to read Epic πολέα for πολλά with Enger, omitting καί here and μοι 1472; 'having borne much through a woman.' καί is not wanted: if put directly the sentence would be ἐδάμη .. τλάς.

l. 1456. Observe the effect of τάς, 'who alone didst bring to death so many, so exceeding many lives.'

ll. 1458–61 are very corrupt and obscure. They are generally taken, after Hermann, to be parallel with 1537–50, a supposition very probable; but if so there are 5½ lines of anapaests lost, and the three lyric lines correspond very imperfectly. It is useless to prune the lines to fit each other; the best one can do is to guess at the sense as near as may be.

AGAMEMNON.

Omitting then δι' before αἷμ' with Herm. and reading with Enger ἢ τις for ἥτις, we may translate: . . . 'Thou hast put forth on thee as a flower a memorable stain of blood indelible ; surely there was strife then in the house, a woe subduing the king.' ἐρίδματος, Epic compound from ἐρι-, 'exceedingly,' δμα-, 'to subdue.' This may be taken in default of better.

l. 1467. ἀξύστατον, 'that cannot be put together, arranged, settled,' and so of pain 'not to be allayed,' 'incurable.' Aristophanes playfully quotes the word (Nub. 1367) of Aeschylus himself, putting it (according to the best arrangement) in the mouth of an opponent; there it seems to mean 'rough,' 'uncouth,' 'boisterous,' lit. 'not to be settled or composed.' (Paley's 'incomparable' will not do at all ; he misses the sense of the passage in the Clouds.)

l. 1469. 'The two sons of Tantalos' are, of course, Agamemnon and Menelaos.

l. 1470 seems to mean, 'and wieldest the sway like-minded of two women, that gnaws my heart.' i. e. 'and who bringest the power of two women equally imperious (Helena and Klytaemnestra) with men, causing such woe to me.'

l. 1472. ἐννόμως is the best supported reading, 'and standing over the body like a hateful raven, she boasts that her song is *just*.' But ἐκνόμως, reading of Farnese, is best sense, 'she boastfully sings a *tuneless* strain ;' the harsh, discordant (ἐκνόμως), triumphant note of the raven makes a much better point.

l. 1476. τριπάχυντον (Hermann's correction for the impossible τριπάχυιον), 'thrice gorged,' explained below in αἱματολοιχός.

l. 1478. 'For 'tis he from whom bloodthirsty longing is nursed in the heart ; before the old woe ceases, the new blood flows.' νείρει, 'in the heart,' unknown word. (Others νείρᾳ = νειαίρᾳ, Homeric adj. 'lowest,' agreeing with γαστρί ; and Hesych. mentions νείρη, 'the belly,' but of two unknown words one prefers the MS. form.)

l. 1480. ἰχώρ, Epic word for the ethereal blood of the gods. Here used for 'blood' simply.

l. 1481. οἰκονόμον (Schn., K.) is the best correction for οἴκοις τοῖσδε, 'haunting the house.'

l. 1483. αἶνον, cognate (internal) acc. to αἰνεῖς, 'a mighty Fate is he of whom thou tellest . . . an evil tale of woe accursed, insatiate.'

l. 1492. 'The spider's web' is of course the cloak in which he was caught and slain.

l. 1493. ἐκπνέων at the end of the anapaestic stanza must be pronounced as dissyllable ; just as θεῶν, πόλεως, βασιλέως, are 1, 2, and 3 syllables respectively when required (synizezis).

l. 1494. After a pause at ἐκπνέων, the sentence is continued in a

NOTES. LINES 1467-1526.

burst of anguish, '(thou liest) alas! alas! on this base bed.' κοίταν, cognate acc.

l. 1495. βελέμνῳ, 'weapon.' It is generally called an axe, though more probably a dagger.

l. 1498. μηδ' ἐπιλεχθῇς, 'but do not think.' ἐπιλέγομαι is an Ionic word, used often in Herodotus for 'to think,' 'expect,' 'consider,' properly no doubt 'to say over to one's self.' This tense does not occur elsewhere, and has been suspected; but there is no more intrinsic difficulty in it than in the deponent διελέχθην, which is common.

μηδέ, 'but not,' is Epic; in Attic it was always ἀλλὰ μή. See Od. 5. 177, 10. 342.

l. 1501. 'The ancient bitter Avenger' is the personified spectre or spirit of justice, which makes demand for other blood in requital for blood shed. See Introduction. p. xii.

l. 1502. 'Who served the hideous banquet' of children to Thyestes.

l. 1504. 'Slaughtering a man for children,' lit. 'upon children,' i.e. the second victim (metaphorically) *upon* the first, that is to say, 'in vengeance for.'

l. 1507. πῶ πῶ; Lit. 'where? where?' Doric for ποῦ. The meaning is, 'Nay, nay!' just as in the colloquial word πώμιλα, 'not a bit.'

πατρόθεν δέ, 'yet from his sires an avenger might aid thee;' you are not innocent, but the ancestral avenger may have had a share in the bloodshed.

ll. 1510-12. Rather difficult and doubtful passage. It begins, 'Yet black havoc presses on, with streams of kindred slaughter (then MSS. read ὅποι δὲ καὶ προβαίνων πάχνᾳ κουροβόρῳ παρέξει, quite impossible Greek, though even Hermann tries to construe it; the easiest alteration is Butler's and Scholefield's δίκαν for δὲ καί, which I have taken), 'thither where advancing he shall give requital for the clot of the blood of children slain for food,' i.e. black havoc presses with murder in the family till he has avenged the murder of Thyestes' children. But one cannot feel much confidence about the reading or sense.

ll. 1521, 2. These lines are clearly spurious; the answer clearly begins οὐδὲ γάρ, the οὔτε is wrong, and the insertion spoils the sense of what follows.

l. 1525. ἔρνος is acc. after δράσας, which regularly takes acc. of person treated, *and* of the kind of treatment. 'But my offshoot sprung from him ... as he hath dealt with her so hath he suffered.'

l. 1526. The τε after πολύκλαυτον marks apposition; so Suppl. 60 Τηρείας ἀλόχου κιρκηλάτου τ' ἀηδόνος. Ἰφιγενείαν, older (dialectic) form with a long; so we find εὐκλείᾱ, ἀγνοίᾱ, ἀνοίᾱ, in Trag. and ὑγιείᾱ even in Com. (Ar. Av. 609). Hence there is no need to read with MSS. Ἰφιγένειαν ἄν· | ἄξια δράσας κ.τ.λ. See next line.

AGAMEMNON.

l. 1527. ἄξια δράσας ἄξια πάσχων. A difficulty has been made with these lines from not seeing that the words are *correlative*, 'the deed was worthy (of the suffering), the suffering was worthy (of the deed).'

l. 1531. μέριμναν, acc. after στερηθείς (which verb takes naturally acc. of thing stolen), 'robbed of thought's ready devising.'

l. 1533. 'I fear the patter of bloody rain, that makes the house to totter; no longer it comes in drops.'

l. 1535. To say that 'Fate sharpens justice for another deed of harm' is quite intelligible, and the imagery quite Aeschylean. So the ordinary correction δίκην may be taken. At the same time the simpler phrase δίκη . . . θηγάναις μάχαιραν (Musgrave) is a rather tempting emendation.

l. 1540. δροίτη, 'bath;' χαμεύνη, 'low couch.'

l. 1544. αὐτῆς for σεαυτῆς, 1297.

l. 1545. ἄχαριν χάριν, 'a graceless gift' (*Mors*.).

l. 1548. 'And who shall utter his praise with tears over the tomb of the man divine, labouring in sincerity of heart.' The ἀλήθεια φρενῶν last and emphatic; it was so terribly absent in Klytaemnestra.

l. 1553. The prepositions as in 1410. 'Down he fell, down he lay, and down we will bury him.' Klytaemnestra is perhaps scornfully parodying the emphasis of the chorus. The absence of augment, and the assimilation of κατ-, is Epic.

l. 1554. Her bitterness and cruel triumph reach a climax in this terrible sarcasm, 'None of the house shall bewail him, . . . but his *dear daughter, as is fit*, shall meet and welcome him at the swift ferry-passage of woes.'

l. 1560. Notice how the last note of this long chorus is the darkness and inscrutability of fate; the inevitableness of the evil consequences of sin. ὄνειδος ἀντ' ὀνείδους, 'reviling for reviling;' the bitterness of Klyt.'s taunt saddens but does not now anger the chorus.

l. 1561. ''Tis hard to discern the right; she spoils the spoiler, the slayer pays his debt, but it remains—while Zeus remains on his throne —that the doer must suffer...'

l. 1562. φέρει φέροντ'. a proverbial phrase, φέρω in the old sense φέρειν ἄγειν, 'to carry off booty.'

l. 1564. χρόνῳ is the MS. reading, which can only be construed with Klausen, 'while Zeus remains, it remains *in due time* that,' etc., and the order of the words is very harsh for this. Paley's rendering, 'while time remains and Zeus is lord,' is good sense, but hardly the Greek. It is better to read θρόνῳ with Schütz (so H., Schn., Eng., etc.)

l. 1565. γονὰν ἀραῖον (H.'s beautiful correction for ῥᾷον), 'the brood of curses.'

l. 1566. Again a certain correction πρὸς ἄτᾳ for the meaningless προσάψαι (ΑΨΑΙ into ΑΤΑΙ), 'the race is fast bound to woe.'

l. 1567. MSS. have ἐνέβη χρησμόν, some alter to ἐνέβης, which gives a poor sense; a far better one is got by altering χρησμόν to χρησμός. 'this maxim (that the doer shall suffer) has with truth trodden *him* (Agamemnon) down.'

l. 1569. Πλεισθενιδᾶν. Grammarians say that Pleisthenes was son of Atreus, and father of Agamemnon, but that as he died young, Agamemnon is usually called son of Atreus. It is certain that Agamemnon is son of Atreus in the Homeric tradition, which seems to be usually that of the later poets in this respect. Perhaps Pleisthenes belongs to another form of the story altogether, and Aeschylus merely uses his name for the *family*, just as he calls them sometimes Pelopidae, or Tantalidae.

l. 1570. 'Making compact that I will bear this, though hard to be borne, but that hereafter he shall go,' etc.

τάδε μὲν στέργειν. It is characteristic of Klytaemnestra's cold-blooded shamelessness that she speaks of '*bearing*' the trouble of the house, she the murderess. The tone is, ' We have been plagued enough, let the hard fate of the house go vex other families with kindred slaughter.'

l. 1573. αὐθέντης θάνατος, 'kin-murder.' See note on αὐτοφόνος, 1091.

l. 1574. The cold irony is at its height here, ' All I want is a quiet life and a humble competence, having cured the house of its *blood-feud*.'

[Exodos, *or last scene* (1577–1673). Aegisthos vaunts his part in the bloody deed, telling the tale of past deeds which have produced this: the chorus rebuke him, and mention the name of Orestes. The quarrel waxes hot, and violence is threatened, when Klytaemnestra intervenes and stops the strife.]

l. 1579. 'The gods look down on woes of earth, aiding mortals,' is perfectly good sense; no need to alter ἄχη into ἄγη.

l. 1582. 'Paying for the crafty crimes of his sire's hand' is explained in what follows; note that Atreus again is called πατήρ, not Pleisthenes.

l. 1585. ἀμφίλεκτος ὧν κράτει, ' being questioned in his sovereignty,' i. e. ' his power disputed.' ἀμφ. must be passive (cf. 881); the passage quoted for the active meaning, ἀμφίλεκτος ἔρις (Eur. Phoen. 500), proves nothing, as the passive meaning is quite possible there.

l. 1589. '(A lot secure), not to die and defile with his blood his native soil.' The MSS. read mostly αὐτοῦ, as the end of this sentence. Even if we construe it ' there on the spot,' it seems unfit and intolerably flat. (See however ἐμήν 14.) Further, the tribrach ξένια is ugly.

75

The probability is that it is a gloss, and one is strongly tempted to think with Schütz that the next line is spurious, and that 1590 originally ran ξένια δὲ τοῦδε δύσθεος πατὴρ πατρί. See next note.

l. 1591. Probably spurious, πατρί belonging to 1590. 'More zealous than friendly,' is only possible as a joke, when applied to a man who under cover of a banquet murders his brother's children; and Aegisthos is not joking. Moreover, the jingle προθύμως, εὐθύμως is suspicious, the name 'Ατρεύς needless, and the rejection of 1591 amends 1590 so neatly.

l. 1592. 'Feigning to celebrate with cheer a day of feasting.'

l. 1594. κτένας, properly 'combs,' here 'the fingers.' The word is used of a variety of things, ribs, hair, rakes, teeth, wherever the metaphor is natural.

l. 1595. The MS. reading will construe ... ἔθρυπτ' ἄνωθεν ἀνδρακὰς καθήμενος. ἄσημα δ' αὐτῶν αὐτίκ' ἀγνοίᾳ λαβών κ.τ.λ. 'The feet and hands he (Atreus) broke up small (θρύπτω, 'to crush,' used with βώλακα, χιόνα κ.τ.λ., *not* 'to break *off*,') sitting above, apart from the rest; but the undistinguishable parts he (Thyestes) taking in ignorance.' etc. And the antithesis between τὰ μὲν ποδήρη and ἄσημα δ' αὐτῶν (which, however, should probably be τάσημα) is clear and natural, and at first sight seems a strong argument for the MS. reading. But the change of subject without any notice is very harsh, and the real antithesis to τὰ μὲν ποδήρη is probably understood in the rapid and vivid narrative. We must then take Hermann's ἄσημ'· ὁ δ' αὐτῶν, and very possibly ἔκρυπτ' for ἔθρυπτ', with Casaubon. The sense will be: 'The feet and hands he broke up small (*or* hid on the dish, ἔκρυπτ'), sitting above and apart, so that none should know them (ἄσημα, proleptic); [the rest of the flesh he put on the dish]; but he in ignorance took thereof (αὐτῶν partitive, or perh. after ἀγνοίᾳ) and ate a meal fatal,' etc.

l. 1599. 'And falls back, spitting forth the slaughtered flesh.' I have taken Hartung's ἀπὸ σφαγήν with the MS. ἐρῶν, i. e. ἀπερῶν σφαγήν, from ἀπ-ἐράω, to 'spit or vomit forth.' Another compound, ἐξεράω, is used in Aristoph. for 'to disgorge.' ἀπὸ σφαγήν would be certain to get corrupted into ἀπὸ σφαγῆς, and ἐράω is transitive, and requires accusative. [ἐρῶν is defended by Prof. Goodwin.] This seems better than the common ἀπὸ σφαγῆς ἐμῶν, 'from the flesh vomiting.'

l. 1601. It is perhaps simplest to construe this, 'spurning the banquet *to aid* his curse.' σύνδικος being properly 'one who pleads with you,' 'an aider in the cause.' συνδίκως governs ἀρᾷ [the common rendering 'jointly,' is worse sense, and has no parallel in the usage of σύνδικος]. The violent crash of the banquet was the symbol (οὕτως) of the invoked destruction of the family. Such symbolism is common and natural in primitive times when good or evil is prophesied or invoked.

NOTES. LINES 1591–1625.

l. 1605. 'For me, the thirteenth child, he drives out with my hapless father.' This is the meaning of the MS. reading; but ἐπὶ δίκ' is almost certainly corrupt; the only traditions we have give at most three children to Thyestes, and the mention of the number seems so needless and inappropriate. I read with Schöm. δυσαλθλίῳ. ἐπί means lit. 'on,' i.e. 'along with.' It is rather needless with συνεξελαύνει, and hence the corruption.

l. 1611. All the MSS. (except Fa., which has been a good deal corrected) give ἰδόντα: the acc. is quite right after τὸ κατθανεῖν, in agreement with the subject. So Eur. Med. 814 σοὶ δὲ συγγνώμη λέγειν τάδ' ἐστὶ μὴ πάσχουσαν ὡς ἐγὼ κακῶς.

l. 1612. σέβω, 'honour,' understatement for 'approve.'

l. 1617. νερτέρᾳ κώπῃ. There were three benches or banks of rowers in a trireme, the θαλαμῖται, or lowest, with least work and pay; then the ζυγῖται, or middle; and finally, the θρανῖται, or highest bench. If ζυγόν, as is probable, refers to ζυγῖται, Aeschylus must be thinking of a bireme, where the ζυγῖται would be the highest. (Klausen.) The νερτέρᾳ κώπῃ is then the θαλαμῖται. 'Dost thou speak so, set to the lower oar, when those on the higher seat control the ship?'

l. 1620. σωφρονεῖν εἰρημένον, 'when bidden to be prudent.' εἰρημένον, 'it being ordered,' acc. absolute, like παρόν, δέον, ἐξόν, προσῆκον κ.τ.λ., the regular usage with impersonals.

l. 1621. γῆρας, acc. 'but to teach even the old, chains and hunger-pangs are excellent physicians of the mind.' (Two MSS. misunderstanding the constr. read δεσμόν.)

l. 1623. 'Hast eyes and seest not this?'

l. 1624. παίσας is found in a Scholiast's quotation of the line, and is in itself better than the other suggestion πταίσας, 'stumbling:' 'lest thou strike them and suffer.'

l. 1625. These three lines must be addressed to Aegisthos, for (1) Klyt. is not on the scene, being only summoned later by the noise to allay the tumult, (2) even if she was here the chorus have said their say to her (1373-1575), (3) it would sadly interrupt the scene to interpolate an appeal to the queen, when the point here is the rising exasperation between Aegisthos and the chorus. Taking Wieseler's μένων (for νέον) and αἰσχύνας, we may leave the rest: it is better than altering τοὺς ἥκοντας. 'Thou *woman*, didst thou abide at home waiting for the warrior's return, and having defiled the man's bed, devise this fate for the leader of the host?'

[If we retain νέον and αἰσχύνουσ' we must take the ordinary correction τοῦδ' ἥκοντος: but we must still, for the reasons given, suppose it addressed to Aegisthos: the fem. part. will then continue the taunt of γύναι.]

77

AGAMEMNON.

l. 1628. There is bitterness in the turgid expression ἀρχηγενῆ, 'the primal source of tears'

l. 1631. 'Stirring our wrath with thy vain howling.'

l. 1632. ἄξει, passive, 'shall be dragged off,' another point of contrast with Orpheus. 'He was sweet-voiced, you howl like a dog; he dragged others after him, you shall be dragged away.'

l. 1633. ὡς δὴ σύ, lit. 'for of course you will be,' 'since surely you will be,' i. e. 'doubtless you will be,' ironical. So Soph. O. C. 809 ὡς δὴ σὺ βραχέα ταῦτα δ' ἐν καιρῷ λέγεις. Or it might be explained as an exclamation, 'how surely you will be !' also ironical.

l. 1637. 'I was of old suspected as a foe.'

l. 1640. βαρείαις, 'with heavy yoke.' ζεύγλαις understood from the verb. οὐ μή or οὔτι μή, properly used with subj. or future indic., e. g. οὔ τι μὴ ληφθῶ, 'no fear of my being caught.' οὐ μή τις ἄξει (Soph. O. C. 177), 'No chance of any one taking you away.' Hence it comes to be used as a very strong negative, and so we find it here negativing an adj. only. 'Surely no high-mettled trace-horse,' well fed and lightly caparisoned, but a heavily yoked one tamed by hunger. [Perhaps however. as οὐ μή is generally used with verbs, we should read with Karst. οὔ τι μήν. So Soph. Phil. 1273.]

l. 1642. μαλθακόν σφ' ἐπόψεται, 'shall see him tamed.'

l. 1645. 'But with thee a woman slew him.' σύν, adverbial, an Epic usage not uncommon in poetry; ἐν, πρός, and others, are so used. But as Klyt. did not *share* the deed, but did it alone, σύν has been doubted. If it is right it must be used loosely to mean ' thy accomplice,' 'acting with thee.' Most edd. read νιν, Schn. suggests σοί, which is not bad.

l. 1649. δοκεῖς, 'art resolved,' personal construction, see 16. ἔρδειν καὶ λέγειν, 'to do and say such things,' no need for κοὐ λέγειν, as most edd. alter.

l. 1650. A line is lost here; 1651 must be given to Aegisthos (not the chorus, as MSS.), for 1652 is clearly an answer to it. λοχῖται, 'comrades,' are Aegisthos' bodyguard.

l. 1653. 'Die, thou sayest; we take the omen,' as Ken. well translates it. τὴν τύχην δ' αἱρούμεθα, 'and we take our good fortune.'

[*Klytaemnestra appears just as they are about to fight, and stills the tumult.*]

l. 1655. The order of the words points to taking πολλά as predicate, 'Even these are many to reap, a bitter harvest.' The commoner rendering, 'Even to reap these many woes is a bitter harvest,' is possible, but would rather require τοσαῦτα.

ll. 1657, 8. Very corrupt. I have taken Madvig's as the best emendation, πρὸς δόμους, πεπρωμένοις πρὶν παθεῖν, εἴξαντες· ἀρκεῖν χρῆν κ.τ.λ., 'Go to your homes, yielding to fate before ye suffer.' This is the only correction which gives a decent sense to πεπρωμένος, a word always used of fate. [If this alters too much, take Hermann's, πρὸς δόμους πεπρωμένους, Πρὶν παθεῖν ἔρξαντες· ἀρκεῖν κ.τ.λ.]

l. 1659. Read with Hermann δεχοίμεθ' ἄν. The best sense seems to be, 'and if these troubles should be found sufficient, we would accept them, though grievously smitten with God's wrath.' (Hermann's δ' ἔτ' οὐ for δέ τοι is unhappy, it would be μηκέτι), i. e. 'if no further trouble occurs, we will be content.' A proudly conciliatory speech, meaning, 'we will forget this outbreak if you keep quiet for the future.'

l. 1662. 'Cull the flowers of a foolish tongue,' a characteristic Aeschylean figure. The accus. and inf. is exclamatory, 'But that these should...' i. e. 'the idea that they should...'

l. 1664. Blomfield ingeniously supplies θ' ὑβρίσαι for the missing three syllables.

l. 1666. μέτειμι, 'will visit it on thee.'

l. 1668. 'Exiles feed on hope;' in this scornful taunt there is dramatic irony, for those who know what is coming in the next play; the exile Orestes returns and slays her.

l. 1669. 'Go on, and fatten, defiling justice; for thou hast the power.'

l. 1671. The cock was the 'home-fighting' bird (ἐνδομάχας Pind. Ol. 12. 13; ἐνοίκιος ὄρνις Eum. 866), and so is Aegisthos, who dares not fight abroad, but is only formidable on his own dunghill.

l. 1672. προτιμάω has a secondary meaning 'to care for,' and the construction follows the meaning; it takes gen. like μέλει, φροντίζειν κ.τ.λ.

APPENDICES.

I.

The Remote Deliberative.

Line 620. οὐκ ἔσθ' ὅπως λέξαιμι τὰ ψευδῆ καλά. All the commentators notice here the omission of ἄν: Paley says it occurs in negative propositions. Kennedy follows Peile in saying the optative is due to indefinite generality: a strange confusion. Enger says the strict Attic rule would require ἄν: Hermann does not notice it. Madvig emends wildly. The true explanation seems to have escaped everybody.

The fact is, that all the passages where commentators have regretted the want of ἄν in Attic Greek have one common character; they are all (not 'negative,' as Paley says, on a small induction, but) *interrogative*, either direct or indirect. The following is a list of those I can find:—

(1) Direct.

Soph. O. C. 170 ποῖ τις φροντίδος ἔλθοι; (sic Laur. Cod.)
„ Ant. 604 τέαν Ζεῦ δύνασιν τις ὑπερβασία κατάσχοι; (sic Codd.)
„ Phil. 895 τί δῆτα δρῷμ' ἐγώ;
Ar. Plut. 438 ποῖ τις φύγοι;
Plat. Gorg. 492 B τί κάκιον εἴη;
Aesch. Choeph. 595 τίς λέγοι;

(2) Indirect.

Aesch. Ag. 620 οὐκ ἔσθ' ὅπως λέξαιμι.
„ P. V. 292 οὐκ ἔστιν ὅτῳ μείζονα μοῖραν νείμαιμι.
„ Cho. 172 οὐκ ἔστιν ὅστις πλὴν ἐμοῦ κείραιτό νιν.
Eur. Alc. 52 ἔστ' οὖν ὅπως Ἄλκηστις ἐς γῆρας μόλοι;
Plat. Euthyd. 296 D οὐκ ἔχω πῶς ἀμφισβητοίην.

Soph. O. C. 1172 καὶ τίς ποτ' ἐστίν, ὅν γ' ἐγὼ ψέξαιμί τι; also closely resembles these and should be classed with them.

[It is true that (2) are not strictly interrogative in form: but just as οὐκ ἔχει τί εἴπῃ (and even ἔχει ὅ, τι εἴπῃ) are allowed by analogy or extension of usage from the strict interrogative form οὐκ οἶδεν or οἶδεν ὅ, τι εἴπῃ, so these instances are really the interrogative optative put obliquely.]

Now it must be plain, considering these examples all in a lump, that what they *vary from* is not the optative with ἄν, but the interrogative subjunctive, or, as it is usually called, the *deliberative*. The subjunctive

APPENDICES.

might be substituted for the optative in all these instances: and in the first two it is usually so read, though against the best MS. authority.

The difficulty then is this: not why ἄν is omitted, for the sentences are not conditional; but why the *remote* form (optative) is used instead of the *primary* form (subjunctive), when the sentences are all of a *primary* character.

The answer is that the optative expresses the remoteness, not as usual (e.g. in past final, or past indefinite, or past deliberatives) of *pastness*, but of possibility: the instinct is to express by optative something *more out of the question* than the subjunctive would have expressed.

Thus e.g. in the first instance τίς κατάσχῃ; would be good Greek, but the question of restraining Zeus' omnipotence would seem to be more treated as a practical one: the optative puts it further off, as a wild impossibility.

Or again, in Ar. Plut. 438 ποῖ φύγῃ would be in ordinary circumstances the expression, and so the older editors all read it: but φύγοι, the MS. reading, and the right one, is the exclamation of supreme terror, treating escape as in the last degree unlikely.

II.

τόπος, τοπή, τοπάω, τὸ πᾶν.

Mr. A. W. Verrall, in a very ingenious paper in the Journal of Philology (9. 115), has endeavoured to show that a family of words—τόπος, τοπή, and τοπάω, all connected with τοπάζω, and meaning 'conjecture,' 'divination,' 'discovery' (the verb 'to divine' or 'discover')—has disappeared from many places in our texts, owing to various corruptions, such as τρόπος for τόπος, τὸ πᾶν for τοπάν or τοπᾶν, etc.

In the course of his argument he deals with the following passages from Agamemnon:—

(1) 161-176.
(2) 681-99 sqq.
(3) 992-3.

In (1) (besides many other emendations) he would read in 174-5:—

Ζῆνα δέ τις προφρόνως ἐπινίκια κλάζων
τεύξεται φρενῶν τοπάν,

which he construes, 'but he that prophetically nameth (κλάζων for κλῄζων) Zeus by titles of victory shall be right in thus divining his character.'

In (2) he would read in 681 ὧδ᾽ ἐς τοπὰν ἐτητύμως, 'with so true a prophecy' (with such literal truth in respect of his divination).

APPENDICES.

In (3) he would read οὐ τοπᾶν ἔχων ἐλπίδος φίλον θράσος, 'unable to discover the welcome assurance of hope.'

After carefully considering his arguments, I must own that in all three passages I prefer the MS. reading. (1) Κλάζων can quite well be used of a loud utterance (cp. 48, 201) : and τεύξεται φρενῶν τὸ πᾶν, 'shall find wisdom altogether,' is a better sense than the one proposed. Indeed 'divining his character' is a totally inappropriate expression; there is no 'divination of character' in piously calling Zeus 'the Victor:' and for the meaning given to προφρόνως there is no authority whatever.

In (2) the emendation is less unlikely: but even there τοπή does not seem quite the right word, as it should properly mean 'conjecture' as opposed to 'knowledge,' and not 'prophecy;' it is properly applied to *finding out truth* by guessing, not *foretelling* it; and the MSS. ἐς τὸ πᾶν ἐτητύμως, 'altogether truly' (not 'on the whole,' as Mr. Verrall says, which is quite different, but like πάνυ or παράπαν), seems perfectly satisfactory.

In (3) τοπᾶν θράσος, 'to discover assurance,' is not at all a happy phrase, while οὐ τὸ πᾶν is just what is wanted to express the misgiving constantly recurring, in spite of the king having just returned triumphant and safe : 'not having to the full hope's happy courage,' as K. translates it.

On the whole therefore I cannot agree in Mr. Verrall's proposed emendations as far as the Agamemnon is concerned. Still I am bound to say that I feel, not merely that the *a priori* probability is great that the τοπή, τοπάω, etc. would disappear from our texts in some places, but also that in some of the passages where he would restore them there is much to be said for the restoration.

III.

Lines 1228 sqq. Mr. H. A. J. Munro (Journal of Philol. xi. 130) has discussed this passage, and rejects Madvig's emendation as too violent. He defends the accusative οἷα after τεύξεται : and in objecting to this I think I was wrong. I still feel however that the sentence as a whole is so harsh as to be very suspicious : οἷα is a long way from τεύξεται : and the other objections seem to me to hold. If οἷα is taken with λέξασα, τεύξεται is unsatisfactory : the things she 'says' and 'obtains' are different.

Mr. Munro's δοκήν for δίκην (with all respect be it spoken for so high an authority), I cannot feel to be likely. 'Lengthening out the ambush of a dark crime'—a version which puts a strain on ἄτη,—is so violent a phrase as to be hardly better than the MSS. text. It gives a construction to ἐκτείνασα, it is true : but the sense and diction is intolerably harsh.

APPENDICES.

IV.

Line 1267. Mr. Munro (Journal of Philol. xi. 139) discusses this line also, and objects to Mr. Verrall's emendation that it should be δέ not τε, and that πεσόντα goes with ἴτε better. I do not see why, as the actions of throwing and trampling are similar in kind and in quick succession, the close conjunction τε is not admissible, though in form one of the verbs is imperative and the other future. The participle πεσόντα seems to me also possible and natural: the things first fell, and then were trampled on. My translation 'as ye lie' was a little free: and I have given ' as ye fall' instead. The meaning is the simple one that one act came just after the other, and the aorist part. is surely common for the first of two such acts.

V.

Further Notes of Readings.

2. δ' ἦν M. ἦν V. Fl. Fa.
82. ἡμερόφατον M. ἡμερόφαντον Fa.
97. λέξαι σ'... αἰνῶ Marg.
105. καταπνε-ει (letter erased) M. καταπνεύει B. Fa. Fl. καταπνείει Ald.
110. ξύμφρονε ταγώ. D.
115. ἀργίας M. ἀργᾶς Blomf.
123. λογοδαίτας M. λαγ. Fl. Fa.
129. προσθετὰ M.
156. ἀπέκλαιξεν M. ἀπέκλαγξεν B. Fl. Fa.
165. τῷδε MSS. τὸ Pauw.
190. παλιρρόθοις MSS. παλιρρύχθοις H. L. Ahrens.
206. πείθεσθαι MSS. πιθέσθαι Turn.
222. βροτοὺς Spanheim.
275. σέβοιμι Marg.
282. corr. Cant.
289. σκοποῖς Schütz; not unlikely.
297. παιδίον ὠποῦ M. πεδίον 'Ασωποῦ Fl. Fa.
304. μηχανήσασθαι Marg.
312. τοιοίδ' ἕτοιμοι B. Fa. τ. ἔτυμοι Fl.
322. ἐκχέας MSS. ἐγχ. Cant.
334. ἐν MSS. ἐν δ' Pauw.
336. ὡς δ' εὐδαίμονες Stanl.
346. ἐγρήγορον MSS. corr. Pors.
350. σὴν ὄνησιν Marg.

APPENDICES.

368. τοῦτο γ' Fa.   τοῦτ' Fl.
384. μεγάλα MSS.   μέγαν Cant.
391. προσβολαῖς Pears.   προβ. MSS.
394. πτανὸν Fl.   πτανόν τιν' Fa.   ποτανὸν Schütz.
408. πολὺ δ' ἀνέστενον Fl.
430. τηξικάρδιος Aur.
457. δημοκράτου MSS.   δημοκράντου Pors.
477. εἰ δ' ἐτήτυμος Aur.   [Probably right.]
511. ἦσθ' Askew.
536. αὐτόχθον' ὂν Klausen.
544. πεπληγμένοι Tyrwhitt.
546. φρενύς μ' Scal.   φρενὸς MSS.
557. στένοντας, ἀσχάλλοντας Marg.   [Very ingenious.]
579. δύμων .. ἀρχαίων is Hartung's very probable emendation. [δόμων was first changed through the influence of τοῖς καθ' Ἑλλάδα misunderstood: then ἀρχαίων necessarily became ἀρχαῖον.]
584. ἥβη Marg. [probable].
644. σεσαγμένον Schütz.
664. ναυστολοῦσ' Cas.   [Unnecessary.]
684. προνοίαις MSS. corr. Pauw.
701. ἤλασε MSS.   ἤλασεν Pors.
715. διαὶ πολιτᾶν Emper.
868. πλέω MSS.   πλέον Dind.
876. ἀνημμένης Weckl.
898. στόλον Fl.   στῦλον Fa.
931. εἶκε Marg.
959. ἰσάργυρον Salmasius.
963. δειμάτων MSS. corr. Cant.
965. μηχανωμένη Aur.   [Perhaps right.]
969. μολόν H. Voss.
990. ὅμως Aur.
991. Ἐρινύος Pors.
1019. πεσὸν Aur.
1084. περ ἐν Schütz.
1117. ἀκύρετος Bothe.
1128. ἐν ἐνύδρῳ Schütz.
1146. ἀηδόνος μόρον MSS. corr. H.
1152. M. ἐπίφοβα originally.
1167. ὁλωμένας V. Fl.   ὁλουμένας Fa.   ὁλομένας Cas.
1174. κακοφρονῶν Schütz.
1198. ὅρκου πῆγμα Aur.   [Perhaps right.]
1227. ἄπαρχος MSS.   ἔπαρχος Cant.
1242. παιδίων MSS.   παιδείων Schütz.

APPENDICES.

1255. δυσπαθῆ MSS.   δυσμαθῆ Steph.
1334. μηκέτι δ' εἰσέλθῃς MSS. corr. H.
1362. τείνοντες Cant.
1364. κράτει MSS.   κρατεῖ Cas.
1368. θυμοῦσθαι first due to E. A. Ahrens.
1396. τῷδ' Tyrwhitt.
1397. τοσόνδε Blomfield. [Probable.]
1408. ὁρώμενον MSS.   ὅρμενον Abresch.
1416. εὐτόκοις Fl. Fa.   εὐπόκοις (corrected) V.
1419. χρῆν Pors.
1430. τύμμα τύμμα MSS.   τύμματι I. Voss.
1471. καρδιόδηκτον Abresch.
1527. ἄξια Herm.
1531. εὐπαλάμων μεριμνᾶν Enger. [Possibly right.]
1545. ψυχῇ τ' E. A. Ahrens. [Probable.]
1605. ἔλιπε κάθλίῳ Marg.
1653. αἱρούμεθα Aur.
1660. δαίμονας MSS.   δαίμονος Cas.
1671. ὥσπερ MSS.   ὥστε Scal.

GENERAL INDEX.

Abstract for concrete, 109, 123.
ἄγγαρος, 282.
ἄγκαθεν, 3.
ἀγοραῖος, 88.
ἀγώνιος, 513.
Accumulation of phrase, 154, 192, 222, 960, 1015.
Adjective, rare use, 10.
— governing accusative, 103, 1091.
αἰχμά, 483.
ἀλλ' ἦ, 276.
ἀλουργύς, 946.
ἄν carried on, 1048.
ἀντίφερνος, 406.
Anachronism, 1355.
Anacoluthon, 97, 100, 816.
ἄπτερος φάτις, 276.
Aposiopesis, 498, 567, 1109.
Art, works of, 241, 416, 801, 1329.
Article, as demonstrative, 7, 397.
— separated from substantive, 1056.
— as relative, 526, 642.
Attraction, personal use, δοκῶ, 16.
— of participle, 1371.
Augment omitted, 189.
αὐτός displaced, 836.
— in compounds, of kindred murder, 1092, 1573.
αὐτοῦ for σεαυτοῦ, 1141, 1297, 1544.
αὐτότοκος, 137.

Beauty of nature, 566.
βοή, 'call to battle,' 1349.

γὰρ οὖν, 524, 674.
γε μὲν δή, 661, 887, 1213.
γε μήν, 1378.

Comparison, abridged, 894.

δίαυλος, 344.
Doricisms:—
 τόλμᾶ, 376.
 πῶ; 1509.
 in chorus, 43, 1072.
δ' οὖν, 34, 224, 676, 1042.
Double meanings, 67, 69, 345, 441, 612, 699, 781, 857, 912.

ἐκκύκλημα, 1372.
ἐξαίρετος, 954.
ἔσκε, 723.
Epic forms and usages:—
 Article omitted, 59, 313, 323, 709, 1395.
 — separated from substantive, 1056.
 — as relative, 526, 642.
 — as demonstrative, 397.
 Genitive of 'hearing of,' 1367.
 — local, 1056.
 Dative, local, 27, 558, etc.; see Cases.
 — after verbs of motion, 357, 363, 1450.
 Subjunctive with εἰ, 1328.
 Syncope, 27, 305.
 Tmesis, 450, 944.
βοή, 1349.
δαμείς, 1451.
ἐπί, dative, 'against,' 61.
ἐπίστροφος, 397.
θύω, 1235.
ἴσους, ι long, 122.
ἰχώρ, 1480.
κῆρ, 206.
μηδέ, 'but not,' 1498.
εἴτε, 50.
ὅπως ἄν with optative, 367.
πολέα (?), 1453.

86

GENERAL INDEX.

πρό adverbial, 253.
σύν adverbial, 586, 1645.
ὡς for ὥστε; see ὡς.
Euphemism, 1288.

'From' for 'on,' 116.

Hearth, domestic, 1056.

ἶνις, 717.
Ionicisms:—
 Τυνδάρεω, 83.
 ἀντήλιος, 519.
 ἐπιλεχθῆς, 1498.
Irony, dramatic, 67, 599, 606, 862, 904. 912, 1225.
— pathetic, 455.

καί in questions, 280.
καὶ γὰρ οὖν. 524.
καὶ μήν, 1178.
— 'and yet,' 1254.
κυρεῖν, 1201.

Lampadephoria, 312.
Licence of drama, 504.

μέν, antithesis suppressed, 924.
μὲν οὖν, 1396.
μέντοι, 644, 886.
Metaphor, rustic, 32.
— grotesque, 494.
— rapid succession, 786, 1031, 1178, 1435.

Names, significant, 687, 1081.
νεῖρος, 1478.
νῦν, 'just now,' 550.

ὅδιος, 104.
οὔ τι μή, with adjective, 1640.
οὐ μὴν γε, 1279.
οὖν, 'in short,' 607.
— in alternatives, 359.
οὔτε omitted, 532.
Oxymoron, 1268.

πνόος, 806.
πράσσεσθαι, 700.
πρέπω, 241, 389, 1222.
πρόδουλος, 945.
Personal construction, 16, 379, 1079.
Personifying instinct, 894.
Play on words:—
 Ἑλένας, 689.
 κῆδος, 699.
 Ἀλέξανδρος, 711 (?).
 Ἀπόλλων, 1081.
 δυσμενεῖς, 1193.
Pregnant construction, 538.
Preposition, adverbial, 253, 760, 1645.

Rhetorical repetition, 8.
ῥύσιον, 534.

Sin only cause of woe, 751.
Slaves in household religion, 1037.
στάξ, 1172.
κατὰ σύνεσιν construction, 308, 562.
συντελής, 632.
'Swallow' for foreigner, 1050.
Symbolic act, 1601.
Syncope:—
 ἀνδαίω, 305.
 ἐπαντείλασαν, 27.

τε marking apposition, 1526.
τέλος, 'task,' 908.
— 'decision,' 934.
τίνω, double meaning, 1324.
τις, εἴ τις Ἀπόλλων, 55.
τί. put for clause, 935.
Tmesis, 450, 944.
Transferred epithet, 237, 920.

φιλήτωρ, 1446.

ὡς for ἐξ οὗ, 1212.
— — ὥστε, 358, 546, 575, 665, 1381.
ὡς δή, 1633.
ὥστε for ὡς, 884.

87

GRAMMATICAL INDEX.

a. Cases and Prepositions.

Nominative:—
Pendens, 1008.
Strange apposition ἅλαι, 195.
After accusative in comparison, 1392.

Accusative:—
Apposition to clause, 49, 225, 1310.
— loose, 643.
Duration, 1.
Internal, 1375.
— cognate, 1, 174, 1111, 1483, 1494.
Adverbial, 280.
Absolute, 1620.
After adjective, 103, 1091.
— verbs of sitting, 184, 664, 834.
— στερηθείς, 1531.
πρὸς κόρον, 381.
πρὸς τὸ βίαιον, 130.

Genitive:—
Comprehensive, 278.
Description, 43.
Local, 1056.
Partitive, 961.
Relation, with 'feeling,' 50.
— — ὕπατος, 51.
— — εὖ, 379.
— — κεκομμένος, 479.
— — οὕτω, 950.
After κάτοπτος, 307.
— negative adjective, 311.
— verb of 'hearing about,' 1367.
— φάτις, 630.
Separation, λελειμμένος, 517.
ἐκ, 'after,' 330.

Dative:—
Ethical, 312, 496.
Instrumental, 521.
Local, 27, 558, 578, 718.
Manner, 521.
Respect, 233.
Time, 521.
With and without preposition, 656.
After passive, 371, 801.
εἰκότως, 915.
ἐπί (motion), 357, 363.
ἐν (motion), 1450.

b. Moods and Tenses.

Indicative:—
Present prophetic, 126.
Imperfect (attempt), 593.
Perfect, βέβηκε, 36.
Future perfect active, 1279.
Aorist gnomic, 717, 966, 1006, 1329.
— momentary, 1243.

Imperative:—
Aorist with μή, 931.

Subjunctive:—
Misgiving, 341.
With εἰ, 1328.

Optative:—
Assimilated, 253, 319.
Generalising, 1042.
Double conditional, 930.
Final with ὅπως ἄν, 364.
Indefinite, 372.
'Potential,' 552.

GRAMMATICAL INDEX.

Optative:—
  Pure optative, 606.
  Remote deliberative, 620.
  With ἄν carried on, 1048.
  — mild order, 1049. 1394.

Infinitive:—
  Consecutive, 15, 481, 569.
  — epexegetic, 217, 307, 621, 640. 956, 961, 1263.

After θάρσος, 980.
Accusative infinitive, oblique petition, 27.
  — exclamatory, 1662.
  — after παρεσκευασμένος, 1421.

Participle:—
  Attraction, 1371.
  Causal, 912.
  Conditional, 964.
  Genitive absolute, harsh, 1298.

INDEX OF NAMES.

Aigiplanktos, 303.
Alexandros, 61.
Apia, 256.
Arachnaios, 309.
Argos, 1.
Artemis, 135.
Asklepios, 1022.
Asopos, 297.
Athos, 285.
Aulis, 191.

Chalkis, 190.
Chryseis, 1439.

Euripos, 292.

Geryon, 871.
Gorgopis, 302.

Helenos, 409.
Hermaios, 283.

Ida, 281.
Ieios, 146.
Iphigeneia, 151.
Itys, 1145.

Kalchas, 122.
Kithairon, 298.
Kronos, 170.

Leda, 914.

Makistos, 289.
Menelaos, 42.
Messapios, 293.
Mykenae, 1.

Orestes, 880.
Orion, 967.
Ouranos, 170.

Paian, 146.
Philomela, 1145.
Pleisthenes, 1569.
Prokne, 1145.
Pylades, 880.

Saronic gulf, 306.
Seirios, 967.
Simoeis, 695.
Strophios, 880.
Strymon, 192.

Tereus, 1145.
Thyestes, 1096.
Timanthes, 241.
Tyndareus, 83.

THE END.

www.ingramcontent.com/pod-product-compliance
Lightning Source LLC
Chambersburg PA
CBHW031448160426
43195CB00010BB/899